MOORINGS OLD AND NEW

ENTRIES IN AN IMMIGRANT'S LOG

Moorings Old and New

Entries in an Immigrant's

Log

by PAUL KNAPLUND

Foreword by MERLE CURTI

1963

THE STATE HISTORICAL SOCIETY OF WISCONSIN

MADISON

SECOND PRINTING, MARCH, 1964

Foreword

It takes temerity to write a foreword to a memoir which so distinguished a historian as Paul Knaplund has given us in *Moorings Old and New: Entries in an Immigrant's Log*. I do so because to be asked to do so is an honor I deeply appreciate and because I can perhaps indicate why in my judgment this book has a much wider appeal and significance than might appear off-hand from the title.

This book is a unique addition to a category of writing which gives us the record of what has been called "transatlantic civilization." Of course, I am not sufficiently familiar with the historiography of Norway to speak of the place *Moorings Old and New* will have in the study of the regional history of that country toward the end of the nineteenth century and in the first years of our own. But I find it hard to believe that any other book on a Norwegian community of this period could more realistically and imaginatively illuminate the economy, social structure, institutions, and common life through a focus on a family, a parish, a fjord and the seas beyond, and on the nearest market town. If I am wrong, all I can say is that Norway is fortunate in having perceptive accounts so telling, so poetical, and yet so thoughtful of one of its distinctive areas. Without using the term national character, Professor Knaplund has described his life on a fishing-farming island within the Arctic Circle and has given us what is bound to interest students of this concept.

In this part of his memoir he weaves folklore and legend into the forces of change, including the Norwegian renaissance, in such a way as to make unforgettable the courage, tragedy, realism, hazards, and combination of fearless and self-disciplined individuality with respect for law and teamwork. This is also sure to intrigue students of personality and culture.

One reason why *Moorings Old and New* is so rich and successful in re-creating the life of a small fishing-farming Norwegian community is that Professor Knaplund is gifted with an extraordinary memory — it might be thought of as "total recall" — and also because, as a keen and thoughtful historian, he has been able to give us insight into continuity and change, into the interrelations between economic, social, political, religious and other cultural forces and the impact of these on members of his family and of the Norwegian community in which he lived until he was twenty-one years old.

Moorings Old and New is, for similar reasons, unique in a large category of writing about immigration to America. We now have at least 330 autobiographical writings by immigrants about their early life in the country of their birth, their reasons for migrating, about what America did to and for them, and, in some instances, what they did for America. Of these autobiographies twenty-seven, by my count, have been written by immigrants from Norway. The occupations of the writers include piano-playing, sailing, logging, farming, journalism, preaching, mining, fighting Indians, trapping, nursing, law, teaching, flying, and skating. The only one, I think, which can in any way be compared with Paul Knaplund's memoirs is the *Logbook of a Young Immigrant,* by Laurence M. Larson. Professor Larson was also a distinguished historian, but his logbook is concerned with an earlier period; it is restricted to the American side of the Norwegian immigrant experience; and it does not have the sensitive, psychological insight into the process by which ties with the homeland were loosened and those with the new country strengthened.

Professor Knaplund's book will, then, appeal to anyone interested in reasons for emigration from Norway to America, in the subtle process by which, in this case, a young man of limited schooling, having no English, journeying alone, compelled to make his own way and to combat loneliness, came to feel and to be an American. It will appeal to the American historian and social scientist because it shows how transformation in culture and in "belongingness" took place without conscious rejection of old loyalties; how it was influenced not only by personality but by the social situations in which this immigrant found himself; and how it took place without participation in the factional disputes in Norwegian-American communities or in playing the role of a professional hyphenated American (a type with which Professor Knaplund had little sympathy but considerable understanding).

Those who have accepted without reservation such books on immigration as Oscar Handlin's *The Uprooted* should especially appreciate *Moorings Old and New*. In admirably supplementing available "immigrant letters," it shows clearly and in a factually straightforward way how one-sided any picture of immigrant experience is that neglects the rural Middle West.

Paul Knaplund's book will also appeal to other readers. For those interested in the history of American education and particularly in the development of scholarship in the field of British imperial and Commonwealth history, the account of his apprenticeship at the University of Wisconsin and of his research experiences in Great Britain will be welcome. I may be permitted to note that his pioneer studies in this field, richly documented with manuscript sources often hitherto unused and breaking many other paths as well, have won the admiration of workers in this field of scholarship all over the world. The point is the more interesting when one recalls that a major reason for this particular emigration was the inability of the narrator to obtain in Norway the education he sought.

More than this, *Moorings Old and New* is a very human book about interesting and unforgettable people such as Hans Christ, the obscure and all but unknown Norwegian-American farmer under whom Paul Knaplund, as a hired man, began his American career. Above all, this sensitive book gives us a remarkable self-portrait of a gifted and dedicated teacher, a renowned scholar, a highly respected member of the community, a man who learned, after the age of twenty-one, to write English with grace and clarity. The writing reveals a nice ability to express feeling about the beauty and harshness of nature, the strength and weaknesses of men. Here, too, is a flair for lucidly relating concrete incidents which are made to give dimension and meaning to larger historical movements. Although a serious book, *Moorings Old and New* is enlivened by amusing and often revealing human episodes. Above all, here is the reflection of a man of great intellectual curiosity, strength, sensitivity, and wise judgment.

So this is not, then, merely a logbook of an immigrant. It is a personal story in the context of large and significant movements and processes. I think it will take a memorable place in historical no less than in autobiographical writing.

MERLE CURTI

Fall, 1962

Preface

of these memoirs came to America from Norway in 1906. He was then twenty-one years old. The son of a fisherman-farmer, he had in his early years followed that amphibious occupation. For brief periods in Norway, he had also been a telegraph messenger and a miner. In America he worked first as a farmhand, then entered school, and for several years did a variety of odd jobs to support himself while getting an education. His ultimate choice was the academic life.

Realizing that American citizenship as well as education would best fit him for a career in America he took out naturalization papers in October, 1913. The presiding judge knew the applicant so he simply asked, "Have you read with care the documents which you have signed?" The writer's affirmative answer satisfied the judge. But the government lawyer, thinking there should be more of an examination, inquired, "Do you believe in polygamy?" and "Does any member of your family believe in polygamy?" Replies of "no" to both questions concluded that ceremony.

The newly naturalized citizen fully appreciated the legal implications of his change of allegiance. But in 1913 ties of flesh and blood still bound him firmly to the land of his birth. In after years these sentimental ties were loosened; they broke one by one while those linking him with his adopted country grew slowly and immeasurably stronger.

In 1906 the author was but one of the hundreds of thousands of Europeans who entered the United States through Ellis Island. It is of such immigrants and their children that a high percentage of the population of the United States consists. None of the new arrivals came from a cultural or intellectual vacuum. Every one bore the imprint of an environment which was the result of long ages of man's efforts to climb the world's altar-stairs, to reach a higher conception of human life and the worth of each individual human being. To a greater or lesser degree this imprint remains and is transmitted to the immigrant's children.

The author presents these sketches of his national background and of the transformation he has undergone because he thinks that they may throw some light on the psychological process of Americanization. Moreover, he believes that Americans may benefit from fuller knowledge of an immigrant's problems, and perhaps come to realize that behind national and racial diversities are great human similarities. The immigrant, too, may profit if he takes an inventory of what America has done for him.

The story is written in the third person because when the author began to recall events of former years, he suddenly understood that both the scene and the actor belonged to the past. The "I" of today is not the "I" of yesteryear. That old "I" has vanished like a winter's snow.

Madison, Wisconsin   P.K.
Fall, 1962

Contents

		Introduction	1
PART	I :	OLD MOORINGS	
	1 :	The Young Fisherman	9
	2 :	Land and Sea	16
	3 :	Lofoten and the Cod Fisheries	34
	4 :	Church and School	56
	5 :	People and Institutions	75
	6 :	Stories and Legends	96
	7 :	Home and Family	104
PART	II :	NEW MOORINGS	
	8 :	A Spring Evening	127
	9 :	Weigh Anchor	131
	10 :	Hans Christ	154
	11 :	School Years, 1907—1913	183
	12 :	Summers, 1908—1913	200
	13 :	Apprenticeship Years	223
	14 :	The Home Port	249
	15 :	Review and Reflections	267
		Genealogical Appendix	271
		Index	272

Illustrations

Map: ARCTIC NORWAY   8
MARTINUS JOHNSEN KNAPLUND   120
KRISTINE ANDREASSEN JOHNSEN KNAPLUND   120
KNAPLUNDÖY   121
PAUL KNAPLUND, 1907   122
HANS CHRIST FARM   123
Map: UPPER MIDDLE WEST   126

Introduction

LIFE AND CONDITIONS
in Arctic Norway during the author's childhood were little
known in the rest of the country, and were virtually a closed
book to the world outside. A land of majestic natural beauty
it is also a land of sharp contrasts, between winter and summer, between grimly stark landscapes and those of bewitching
appeal. In the lifetime of the author's parents, and even during
his own childhood, most people in northern Norway led a
toilsome existence and faced the fearful perils of stormy seas.
But they were deeply attached to this region where their
forebears had settled before the Christian Era. Though they
might migrate to far-away lands, the imprint and memory of
their childhood home remained enshrined in heart and mind
till life's last day.

In the latter half of the nineteenth century a large number
of Norwegians emigrated to the United States and settled in
the Middle West. Norsemen played important roles in the
early development of Illinois, Iowa, Wisconsin, Minnesota,
and the Dakotas. In this pioneer period when the prairies were
brought under cultivation communications were undeveloped
and markets were distant. For the Norwegian immigrant
farmers the physical hardships were intensified by their un-
familiarity with the customs and language of their new home.
Moreover, they were haunted by intense loneliness. They
had slipped their old moorings and many felt adrift. The late
Professor Knut Gjerset of Luther College, Iowa, who at the
age of five was brought to Minnesota by his parents, said
that the most vivid of his early childhood memories was of

1

his mother weeping. The yearning for the home left behind in Norway was quite overwhelming. The prevalence of mental breakdowns among the wives of Norwegian settlers in the Red River valley offered tragic testimony to the severity of those heartbreaks.

Nostalgia intensified by the privations suffered in "the land of promise" caused immigrants to idealize life in the old country. Forgotten were the low wages and the paucity of opportunities; remembered were the friendliness and neighborliness prevailing there. Ways had to be devised to make life in the New World endurable. Quite early the immigrants discovered that by settling with others from the same region in Norway they could co-operate in meeting the problems of a pioneer community. They quickly learned the techniques of American farming; they were willing to work hard for long hours; and they were accustomed to do a variety of other jobs such as carpentry, blacksmithing, and harnessmaking. Before long the immigrants found that they could more than hold their own in competition with native-born Americans — "Yankees" — and with farmers of other national origins. This discovery created satisfaction and helped to foster an "at home" feeling.

In time clusters of Norwegian immigrant settlements became training centers from which new arrivals spread into other more remote areas. Prominent among these centers were the Fox River settlement in Illinois, those in Wisconsin's Rock and Dane counties, Winneshiek county in Iowa, and Fillmore and Goodhue counties in Minnesota. Many of the immigrants had been cottars in the old country. They welcomed the opportunity to become freeholders in America. Since they were pioneers in transforming a wilderness into thriving communities they rightly looked upon themselves as builders of America. The farmstead self-sufficiency prevalent a hundred years. ago in many sections of Norway did not suit the conditions in the Middle West. Here farming became a specialized branch of the national economy, and the immigrants adjusted to this situation. They became *American* farmers.

With the creation of their own church organizations the newcomers met not only spiritual needs but promoted social and intellectual activities which diverted their minds from their hard toil and loneliness. The Norwegian state church showed little interest in the emigrants, and some of its leaders considered them deserters or even traitors to the land of their fathers. It took some time before the Norwegian settlements were well enough established to issue calls to ministers ordained in the old homeland. Arriving in their new parishes these ministers found the conditions more primitive than they had anticipated, and they were often shocked to discover that their parishioners had acquired egalitarian opinions not commonly found in Norway. Moreover, they had as colleagues, or perhaps more properly "rivals," ordained laymen who represented a Norwegian evangelistic and pietistic movement which had gained strength early in the nineteenth century.

Soon religious factional strife arose among the Norwegian Lutherans. The questions of ritual, clerical vestments, and the administrative power of ministers were hotly debated. Theological issues such as absolution, predestination, and the priesthood of all believers aroused sharp controversy. When, under the influence of the German Lutheran Missouri Synod, some pastors trained in Norway defended slavery, they were bitterly assailed. The overwhelming majority of Norwegian immigrants devoutly believed that human bondage was unchristian.

Efforts to unite Norwegian-American Lutherans with their Danish, German, or Swedish co-religionists failed. Not only that, the Norwegians could not agree among themselves. By the end of the nineteenth century, though all groups claimed to be orthodox Lutherans to whom Luther's *Small Catechism* was almost as sacred as the Bible, they were split into about half a dozen church bodies. However, whether they were conservative or liberal, the Norwegian Lutherans refused to co-operate in religious matters with American Congregationalists, Methodists, or Presbyterians. Some of their sons and daughters, however, were attracted by the generally cheerful atmosphere of these other Protestant churches, and denominational lines were frequently crossed by their marriages. Thus a quiet, unobtrusive Americanization process went on.

Although some Norwegian Lutheran congregations maintained elementary schools where the teaching of the language and religion of their fathers was stressed, the vast majority of the immigrants' children went to public schools. In classrooms and on playgrounds they learned the national language of America. Homes became bilingual, and despite the earnest efforts of the older generation the Norwegian language steadily lost ground.

To supply the need for pastors the Norwegian-Lutheran church bodies soon established academies, colleges, and theological seminaries. In the early days all of these were bilingual and so afforded young immigrants an opportunity to get an education which fitted them for life in America. Not all who studied at church academies or colleges went into the ministry. Though normal schools and state universities were often suspected of being godless institutions, many Norwegian-Americans continued their education there.

In addition to the church and church schools Norwegian-language newspapers helped ease the loneliness of the immigrants and acquainted them with their adopted country. Among the American cities with relatively large groups of Norwegian immigrants Chicago and Minneapolis were pre-eminent. Here they organized dramatic and literary societies and musical and fraternal organizations which promoted fellowship and counteracted nostalgia.

As strong opponents of slavery, a large number of Norwegian immigrants volunteered for service in the Civil War. They were especially numerous in the 15th Wisconsin regiment commanded by Norwegian-born Colonel Hans Heg. Mortally wounded at Chickamauga, Heg became the great hero of his compatriots who felt that they, in this crucial conflict, were doing their share to keep "America strong and free."

The early eighties witnessed a heavy Norwegian emigration to America. This was a period of sharp political conflict in Norway between the Storting (parliament) and the king. The king claimed absolute veto power over constitutional amendments. The basic question was whether the executive branch of the government should be controlled by the king or by the elected Storting. The latter won.

It is not surprising that the immigrants, having participated in political discussions in their homeland, showed an early interest in the politics of the land of their adoption. One of their numbers, Knute Nelson, served Minnesota as congressman, governor, and United States senator between 1883 and his death in 1923. His success encouraged compatriots to seek political careers. The Norwegians and Swedes who at this time were quarrelling bitterly in the old world co-operated so well in America's Middle West that early in the present century it was said that the Minneapolis Odin Club governed the state of Minnesota.

By the time the author arrived in that state the assimilation of Norwegian immigrants and their descendants was well advanced. But many of the pioneers were still living, and during the years 1907–1915, when he stayed in their homes, he learned about olden times. Those early settlers described the conditions which met them on their arrival, told how America had been developed by them, and spoke of the ways in which Norwegian immigrants had become integrated into the economic and social life of this nation.

Red Wing Seminary, a school established and operated by one of the Lutheran church bodies, provided the author with educational opportunities not available to him in Norway. This school, though little known, had devoted teachers who rendered invaluable help to immigrant students. After graduation from Red Wing's college department this writer was admitted to the University of Wisconsin as a graduate student. Its history faculty was world famous, and these historians treated the author with a measure of sympathy and interest which he had never imagined could be found in a large secular institution. Ultimately he became a member of the Wisconsin history faculty.

In later years when he went to Europe for research or visits, he often heard the charge that America was the land of cold-blooded and heartless materialism. While it is true that thousands of immigrants were disappointed and became discouraged failures in this country, the author could give many examples from his own experience to refute those charges. He was content in the knowledge that this great country, which had become his own, had made him and countless other immigrants happy and useful. It would be the land of his children and of his children's children.

Part I

Old Moorings

IN MEMORIAM

KRISTINE AND MARTINUS JOHNSEN KNAPLUND

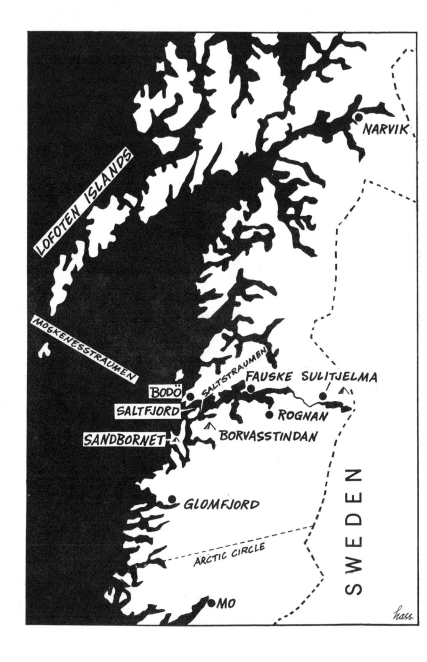

Chapter 1

The Young Fisherman

IT WAS MID-SUMMER
in Arctic Norway. The day had been perfect with a
cloudless sky. The stiff morning breeze from the eastern
mountains died down as the sun rose in the heavens, dead
calm and warm at midday, and in the afternoon a salty ocean
breeze grew brisker the deeper it penetrated the narrow
irregular fjord, which wound its way between mountains for
half a hundred miles from the coast toward the Swedish
border. Twelve miles from its entrance the fjord was blocked
by an island leaving only narrow passages for the tide to flow,
producing a current swift and dangerous especially at new
and full moon.

Two hours before midnight the slanting rays of the sun
illuminated sea and land with a peculiarly soft eerie light.
The sea breeze had subsided and near the eastern end of the
island the tide flowed placidly between rocky shores. Stillness
was descending on the earth, a stillness broken only now and
then by the bleating of sheep, the lowing of cattle, or an eider
duck calling its young. Suddenly ducks and ducklings were
disturbed in their mysterious explorations of crevices and
seaweed by a rowboat which, hugging the shore of the island,
headed westward against the tide. The boat moved slowly,
sticking close to the winding coast so as to benefit by the
eddies in the many coves. It was propelled by a lone oarsman
who pulled with the slow, even stroke of one accustomed to

rowing from early childhood and to conserving his strength for long exertions. Soon the boat came abreast a clearing where remnants of stone fences and man-made ridges gave evidence of cultivation and abandoned fields; foundations of houses and a boat-landing offered further testimony that this sheltered spot had once had human habitations. At the landing place the boat turned in; the keel scraped the rocky bottom. The man stepped ashore, fetching a lunch basket and an anchor from the bow of the boat. Deftly he tested the anchor line, fastened a thin rope to one of its arms, balanced its shank on the gunwhale, and shoved the boat off. A quick jerk on the landing rope dropped the anchor at the proper distance from shore; the rope was wound around a rock and the boat was safely moored.

The rower now picked up his basket and started climbing a steep path leading to a plateau. He was a youth of medium height, strongly built, dressed in the outfit of a fisherman. A battered cap sat carelessly on his bushy hair. The face was blond and ruddy as befits one exposed to sun and wind, the nose rather prominent, the eyes greyish blue and deeply set in their oval frame. Despite its boyishness of outline, the face was serious, almost solemn, as if something weighed on the young mind. A salmon fisherman, he was returning home from a visit to a trap in a bay on the mainland. To reach it he had crossed the island and then rowed a distance of about two miles. Sometimes he would just visit the trap; at other times he might spend the whole day there, depending on whether duties on the small parental farm required his attention or whether he was to market the fish. The trap site was not particularly good. Many days it yielded no catch. This was one such day, hence he had no burden to carry up the winding path and across moor and marsh to his home on the north-west corner of the island.

Slowly the young fisherman ascended to the moorland. The path thither lay in the shadow, but the plateau was bathed in sunlight. Unencumbered save for the empty basket, he now moved more swiftly. At the same time he looked intently at the familiar surroundings, as if everything deserved scrutiny and had a new meaning. He crossed a wold where in years gone by he had run races or played ball with other boys. It was a bit of an oddity, level, smooth, set in a frame of hills and marshes. This open tract of land had evidently been treeless even in olden times when the nearby marsh was a pine forest, doubtless a playground for the youth of bygone ages as well as those of the present. On a hillock was an immense boulder standing somewhat precariously on a few small rocks. To climb it had been one of the fisherman's ambitions when he was very young; he recalled that beneath this rock an arctic hare had once found refuge when chased by many little boys through the deep snow on a bright winter day. They had fancied themselves great hunters and had returned to their homes with tales of what they would have done had they had a gun. A plover whistled mournfully from a knoll; a skua rose from the marsh and disappeared.

The skua, a curious bird, stirred a chain of memories. Every summer a pair seemed to make their home in the marsh. Time and again boys searched in vain for their nest, but no young had ever been observed. The skua was an unpopular bird as well. It foraged on the fishing grounds, but instead of diving for herring, scraps of bait, or entrails of fish, it always waited till the herring gull or the slender, graceful tern had caught something. Then the skua would swoop down on the other bird, forcing it to drop its catch which the marauder quickly snatched in mid-air. A cowardly and contemptible bird, the skua had been named "thieving Joe."

As he entered the marsh the young man came upon a ptarmigan with a large brood. The fluffy young scattered quickly, hiding under heather and juniper while the mother hen, feathers ruffled, stood ready to battle the intruder. As he looked at the brave brown little hen, a bird which in its white winter dress was considered the most beautiful of the northland, the youth recalled that many years ago he had been frightened by such a one, an episode older brothers and sisters seemed unable to forget. Crossing a swampy stretch he noticed a lemming appear suddenly and then flee swiftly to its hole. There was an unsolved riddle about the lemming. In the late summer ten years earlier the island had been overrun by hordes of these small black and yellow rodents. For some mysterious reason they had quit their mountain home, swum the sound separating the island from the mainland, and in an incredibly short time they so multiplied that they became as innumerable as the locusts in the plagues of Egypt. Armed with sticks and accompanied by a poodle, he and the boys of his gang had killed lemming from morning till night. It gratified the bloodthirsty instinct of the young males and gave them an excuse not to help their elders dig potatoes. Were they not doing useful labor in ridding the island of a pest? Parents had told the boys that with the frost the lemming would disappear. This had happened before, but the younger generation argued loudly that unless exterminated the lemming might find good winter quarters, start breeding in early spring, and by mid-summer be so numerous that all the grass and barley would be devoured by them — and so the hunt went on. Events proved the parents right, but the year of the lemming invasion stood out as a great event among childhood memories. Whence the lemming came and where it went remained a mystery.

Having crossed the low-lying swampy section of the island the youth turned from the path leading to his home and began climbing a high hill whose summit afforded a magnificent view of the surrounding country. He had told his mother he might spend the night at the trap, and acting on a sudden impulse he decided to have a look at the familiar scenery. On this hilltop he, Brother John, and their friends had gathered as children on the eve of St. John's Day for midsummer celebration with a blazing fire, an age-old ritual of the northland dating back to heathen times. The climb was short and easy, and the summit was reached as the sun was slowly disappearing in a large cleft of a mountain to the north of the fjord. With an unobstructed horizon the sun would have been visible throughout the night, but the mountain hid it for about two hours. For a brief spell in the summer this region had mornings without beginning, evenings without end. As the sun disappeared, complete silence stole over the island — the hush of the arctic night at midsummer. Land and sea, mountains and marshland, fields and houses were bathed in a peculiarly diffused light which left no shadow. The drone of the tidal current and the splash of waterfalls on yonder mountain emphasized the quiet of the night. The birds — larks, finches, cuckoos, thrushes, sparrows — were roosting peacefully on nests or in birches whose fresh fragance filled the air. Eider ducks swam silently along the shore leaving streaks of ever-widening ripples on the water. A small ship, its sails flapping, drifted lazily on the fjord. Even the gulls sat peacefully on the rocks. On a gray mountain to the south water glistened in the sunlight; the tiny glaciers and snowdrifts had a pinkish hue. Nowhere could be seen the cold gleam of a dying day, rather it was as if even the hard granite had borrowed the soft tint on the cheeks of a sleeping child.

As the youth gazed, the pale blue sky and the soft mellow light seemed at first to gather the isolated aspects of the landscape into one sublime unity of which he was a part. But gradually units became separated, the fjord and the distant ocean, jutting headlands and skerries, the mountains, the island with farms, marsh, and moor. The familiar sights, land and sea, the nearby church and school, the farmsteads, boathouses and boats, had this night acquired a new significance for the silent, serious youth. So had the people who dwelt in this land as well as those who rested in the graveyard close by the church. So had the stories and legends interwoven in the texture of the lives of these people; and so had the home with parents, brothers and sisters. Everything, even the memories, had today taken on a different meaning because he had decided to leave this land, the home of forbears for countless generations, the land of family and friends, of childhood and youth. Like a ship he would weigh anchor, cast loose from old moorings, cross the ocean, face the unknown in America — a land so distant that it seemed enveloped in a mist, mythical like the island in the sea of which tales were handed down from long ago.

When he was very young three cousins and a few others from the neighborhood had emigrated. Such action had then seemed one of dark, doleful significance. Letters from the emigrants had been infrequent; those that came told of life and conditions so different from anything found in the northland that they were like messages from another planet. Tales of California and the Klondike conjured up pictures of gold as abundant as in the City of God described in the Bible; stories of Indians and cowboys, of plantations with "darkies," and of prairie farms which required neither drainage ditches nor fertilizers had seemed more like figments of the imagination than anything based on fact.

In the previous winter a preacher who had spent some years at a Norwegian seamen's mission in Australia had described the feeling of loneliness and desolation which gripped one living far from his homeland. He had quoted:

> Wherever you go
> Be it east
> Be it west
> It will not
> Be your fatherland.

At high noon in bustling cities as well as at midnight in a lonely hut the ex-patriate would feel the call of the land whose soil was hallowed by the tears and toil, the blood and graves of ancestors. And the youth knew that the preacher spoke the truth, that while ships are free when they cast off to sail on the trackless ocean, the spirit of man has moorings which are not severed until the final curtain falls. He therefore wanted to carry pictures of the old land, its life and its people with him so that when oppressed with loneliness he could be transported and for a moment by day or by night live as he had in bygone days. As a boy he had spent much time alone, roaming by himself in hills and mountains and finding pleasures in recreating the lives of heroes of his books. Later, during long summer days as lookout at the salmon trap, he had reflected on many things. Thoughtful beyond his years, he had become unusually self-contained in matters of the spirit. And now he had decided to take with him to the new world treasures from the old which would always be his very own; he would keep within himself a retreat, a secret garden with flowers and greensward which could not be trampled upon and crushed by callous intruders. He knew that in the foreign land he would be a stranger among people whose language he did not know, whose habits of thought and ways of thinking were not his. He would be lonely, perchance suffer disappointments, defeats. Privacy and solace could then be found only in his own soul. For this purpose he had resolved to store up these pictures and impressions of familiar scenes, of the people with whom he was one in flesh and blood. For this purpose the youth had sought the solitude of the hilltop at midnight; from amid the ashes of old midsummer fires he scanned the wide horizon, visualized the life of the past, relived his own. During this summer night he collected treasures not made with hands, lasting, incorruptible; he gathered the gossamer threads of which old men weave their memories.

Chapter 2

Land and Sea ·

As the youthful dreamer looked around he became aware of the fact that all his life he had been surrounded by mountains. They had been a part of his existence from the very beginning, barriers to light and sunshine, walls that blocked the view but stimulated the imagination, towers reaching to the vault of heaven, ladders to the City of God. In this land the mountains, like everything else in nature, were personified by the people, each peak was a "he," each had character and individuality.

To the south was a row of remarkably symmetrical peaks. When he was but a baby he had had them pointed out to him, and when he was big enough to crawl up on a chair he had viewed them from the south window in the living room. There were nine peaks in all, and at noon the sun stood over the one in the middle. Just to the east of it the sun disappeared on November seventeenth not to be seen again until January twenty-fifth. As a boy he yearly saw the sun vanish — life giver that it was, sun was a "she" in the local dialect. Gradually it dipped lower and lower, one day it failed to clear one of the peaks, a day or so later another, and finally came that last day when only a glimpse could be had of the upper rim. And then no sun for more than two months. Sensitive to changes in nature, he had been oppressed by the dark period — with joy he had welcomed the first glow which hailed the return of the sun.

He had watched these peaks when the moon appeared to be

close to them — if only he could be on yonder high peak he might perchance reach the moon. As a child he had wondered but had been too shy to ask about that; an older brother might laugh and tease him. He had linked Biblical stories with one or another of these peaks. It had seemed fitting to have white-robed angels move up and down a mountain glittering with snow.

Beyond these mountains lay the southland, a land that invited dreams. He knew that in southern Norway the sun shone on Christmas Day. Sister Constance who had been in Christiania had told him about that — this seemed so strange. But farther, much farther south were lands with oranges, dates, palms. He had read about these and often speculated upon what they might be like.

On the eastern rim of the horizon loomed a gigantic mountain with a large glacier, the Blue Man's Ice. That man of the glacier, strangely enough, was a sower; at least so said Father. But the sower with full equipment, bag of grain on his back, a pan of grain in his left hand, was visible only during the warmest summers. At midsummer, of course, just a small portion of his body had emerged from its icy covering, but he was watched closely, and if the Blue Man finally acquired all his paraphernalia, the barley was sure to ripen.

The glacier was part of Sulitjelma mountain. East of it lay Sweden, a neighbor yet a foreign country. That idea had always been intriguing. To be in a land not one's own had seemed almost uncanny, and now he had decided to go much farther away to a land more foreign than Sweden. After all, a Norwegian could talk to and be understood by a Swede. Although they had often quarrelled, and just now it seemed as if they might fight one another again since the Storting of Norway had recently dissolved the union with Sweden, the Swedes were considered cousins. America and Americans were quite different. At times the thought of them made him shudder.

Sulitjelma had another distinction than that of a boundary and the place of the "sower." Somewhere between its ranges lay a copper mine. Neither the young fisherman nor any of his family had been there, but they had heard much about the life at that mine. A Sodom it must be. The miners were a wild lot, mostly Finns and Swedes, and of late some Norwegians he knew had worked there in the autumn from August until Christmas, when they quit to get ready for the fishery at Lofoten. The regular miners he had seen frequently at their semi-annual visit to the town of Bodö. Rough men they were, and a horror to the local police force of but two constables. When the miners were in town, brawls were frequent until all their money was spent — just enough left to pay the fare back to the mine, and often even that had to be raised by sale of the watches and fine clothes bought when they had first arrived in town.

Far to the southwest could be seen some of the mountains which lined the coast — row upon row of them, both on the mainland and on the islands along the shore. But the land was not all mountains. From the hilltop he could see the small islands which with skerries and submerged rocks formed an outer barrier all along the coast. Against this barrier broke the mighty waves of the Arctic Ocean. With awe and admiration he had watched great white-capped rollers dash against the granite cliffs and shatter into a fine spray which carried inland for miles. The roar of the coastal breakers on stormy winter nights was like the roar of distant cannon. In the shelter of home the sound engendered a feeling of safety, snugness. That, like much else he knew, he would miss in America.

The nearby landscape was a beautiful one, peaceful with summer lushness of meadow and hillside, the frame of mountains mirrored in the calm waters of the fjord. Across from the island on the north side of the fjord the land rose more steeply than on his island. Since this section was sheltered from the north wind by high mountains, trees, flowers, grass, and crops grew with amazing vitality — and this within the Arctics, twenty-three degrees from the North Pole, a latitude where Greenland is covered by glaciers. This was a new thought to the lonely watcher. Hitherto he had taken so much for granted. What a fair land this was — how enchanting its summer nights! And this was to be his last summer in the northland for perhaps many, many years!

Nights such as these compensated for the long dark ones· from September to March. During the winter the heavens yielded only a semblance of light. Often the sou'wester blew with hurricane force for days on end, dark clouds scudded across the sky, rain beat against the window, and the house shook. Yet, stormy nights were considered really bad only when brothers were away sailing or fishing. The worry for their safety was painful. On stormy evenings with everybody safe at home, Father would tell stories about olden times and events at sea.

On the shores of this fjord ancestors had lived for generations, indeed centuries. Family records in the parish register had never been examined, but Father, who had the instinct of an historian, knew genealogies and old family stories of the past 150 years. In his youngest son he had had an eager listener. This son now picked out the various places where forbears had lived. Here a great-great grandfather had been the one to clear and build a farm, there a great-aunt had fallen over a cliff. On the furthermost point at the entrance to the fjord a grandmother was born, Mother's mother whose life had been both intriguing and sad. A belle of the parish, she was much sought after, but one husband after another had met with accidental death. She had established a record for the region — four times married and four times a widow. Her grandson, born after her death, now looked at the four different places which had been her homes and reflected on the strange vicissitudes in the life of Katherine Arnsberg. As far as eye could see on both sides of the fjord there was hardly a spot without some connection with family history past or present. Most of the more than twenty different groups of farms, each separated from the other by pasture and woodland, included an uncle or cousin among their occupants.

Thus he was attached to this region by many and very

deep roots. But these roots were most firmly imbedded in the soil of the island where he was born and had lived his twenty years. There was nothing remarkable about the island except that he belonged here; this spot had become a part of himself. Here he had explored every square foot of ground. He knew where the cloudberry grew, where the blueberry and the whortleberry could be found in the greatest abundance. The berry crop of the barren and windswept island was limited, but strawberries and currants grew in secluded places, and in a little valley the choke-cherry could be found. He had many associations with these spots, several of which were, he believed, known to him alone.

In the winter he had skied and coasted on the hills and skated on the frozen marsh. When he was a very small boy his skis had been barrel staves, but at the age of ten he became the proud owner of a pair of real skis, a present from Brother Bernt. What a red-letter day it was when they arrived, how pleased he had been with his new treasure, and how angry when a boy at school had attempted to steal them. Ski-jumping was not common on the island; the skiers were content with sliding down hills and with cross-country runs. Regular skates he had never owned. Brother John and he had made crude ones from sections of discarded scythes fastened in pieces of wood and tied to shoes or moccasins with elaborately arranged cords. They were not suited for either speed or figure skating, but since this was the kind all the other boys used, store skates were not missed; the crude homemade ones had given much pleasure. Skating in the moonlight, especially when the sky was illuminated by the flickering aurora, had left memories to be cherished forever.

The part of the island now a marsh once had been a fine forest. Old pine roots had been dug up by the hundreds, and some of them showed evidence that the deforestation was at least in part due to fire. But most was no doubt caused by the need of fuel. One lone small pine was all that remained on the island of that type of tree. In dales and on hillsides the birch, alder, aspen, and rowan grew, but they were stunted by the severe winds of autumn and winter. The childhood home of the young man's father had been in a section of the parish where trees grew well. He had missed them very much, and on retiring he had tended with loving care the trees growing on his share of the old common land. It had been a struggle not against nature alone, but against poaching cottars and their goats which fed on the saplings.

The island was about four miles long and two wide with groups of farmsteads on the eastern and western ends. The western settlement was the larger by far, consisting of six farms on two of which dwellings of thirty cottar fishermen clustered by the shores of the tide current. The cottars fished in the summer in the current which usually had heavy runs of pollack. For the rest of the year they participated in the great seasonal cod and herring fisheries often far from home. Each cottar had a plot of ground sufficient for a potato patch and feed for a goat, some sheep, or a cow. For this land he paid a small ground rent in cash and a few days labor during haying, harvest, or potato digging. The prospective emigrant was the son of one of the four farmers who had no cottars on their land and whose farmsteads were at the foot of the hill where he sat.

Meditatively he examined these farms. Each consisted of about twenty acres fenced off for cultivation, plus some 300 acres of marsh and woodland. Only a part of what had been enclosed was actually cultivated. An embankment formed by an old coastline had relatively fertile soil rich in lime, but behind this narrow strip the soil was waterlogged and the imperfectly decomposed moss offered poor prospects for crops even after drainage ditches had drawn off the surplus water. Each farmer had a horse, four or five cows, some sheep, and small patches of barley and potatoes. Barley was a rather uncertain crop, but potatoes produced about tenfold; with salt fish it formed the staple diet. The story of the original clearing of these farms was hidden in the remote past. That it must have been very long ago, more than a thousand years, was evidenced by the huge mound, the accumulated débris of centuries, which marked the old common building-site of the four farms. Christianity was forced upon the people of this region by King Olav Tryggvason about the year 1000. Until the late eighteen-sixties the houses of all the farms were clustered on the mound, but with the consolidation of holdings only those of the so-called home farm, which belonged to the youth's father, remained on the old site. Hay for the cattle, potatoes for the household, and a little barley were raised on these farms. The only cash income from farming came from the occasional sale of an old ox or cow or a few bags of potatoes at seventy-five cents for a bag of 220 pounds. Money for fuel, flour, and taxes must come from fishing.

These little farms were fairly representative of the district of the outer fjord. While more waterlogged and less suited for grain growing than most, they were less rocky and yielded a better hay crop than many others. To the young man his father's farm seemed attractive both in comparison with others and because it was allodial (odel's) land, a farm held not only as freehold but one which for generations had been in the family. This was always a source of pride among the people of the north. They might be amphibian and spend much of their lives on the water, but their roots went deep in the stony soil. Furthermore, a yeoman rated much higher than the cottar or one whose subsistence depended solely on fishing. Until shortly before the turn of the century every freeholder irrespective of the size of his holding had the franchise, while cottars and fishermen did not unless their income was above a certain level. By and large the son of a yeoman was contented with his lot.

But a spirit of restlessness was inborn among the men of the northland. For some the urge to roam was satisfied when they participated in the periodic cod and herring fisheries, while others went farther afield, sailing the seven seas. Of his five brothers, four had followed the sea, one was a businessman, but he, the youngest, was poorly suited for either business or a craft and wholly unfit for the fisherman's or sailor's calling. His first love was books, his second the land. For financial reasons the former was beyond reach, and the prospects for land ownership were never bright in this arctic region.

Now he peered narrowly and critically at the farms of the island. Despite hard, back-breaking toil it was impossible to gain a livelihood from farming alone. Other countries offered better opportunities. Years ago Bernt had brought home literature on Queensland which told of free passage to immigrants. The prospectus was alluring — such marvellous grain, fruit and vegetables — but the land was far away and near the tropics so Bernt had not gone to Australia. From America had come many strange reports of the great prairies where the soil had no rocks and required neither drainage ditches nor fertilizer. All it needed for a harvest was plowing and sowing. It seemed incredible, so much so that an old cousin of his father's had declared she did not believe a word of these stories about the great American farms and the fertility of their soil. "That's all stuff and nonsense," said Maren Anna, "anyone with the least bit of common sense would know that grain could not grow without fertilizing the soil." And people listened to Maren Anna because she was so positive in her opinions. But there were reasons for believing that she was wrong. He had seen pictures of prairie fires as well as of farms on the great American plains, and as he gazed at this rugged northern landscape he tried to visualize what it would be like in a country without mountains and far from the sea. Newspapers carried enticing advertisements setting forth the advantages offered by western Canada where 160 acres of rich prairie land could be had absolutely free. The bait was tempting, but being of a cautious temperament he was not willing to gamble with the unknown in Canada; he preferred the land where many of his countrymen had found homes.

The tiny fields of the farm at home had always fascinated him. From time immemorial they had grown things. Within the last century the rotation of crops had been regular — barley one year, potatoes the next. The cultivation of potatoes established intimate contact with the soil. After the field had been plowed and dragged with the harrow, the potatoes were planted in furrows made with a pointed hoe. So that the furrows should be straight a rope was stretched the length of the field, and the one who made the furrow followed it with great care. After the potatoes had been planted they were covered almost lovingly to just the right depth. No sooner were the new plants visible than the weeding and hoeing began. Literally every particle of soil and every seashell in that field had been through human hands. He remembered how puzzled he had been by these shells in a field forty feet above sea level. They were identical with those found along the shore at low tide. Had the relation between sea and land actually changed? Then he remembered that the Bible spoke about the sea first, out of which appeared the dry land. These shells probably dated back to that remote period. They had been conundrums to him as well as to generations of other children. All had handled them, wondered, speculated. It seemed as if these children had left something of themselves in these fields, and so had he.

Mountains, land, and sea, these made up the physical world around him. By ship his forbears had come to the northland, the riches of the sea being the chief attraction. From the sea had come food and the only commodity exchangeable for grain and other articles needed for human consumption. The mountains fascinated, the sea alternately enthralled and terrified. It was bountiful — from it came the cod, pollack, halibut, herring, and salmon so indispensable for all the inhabitants. It gave much, but it also took its toll of human lives, causing ceaseless anguish and sorrow. Inviting on a calm beautiful summer night, thrilling when one skimmed over its surface under full sail, even this fjord could be repellent when lashed into fury by a sou'wester, or in the winter when the icy blasts from the Blue Man's Glacier caused steam to rise from the fjord like drifting snow, not warm soothing steam, but frosty vapor that chilled one to the marrow.

The fjord was a charmer; its shores were alive with mysteries. The rise and fall of the tide had seemed the greatest mystery of all. Slowly, imperceptibly, relentlessly the water would rise and destroy all walls and landmarks made by childish hands. And wonder of wonders, the barnacles which had seemed only crusty protuberances on the rocks, sharp ones that cut bare feet, sprang to life when the tide came in. From tiny lime ridges appeared slender tongues that moved in the water. That the sea brought life to seemingly dead things was curious indeed.

The mysteries of the incoming tide were as nothing compared with those left when the tide receded. There were so many strange and fantastic beings among rocks and seaweed — crabs, anemones, urchins, clams, snails, starfish and, under the rocks, myriads of creeping things. The different kinds of kelp and other seaweed had invited examination. Some were gathered in large quantities in the spring and used as food for the cattle. The supply of hay then generally ran low, especially in years when snow covered the ground until June. And when the bouillon of cod's heads was poured boiling hot over certain kinds of kelp, the cattle found the seaweed palatable. Later in the season stranded jelly-fish had stirred his curiosity. Exquisite were the pale blue geometrical patterns on some of them, and one had felt friendly to them until physical contact caused skin to prickle and eyes to burn. For the salmon fisherman the jelly-fish and floating seaweed were sources of constant annoyance since they clogged the lead as well as the net in the trap.

The eider duck was a common sight along the shores of the fjord. Omnipresent, it was regarded almost as a barnyard fowl. In winter as well as summer flocks of these heavy, lumbering birds hunted for food in the tide current or rested on the rocks. Though the bird was protected by law, its nest might be plundered, so favorite breeding places were safeguarded by the owners of the land who kept close watch during the nesting season. Since the tide current was rich in fish life, it was a favorite haunt for the eider duck, but the choicest breeding places were on lonely islands along the coast where the eggs and down of the eider duck constituted an important source of income for many islanders. The down which lined the nest was plucked by the bird from its own breast. This down was finer and fluffier than any from a dead bird and hence repaid the labor of ridding it of seeds and sticks which blew into the nest. At the regular breeding places the owners would take down from the nest once before the eggs were hatched, thus compelling the bird to pluck itself twice. With careful handling the birds returned year after year and would take possession of sheds and other outbuildings and even explore the possibilities of entrance halls as shelters for their nests. Knowing the habits of the eider duck the young fisherman had regarded it with special affection. He would miss its quiet, friendly quacks and the sight of the brown ducklings which were often carried on the parental back considerable distances before they reached the sea.

The other diving birds were relatively few, and the famous arctic bird rocks were found only along the outer coast. The cormorant was admired because of its black, shiny plumage, and the loon disliked because of its weird cry. Heard in the dusk of an autumn evening, it sounded like a human being in distress. Of the many other birds which gathered to feed on fish in the tide current, the arctic tern and the great black-backed gull had been particularly attractive. The tern was quick and graceful, and the gull was majestic whether at rest or soaring on the look-out for food, its black so absolutely black and its white so pure. The gulls acted as scouts for the pollack fishermen. When with raucous cries they clustered and dove in the tide current, the fishermen knew that the herring or other food for pollack was present. This bird life with its sight and sound was a part of the seascape as much as was the kelp, the jelly-fish, and the fauna of the strand. All this was fascinating — something forever to be remembered by one brought up on the shore of the sea.

Swimming had not been a favorite pastime for the water of the fjord was cold even in July and August. But though there had been no gay swimming parties at midday or midnight, there were many memories of fishing on the fjord. In days gone by Salten had rated among the famous herring fjords of northern Norway. Year after year late July or early August had brought the cry "herring has been sighted," a cry which caused the men to leave haying to women and children and rush for their boats. The herring was caught in the center of the outer fjord by fishermen who drifted with their nets at night, but the real excitement began when the school of fish chased by whales came close to shore. Then the seine crews got busy. On one great occasion in the early eighties the entire northern coast of the island had been girded with herring seines. What a turnout that had been; the spouting of whales, the screaming of gulls, the splashing of oars, and the shouting of hundreds of eager, excited men had reverberated between the mountains throughout the August night! It was a great year for the landowners as well. In payment for the use of their land they received a minute percentage of the catch. Each of the four farmers who held the fishing rights of the shore had then pocketed $ 500, a fortune for men who seldom saw even a ten dollar bill.

The herring is a fickle fish. The annual visits in the eighties had led the people to believe they would be as regular and dependable as those of the cod to the Lofoten islands. Fortunes were invested in boats, seines, and warehouses. Then the herring disappeared. Year after year the crews gathered at the usual time, scanned the horizon for signs that the herring was approaching, rowed about investigating with line and lead to see if it had sneaked into the fjord unheralded by gull and whale. Disappointment followed disappointment, and in the wake came financial ruin. It was a melancholy story even for one so young as the future emigrant. He had often heard the sad tale of foreclosures and bankruptcy. Four uncles had travelled that dreary road and from his look-out on the hilltop he could see the unpainted, dilapidated seine sheds of their establishments. They were now old men living on the memories of the past, especially memories of that great herring year of 1883.

For many seasons elder brothers had participated in the too often futile quest for the herring. Since childhood he had listened to the stories of past successes and present failures. They had made a deep impression, and he resolved not to tread in their footsteps.

It was different with redsnapper, pollack, and salmon fishing. His earliest recollections as a genuine fisherman were connected with the redsnapper. Too young to handle a pair of oars in the little boat used on calm days in the sheltered fjord, he and his next older brother, John, had each pulled one oar while Father fished. Some spots were only half a mile from shore, yet to an eight-year-old it had seemed quite a row to get there. The expeditions generally started early in the morning, which by mid-August meant leaving while it was still dark. The prospect of fishing had been attractive the evening before, but at 4 A.M. the glamor vanished. A hasty cold breakfast of milk and sandwiches and then off for the fishing ground. The habitat of the redsnapper was generally at the hundred fathom mark. The fishing line was equipped with a reinforced wire bow which had a short line with a hook at both ends and a heavy iron sinker in the middle. To detect a strike, the line had to be kept vertical, and it was the duty of the youthful rowers to hold the boat steady and off the line, a difficult task for young boys.

In retrospect, however, the fishing seemed pleasant. Since the family did not depend on fishing for a livelihood, Father had as a rule gone out only on still, sunny days. Then the calm fjord and the mirages on the western horizon with ships and islands suspended in air had been a source of constant wonder. It was exciting to wait for a fish to strike, and when it did to guess whether it might be the desired redsnapper or some other fish hardly fit for human consumption. At first the boy had been astonished to see the redsnapper appear with the stomach in its mouth and to learn that if it came off the hook part way up it would soon be seen floating on the surface close to the boat. It was fun, too, to speculate on which of the boats on the fishing grounds would get the most fish. The fishermen watched each other to see how far from the bottom the fish could be found for this distance varied from day to day and even between morning and noon. Because the light was dim at a hundred fathoms a difference of a few feet might make a great deal of difference in the luck of a fisherman.

Father would relate these and other secrets of the fishermen's lore while he waited for the redsnapper to bite. He followed a definite ritual in this fishing. When the fish was caught it was taken off the hook, the hook was rebaited while the boat was rowed back to what seemed the most likely spot on the grounds. Then as the line went to the bottom the fish just caught was cleaned and scaled. Though Father never ate nor drank on the fishing grounds, the boys were encouraged to have an ample lunch. Father himself might fish eight or ten hours without any refreshment, a habit he had acquired in his youth when fishermen generally had a very light lunch early in the morning and a hearty meal of boiled fish and fish liver at night — that was all. The redsnapper fishing was a fine school for training boys to be patient. Thirty fish were rated a good day's catch, sixty-three a record. Often they caught only a dozen. What was not eaten fresh or salted for home consumption was generally exchanged for firewood with farmers from the valleys. Sold fresh, the redsnapper usually fetched two cents apiece; salted the price had been a good deal lower. Those early days with Father and John lived in his memory, and so did the feeling of importance he had enjoyed when he landed with a good catch, and the pleasurable anticipation of an ample meal of redsnapper, liver, barley bread (flatbröd), and coffee. For some strange reason, potatoes, always a staple with salt fish, were in those early days never served with fresh fish. This was probably a custom handed down from the time when potatoes were a rarity — not farther back than in grandparents' time. But recently the custom had changed and potatoes were now served with fresh fish, too. This was among the innovations of the youth's own lifetime.

By the time the boy was twelve, he had fished alone with his father for John was then away sailing with the elder brothers in the small ship which the family owned. In those days father and son had grown better acquainted despite the more than fifty years difference in age and the fact that both father and son were naturally reserved.

The tide current which almost encircled the island enjoyed

fame as one of nature's great marvels. The inhabitants of the district contended proudly that their "Salt Current" (Saltstraum) was more of a phenomenon than the Maelstrom at the western islands of Lofoten. Among famous visitors to Saltstraum had been King Oscar II of Norway and Sweden and Emperor William II. The young man recalled with some regret that attendance at church the Sunday Emperor William was there had prevented him from getting a glimpse of the famous kaiser. Visits by tourist steamers and millionaires' yachts provided interest and variety for this secluded corner of the world, made it seem important, and somehow caused the local cottars and farmers to feel that they, too, were important because they lived there. Did they not have the privilege of viewing every day what the great ones of the earth travelled long distances to see? Hands in their pockets, chewing tobacco slowly and deliberately, the fishermen would stand on the cliffs by the narrows and watch the swirling current. In the summer when the water of the fjord was brackish from the melting snow, it put on a great show at spring tide. Foaming and thundering, it spewed spray like a waterfall; the uneven cavernous bottom produced sudden upthrusts of swirls of water and gigantic whirlpools which deflected ships from their course and sucked even large boats into the deep. What power! The mail steamers arranged their schedules to fit the change of the tide, and a special signal system guided ships carrying ore from the copper mine at Sulitjelma. Not even the whale could breast that current. Mighty it was, and also mysterious — ruled by a force beyond this globe; it was so regular, so untiring; it fascinated yet repelled.

The Saltstraum was responsible for the island's relatively large population of cottars. The whirls and sudden spouts of the rushing water brought both fish and hazards, and a special type of boat had been invented, a boat that could be easily maneuvered amid the whirlpools of the current. The cottars had become real experts at this art. When schools of pollack appeared the fishermen would rush even into the most dangerous parts of the stream; one of the two men in each boat would cast the line in the right place while the other calmly and skillfully maneuvered the craft on the rim of a large whirlpool which threatened to pull the boat under at any moment. In the course of years the Saltstraum had taken many lives.

None of the youth's own family had become skillful pollack fishermen, nor had Father ever encouraged his boys to fish in the tide current. From their earliest youth he had urged them to be cautious. Even so, the current with screaming gulls, jumping pollack, and fishing boats rushing, twisting, and turning had always formed a part of life's fascination in that arctic area.

One summer day many years ago a sailing boat had cast anchor by the island. From it had come two men in a skiff. They rowed along the shore, studied its general contour, and paid special attention to a point which formed the western end of a wide-sweeping shallow bay. Then they approached the four farmers who had the fishing rights to this shore. They were salmon fishermen from southern Norway — they believed they had found a good site for a salmon trap, and they requested permission to start fishing. This was granted on condition that the farmers would get 8 per cent of the value of the catch. Thus salmon fishing was introduced in this section of Saltenfjord. A few years later the farmers bought the trap and then another for a second site. This was the type of fishing in which the youth had been engaged for several years. At the turn of the century a brother had leased a trap site on the mainland, the site the youth now had, and care of these traps in addition to the work on the farm kept him busy from early May till the end of July.

The salmon traps were nets equipped with cork floats and rocks as sinkers. Anchored a distance from shore, the nets were so arranged that the salmon drifting along with the current would first encounter the lead, following that he would enter the trap which was contrived in such a way that the fish kept running into false openings until the fisherman came and emptied the trap. Salmon thus caught had been on their way to spawning grounds, rivers farther in the fjord.

To ensure that the fish should not become extinct a law regulated the size of the meshes of the net so all salmon below four pounds could escape; the law also stipulated that the traps should be closed or taken ashore between 6 P.M. Friday and 6 P.M. Monday. This had of course resulted in grumbling among the fishermen; nevertheless they faithfully obeyed the rule. Over the weekends the nets were usually brought ashore, cleaned, repaired, and to prevent the hemp from rotting they were twice a month soaked in a tanning extract made by steeping birchbark in water.

In his early teens the youth had taken his place with the older men in all work of salmon fishing. He had enjoyed their companionship and talk. One of them had sailed on the high seas for a year. He had taken trips to Hamburg, Bremen, and Rostock — short voyages for a true sailor, but because Haakon had a knack for story-telling, his brief experience as a sailor supplied him with material for stories the rest of his life. Everybody knew that most of these yarns were made of whole cloth for Haakon had the reputation of being a great liar and rather malicious to boot, but his stories were well told and held enough of truth to provoke discussion.

This particular season, 1905, with the crisis in Norwegian-Swedish relations, had proved quite exciting, and news was gleaned on the frequent trips to Bodö, where the salmon was sold either to housewives or to buyers who shipped the fish to England. The town was reached by crossing the fjord and then walking about two and a half miles; the fish was usually transported in a wheelbarrow which the men took turns pushing. Sometimes they had loads of 200 pounds or more so the trip called for real exertion. Bodö had about 4,000 inhabitants and was the capital of the province ("amt") of Nordland, which with an area of 15,000 square miles was one of the largest provinces of Norway. It was a bustling little town in the summer; tourists on their way to the North Cape rushed ashore from the coastal steamer to get a look at the surrounding country from a mountain close by; fishermen crowded the streets on their way to the various fishing grounds; and once every summer the miners from Sulitjelma would "paint the town red." To the boy from the country it had seemed a real metropolis.

On his first visit to Bodö the youth had had his full share of that feeling of inferiority which grips the country-bred child in town. He had heard about the officials in their gold-braided uniforms, about stores so well stocked with merchandise that they were veritable emporia compared to the country store near home, and about the splendor of urban dwellings and the carriages of the townsmen. Yes, he had been impressed, but the dust and dirt had not pleased him and he had been glad to return to his home in the country.

Now for several summers he had been a regular visitor to Bodö, sometimes as often as five days a week. The feeling of inferiority had vanished. To be sure, he saw that the townspeople were better dressed and that they ate wheaten bread while his was of rye or barley, but these were minor matters. With two companions he brought the fish to town, and when it was sold they went to a lunchroom for skimmed milk to wash down the sandwiches they had carried from home. The youth knew few people and was anxious to leave as soon as the business was finished. Haakon and Hans, on the other hand, were eager to collect new stories from the sailors and fishermen who gathered in stores or at street corners. Since these men were long-winded and circumstantial the homeward departure was often long delayed.

Far from envying the city dwellers, the youth had come to pity them; he had acquired the farmer's and fisherman's pride in having no boss, no time-clock to punch. He was his own master. Sailing home in the afternoons with the cool sea breeze he had thanked his lucky stars that he did not have to stay in Bodö; striding across the meadows on the parental farm he rejoiced that he was not a townsman. Land and sea had shaped and molded him. From ancestors and his surroundings he had acquired a deep and abiding love for nature and all the things God had made. These had fortified him with impressions so deep and lasting that wherever he went they would be with him — yes, even in far-off America.

.

Chapter 3

Lofoten and the Cod Fisheries

ROCKY, ROUGH, MOUNTAINOUS, deeply indented by the sea was the landscape which the young man viewed. The soil was poor and the growing season was always short — three months of uncertain summer after the nine months of winter. Often snow began to fall in the middle of September, and not infrequently it remained on the ground until midsummer. With ceaseless toil and limitless patience this land had been cleared of rocks, drained, and brought under cultivation. Truly, it had been won by the Norsemen; it belonged to them, and their attachment to it was deep, boundless. This pull of the land, unfathomable, half spiritual, had been felt since childhood. To break away meant laceration of the soul.

Almost equally strong was his attachment to the sea. Here he had sailed and fished, or just drifted and dreamed. The sea was fickle, variable, temperamental; it bewitched and it challenged, it was generous and exacting in turn. Sometimes its bounties were bestowed in ample measure, then again it yielded nothing, and day after day nets and lines were empty. Today the boat might glide over friendly, sunlit waves, tomorrow the ocean would be an angry death-dealing fury to be fought with every ounce of strength, with all the skill which years of experience could muster.

It was the fish in that sea which had lured the first settlers northward even to the North Cape, less than 1,300 miles from the pole itself. Of the many species of fish taken from the sea, the most dependable and valuable was the cod. Caught the year around in small quantities, the cod twice each year appeared in shoals which filled the sea. At midsummer it followed the caplin to the coast and into the fjords of Finnmark. As it feasted on the hapless caplin, fishermen caught the cod by the millions and cured them for the overseas markets.

While the cod fishery of Finnmark was important, at no time in the history of Norway had it played a rôle comparable to that at the Lofoten Islands. Several factors combined to make the Lofoten fishery unique in the economic and social life of the country — its season was during the stormy winter months from January to April; the locality, close by one of the most magnificently picturesque regions found on this globe; the long history of this fishery, whose origins went back to the dim era before written records; and the fact that it had never absolutely failed so that it always attracted fishermen from below Trondheim to the northeast boundary with Russia at Jacob's River. Thus had Lofoten won a special place in the annals of Norway.

From childhood the young man had heard about Lofoten. The life at these islands and the cod spawning on the ocean shelf in the lee of them had produced an inexhaustible wealth of stories and memories for fishermen and sailors. Lofoten had become a source of dreams and fables for the child, a place where youth was tested, where the boy passed from adolescence to manhood. Fascinated he had listened to the Lofoten lore told by a father who for forty winters had fished there, by five older brothers who had been at the grounds every winter since they reached the age of fifteen, and by a host of friends and relatives. The fishing stations, lighthouses, methods of fishing, all had been described long before he had his first glimpse of the Lofoten Alps.

These mountains were so different from anything he was likely to see anywhere in the world that purposely he had fixed in his mind pictures of them as they loomed in the distance from the southern side of the Vestfjord, as they appeared near at hand, as they looked garbed in the white mantle of winter or in the gray and green cloak of summer. They were majestically impressive and awe-inspiring from any distance and at any season of the year. On his first trip to Lofoten he had stood in the bow of the steamer as it passed the island of Landego and watched the Lofoten "Wall" come into view from its eastern limit, the entrance of the fjord leading to Narvik, to the westernmost of the series of islands forming a great arc some sixty or seventy miles from point to point. At Landego only a row of jagged peaks was visible; they looked like spires resting on the sea. As the ship drew nearer the mountains assumed the appearance of a vast continuous wall with bastions and turrets. Out of the sea they rose skyward for two or three thousand feet; they were smooth and steep and had challenged the skill of the most experienced Alpinists. The ship seemed ready to crash into a granite wall before channels were sighted, channels that led into snug harbors.

Benefiting by the warm waters of the Gulf Stream and sheltered from the cold northern winds by the high mountains, the Lofoten shores of the Vestfjord enjoy a relatively mild winter temperature whose mean is barely freezing at the western end of the island chain. A score of fishing stations and villages dot the area. Two of them, Svolvaer and Kabelvaag, were fair-sized towns, but the other stations consisted of only a few stores, some fairly pretentious dwellings, ware- and boat-houses belonging to the owners of the stations, frames for drying fish, and in several places hundreds of cabins occupied by fishermen during the fishing season. Since the resident population was small, schools and churches were found at only a few of the stations. The first impression of these islands was, what an abundance of rocks! Everywhere rocks of all shapes and sizes, and mountains towering above men's tiny abodes looked as if the gods in a sportive mood had experimented with fantastic types of architecture. The mountains alternately oppressed human beings or carried them upward into realms of dream and fantasy.

At sixteen the youth had spent his first winter at Lofoten as a telegraph messenger. Since then he had worked there three other winters for Brother Bernt, who was manager of one of the stations. He had learned to know hundreds of fishermen, listened to their stories, talked with them both when the catch was good and when they returned with empty boats, joined them in services at the local meeting house, sympathized with them when comrades had drowned ("remained" was the idiom) on the grounds. By birth, upbringing, and experience he was one of them; he knew and understood them. He regretted that no more would he watch Lofoten fishermen depart for the grounds in the gray dawn of a winter morning and return as dusk settled over the harbor. He would miss them.

On his first trip across Vestfjord he had recalled the historical rôle of the Lofoten fisheries. None would ever know who was the first man to learn of the annual migration of the cod to those waters. One thing was certain, it was very long ago. Even in the tenth century powerful chieftains lived on these islands, and early in the twelfth century a king of Norway had built log cabins for the transient fishermen. In the middle ages the dried cod of Lofoten had been the great staple of Norwegian export, a source of wealth to the merchants of the Hanseatic League who then controlled the trade of the north and who cheated the fishermen mercilessly. The false scales used by these merchants were, he knew, among the prize exhibits at the Hanseatic Museum in Bergen. When the power of the great Hansa was broken many of its employees became citizens of Bergen, and as exporters of dried cod they continued their old German practice of robbing the fishermen. By bribery or political pressure at the then capital, Copenhagen, they prevented the establishment of trading posts in northern Norway. Every summer the men of the north, their dried fish stored in the holds and piled high on the decks of their broad-beamed, square-rigged vessels, took the catch to the Bergen merchants. The latter by agreements among themselves fixed the price on the fish they bought and on the grain, hemp, cottons, and other goods which they sold. Somehow the fish, fish-oil, and salted roe never seemed adequate in the barter with wily merchants reared in the Hanseatic tradition. From the time the ships from the north dropped anchor till the crews left for home, the men were preyed upon. Peddlers, jugglers, brothel keepers joined the more respectable burghers of the city in defrauding the men from the northland of the fruit of their toil at the Lofoten fishery. The fishermen were always in debt to the merchants of Bergen.

It was the cod which had saved the population of northern Norway in time of war and famine. During the Napoleonic period when British ships blockaded the Norwegian coast and a succession of cold, rainy summers ruined the domestic harvest, the cod and the cod's liver kept the people alive. In that period, 1807–1814, fishermen arrived at Lofoten with practically no bread in their provision chests. On empty stomachs they left in the morning for the fishing grounds, but in the evening they feasted on the cod and its liver. Fish and liver were boiled in the same pot, the oil was skimmed off, in it they soaked what little bread they had, eating both oil and bread. It was a monotonous but healthy diet, one that preserved the strength of these men despite the hardship of fighting arctic seas. At home wives and children subsisted on dried and salted fish, thin gruel, and milk. The potato had not yet been introduced. The fishing population had survived fairly well through the famine years — the cod was the lifesaver.

Father had been inducted as a full-fledged fisherman in 1847 when he was only fourteen. At that time all boats were without cabins, open and square-rigged. On the voyage to and from Lofoten the crew slept either in the boat with the sail as tent or in boathouses or other outbuildings along the route. Famous among these stopping-off places was Grötöy on the southern shore of Vestfjord where hundreds of fishermen might gather to wait for favorable weather before risking the trip across this wide and turbulent sea. The hardships of the voyage were increased by the difficulty of making fire. If the tinder got damp it might prove well-nigh impossible for stiff and numb fingers to start a much-needed blaze. Indeed, life on the voyages to Lofoten in Father's youth was practically identical with that of the Viking era; even the boats had not changed much in structure and equipment during the intervening thousand years.

Conditions at the fishing stations, too, were as primitive as they had been for many centuries. In 1847 lighthouses were non-existent. The only warnings of treacherous reefs were the sight and sound of breakers; it took a keen eye and a steady hand to guide the boat on a winter night through the winding channels of the Lofoten harbors. At the stations the men lived in small cabins with dirt floors and open fireplaces. Crowded at all times, the cabins afforded little more than standing room when storms drove additional boats into the harbor. Cabin rent, rent charged on the frames where the fish was dried and on facilities for producing fish oil, and profit from their stores made many of the station owners rich. They formed an aristocracy which vied in pomposity with the officials of church and state. Proudly, Lofoten families such as the Normans and the Ellingsens traced their genealogies back to the nobility of medieval Norway. There was a feudal and at times even patriarchal tinge to the life of the Islands.

Since the Lofoten fishing took place in the dead of winter the weather was always uncertain and generally stormy. Though the great mountain wall was a shield, it also obstructed the view to the northwest whence came the most disastrous storms. The morning might be calm and bright, and before daybreak the fishing fleet went out to pull the nets. Suddenly in the dim light of the short day snow would be seen churning on the peaks and almost at the same moment the blow came; roaring through the passes rushed the nor'-wester whipping the sea into a foam with spray that froze on oars and tackle. Since the boats were not rigged for tacking there was no choice but to try to reach harbor by rowing against the off-shore gale in the raging, blinding snowstorm. To lighten the boat, fish and nets were dumped overboard, often to no avail. Ice loaded the boat and encrusted the men. They rowed till arms were numb. If they failed to reach an island, as a last resort they would make a desperate attempt to run before the wind across the thirty-mile stretch of the Vestfjord on the chance of finding a harbor on the mainland. With all reefs down they scudded through the Arctic night, snow blanketing the sea. As they neared land their only guide was the foam and thunder of breakers. The least error of judgment, the slightest of wrong move with the tiller, would result in a capsized boat, a futile clinging to the keel, peace among the kelp, and the ocean chanting *requiem aeternam.*

Father had never "ridden the keel," but Grandfather once had and been saved at the very last moment. Among Father's stories the one which left the deepest impression was that of the experience he had in 1863. With Mother's brother, Uncle Salomon, he started fishing at the very westernmost of the Lofoten Islands, an independent group called Röst which differs from the real Lofotens in being low-lying, surrounded with hundreds of reefs and skerries. Because of the great hazards of fishing at Röst the grounds had been abandoned for several seasons until Father and Uncle Salomon decided again to try the fishing there. On their first voyage, the day at dawn seemed favorable as four boats set sail from the harbor of Helligvaer. When twenty of the forty miles of open ocean had been crossed, darkness descended and with it came an arctic blizzard. Of the four boats, two were fairly large, two were small, all were square-rigged. At the head was one of the larger boats whose helmsman was the only one of the company who had ever visited Röst. Behind the leader followed the two small boats sailing side by side with Father steering one of them. Uncle Salomon with the second large boat sailed at the rear. On land Uncle Salomon was "crazy as a loon," but with his hands on the tiller none in the north-

land, said Father, was calmer, swifter, and surer in his judgment than Uncle Salomon.

The four boats raced before the wind toward an unknown,
uncharted, unlighted coast, with sight and sound muffled in
a maze of swirling snow. Suddenly a breaker came from nowhere, roaring, foaming, bent on destruction. The helmsman
on the boat beside Father's judged wrongly, the boat capsized
and Father could neither stop nor turn. But the lookout on
Uncle Salomon's boat saw the accident; in a split second orders
and action followed. Down went the sail, straight on the
overturned boat steered Uncle Salomon, his crew hanging
over gunwhales to seize the men in the water. They were
pulled in from both sides; all but one was rescued — gone he
was, and no search was possible.

The second year Father went to Lofoten, 1848, was tragic in
the annals of that fishery. January had been stormy, and a
large part of the fleet from the south was delayed in crossing
the Vestfjord. One Sunday morning in February the outlook
seemed promising. The fleet left Grötöy in fair weather; half-
way across the Vestfjord a fierce sou'wester overtook it.
Father, who had already reached his station, Oersnes, went
that day to the neighboring station of Henningsvaer, about
seven miles farther west, with some gear for another boat.
After·more than forty years the events remained fresh in his
memory. "It was quite calm when we started," said Father,
"But the western horizon looked strange and one of the men
said jokingly, 'Today it dawns in the west.' That opening
in the leaden western sky meant a wind of terrible force was
coming. Shortly after we had reached Henningsvaer it was
upon us. Never have I experienced such a blow — it was impossible to stand upright, and it seemed as if all of the Arctic
Ocean was rushing in. Skerries which usually made a good
breakwater for us simply disappeared, and mountainous
waves tore the boats and ships from their moorings. The
boats which had crossed the Vestfjord came riding in with
only the bare mast, and we men on shore formed human
chains to grab the boats and pull them and their crews to

safety. But despite all we could do, boats capsized and many of those men drowned in the breakers. In that single day more than a hundred lives were lost at Lofoten."

In the days of small open boats drownings were frequent. With no mail or telegraph service, information did not reach the bereaved till spring came. Day after day the families of fishermen scanned the horizon for the well-known sail. Sometimes it failed to appear. The loved one was lost; he had "remained." Finally the news of the tragedy would be brought by a friend or neighbor. Quietly as behooves a bearer of dread tidings, a boat would slip in to the landing; out of it would step tight-lipped men. They felt deeply, but their words were few. Silently they carried ashore the sea chest and gear of the drowned man. Gravely they told the story of that terrible night when husband, father, son, or brother fought his last fight with the Vestfjord.

For hundreds of years throughout the arctic nights the men of the north had faced cold, storms, and an angry sea in order to obtain a modest livelihood. Generation after generation of boys had anticipated the time when they could prove themselves men at the Lofoten fisheries. It had been a stern school for all, a superb training in seamanship and in communal living. The fisheries had brought joy and victories, but they had also brought stark tragedy and defeat. The Lofoten Alps had been beautiful and majestic on winter nights when the aurora flashed across the sky, seeming to touch the peaks, but they had also appeared like angry, man-eating giants bent on the destruction of feeble mortals when a howling nor'wester rushed from their cliffs and caverns and tossed fishing boats like cockleshells amidst mountainous waves. Teeming with life is the sea that washes the islands of Lofoten; much it has given the men of the north and much it has taken away.

Marvellously regular has been the visit of the cod to the spawning grounds at Lofoten. About the middle of January it moves in on the ocean shelf which stretches from three to twelve miles from shore into the Vestfjord. The fish often appeared simultaneously along a front sixty miles long. From whence they came no one knew, and by the middle of April they had vanished. While on this shelf the cod is constantly pursued by man with nets, hand lines, and long lines. When Father first went to Lofoten nets and hand lines were used; later the long line became the most common method of fishing. This gear was cheaper and more quickly replaced than the nets — hence its popularity. The square-rigged boats built on the model of the Viking ships were gradually superceded first by boats having fore and aft sails, handy for tacking, and later by motor-boats with dories. The last type of fishing craft put in its appearance about the time the young man first visited Lofoten. When he was a small boy a fleet of newly-built square-rigged boats with white sails had emerged from the tide current by his home every winter; generally they came on a bright day with a brisk east wind. The boats were lithe and beautiful, like white-winged gulls skimming over the water. He had watched them till they disappeared from view. Built in Saltdal at the head of the fjord where timber was plentiful, these boats would be used by their original owners for one season, tested in every way, and then sold to fishermen from other parts of the country. Of late no such fleet had been seen on the Saltenfjord.

Many other changes had occurred at Lofoten in the nearly sixty years since Father first went there. Lighthouses now showed the channel at every harbor, and the fishermen's cabins were larger, lighter, and fitted with floors and stoves. But the beds were still bunks with boards instead of springs, and for three months or more the cabins often housed ten or twelve men in one room. Now every station had regular mail service, as well as telephone and telegraph over which came reports daily of fishing and weather conditions in the entire area. The villages had reading rooms, and stations without church or chapel had a meeting house for religious services, lectures, and discussions. Several small hospitals had been built, and the fishermen received medical attention and hospitalization free. "Yes," mused Father, "things have certainly improved since I was young."

New fishing methods necessitated government regulation.

The introduction of long lines forced division of the fishing grounds between fishermen using nets and those using lines. Rules were drawn up fixing the morning hour when the fishermen might start and prohibiting fishing on Sundays except when inclement weather on Saturdays prevented the boats from going out. Not Sabbatarianism but the desire to preserve the fish was responsible for the ban on Sunday fishing. Unfortunately this regulation was often violated. Net fishermen whose gear could operate without attention for two or three days grew suddenly timid on Saturdays; after much scanning of the horizon they frequently decided that the weather seemed too threatening to go out, so the nets were left on the grounds till Monday. Otherwise the Lofoten fisherfolk were scrupulously law-abiding; men of their own choosing acted as inspectors and assisted the police officers in trials for violation of regulations.

The fishermen's self-discipline and respect for law had filled the young man with pride in his race. At the station where he had been about a thousand fishermen and sailors gathered each winter. They came from as far south as Bergen and as far north as the North Cape. In age they varied from fifteen to sixty, the overwhelming majority being young. There was only one policeman, and except for collecting data about the number of boats and ships and the daily catch, his job was a sinecure. Brawls were unknown; in four seasons the young man had seen only two men drunk, one of whom was that year's policeman and the other a baker on holiday. This, too, represented an improvement since the time when liquor was sold at the fishing stations. Then men disappointed with the catch or bored by storm-enforced idleness occasionally sought to forget their troubles in the age-old remedy, became bellicose, and went berserk. But prohibition together with the growth of the temperance movement had put an end to the fights at the fishing stations. The fishermen's hatred of blind pigs was so strong that in 1895 they had risen against illegal purveyors of liquor at Stamsund. The men raided the blind pigs, poured their stock into the ocean, and tossing into the sea the owners who resisted, routed them all.

In normal years nearly 6,000 boats with crews totalling about 35,000 men gathered at the Lofoten fishing stations. Several hundred small ships varying in size from 20 to 100 tons took aboard the fish that was salted. Hundreds of men were employed in the factories which extracted the oil from the cod's liver. Other hundreds worked in the stores for the owners of fishing stations or served the needs of the large transient population. In Father's time the fishermen "boiled" the liver to extract the oil, and cured their own fish. The usual method then was to tie the fish (cleaned and minus their heads) by the tails in pairs and hang them over poles placed on frames along the shores of the harbors. This, the celebrated "stockfish," was neither split nor salted; it was dried in the air, and it was usually sold to Italy. The other method of curing the cod was to split and salt it heavily in the holds of vessels gathered at Lofoten for that purpose. In the spring the fish was removed from the holds, scrubbed in sea water, dried on rocks, taken to Christiansund, Aalesund, or Bergen and from thence shipped to Spain or South America. Cod-liver oil was extracted by placing the liver in steam-heated containers. With amazement the young man had watched employees at these factories drink the oil like water; healthy the men looked, but somewhat greasy as well. The cod's roe, a great delicacy early in the season until it became too "ripe," was salted in barrels to be used as bait by the sardine fishermen of France. Thus the cod gave employment and income to hundreds of thousands, and provided valuable products for export to foreign lands.

Before the advent of the motor-boat, the individual fisherman owned his own gear, whether net or long line, and the catch was divided in equal shares, one of which went to the boat's owner for its use. Boats fishing with nets generally had crews of six — those employing long lines, five men. It was a democratic arrangement, each man had fixed duties, and the skipper was simply the first among equals. Only a man tested in the skills of sailors and fishermen could get a good crew, and if he failed in an emergency he might be removed from his post by his own men. Birth, wealth, and social position mattered little among the fishermen; only the real leader, the proved expert, won recognition. On the whole they were a brave, honest, independent, clear-eyed group of men, men who never deserted a comrade, who without question or hesitation risked their own lives to save others.

They were as keen and merciless in their criticism of mistakes in the handling of a boat as they were generous in their praise of heroic deeds. The coward and especially the "nithing," the one who was both cowardly and deceitful, received short shrift. The brave and honest man who had saved lives at sea and was known never to have lost his nerve or failed in an emergency had his praises sung from one end of the land to the other. The nithing was rare, the hero not uncommon. Among the heroes of the sea those in the life-saving service were treated with special respect. Smacks designed to sail in any kind of weather cruised among the fishing boats on the grounds most exposed to the fury of the Arctic Ocean. If a storm arose, close watch was kept of every boat, and if one seemed to be in difficulty or capsized, the life-saving craft was on the scene in no time, oil was poured on the sea, and lines were thrown to the men in the water. Although the work was exceptionally hard and dangerous, there was keen competition for posts in the life-saving service. Better men than those found in that service have never sailed the sea. To the casual observer the fishermen might appear slow, even sluggish; and slow they often were on land, hands in their pockets, chewing their tobacco and voicing their opinions with measured deliberation. But watch them aboard their boat! They understood its action under sail, how to handle it in storm amid shoals and breakers. Alert and keen they were, action followed order with lightening-like rapidity. On land they might be uneasy, even self-conscious; on the sea they felt at home.

The tenderness of these rough, horny-handed men was as great as their loyalty and courage. The youth recalled how while a messenger boy at Lofoten he had been clumsy with an axe and cut his foot. A crowd gathered immediately; a total stranger carefully removed the boot; another bandaged the wound with real skill; and a third, who believed he could stop bleeding by some mysterious incantation, rushed to his cabin to get the necessary materials. Another day when two men were overcome by coal gas in the cabin of their boat, volunteers to get a doctor and move the men to a hospital far exceeded the needs. That they lost a day's fishing thereby was a minor matter. Perhaps the most striking evidence of the value placed upon human life and the sympathy felt for the families of drowned comrades was shown when a boat capsized with the loss of two lives. The news spread quickly, and scores of fishermen met at the store as they usually did when something important had happened. Most of them had never seen the drowned men, but one thought seemed to fill everyone's mind: "What if this news were for my family?" All had the deepest, most sincere sympathy for those struck by sorrow.

With few exceptions all the fishermen were poor; many lived on the brink of destitution. They were in debt at the store at home for provisions to tide the family over the winter months, and although they generally brought a fair amount of supplies to the station with them various things had to be bought in Lofoten on credit till the fish had begun to run. The run might be a bit later than usual, perhaps it failed at this particular station, or, worst of all, as the run started, a week or two of storms made fishing impossible. To the failure of the catch was added the certainty that much gear would be lost. Life seemed dark indeed. Slowly by twos and threes they gathered at the store. Gloom prevailed. The storm, which like all hostile forces in nature had a masculine gender, was an implacable enemy; "he" would keep on blowing till the cod had gone. The season would be a total failure. Dejectedly they watched clouds scudding across the murky sky. But after a while some one in the crowd would begin to reminisce. "Now, listen," he would say of such and such a year "the outlook was just as dark as it is now at about this time in the season, but the fish were late and we made a good catch," or "I remember one year when at this station we got nothing but we moved further east where there was a great run, and we came home with money in our pockets." If it were very late in the season, the messenger of cheer would recall what a marvelous success the fishing in Finnmark had been one year when Lofoten had failed. Thus gloom was dispelled and the men returned to their cabins with new hope and courage.

Fishermen the world over experience many sudden and drastic changes of fortune. Those at Lofoten were no exception. Although the cod came every winter the catches fluctuated a great deal. In 1895 the catch numbered about 35,000,000 fish; some four or five years later the total was only about 15,000,000. The whole industry seemed a game; days, even weeks, of idleness might be followed by a spell of the most intense activity. Having hauled in nets or lines for a long period without a fish, the fishermen might suddenly find them so weighted down that the boat could not carry the catch. Similarly, northern Norway is a land of extremes, months of light are followed by months of darkness. The stillness seems so absolute, the storms so violent; the line between paucity and plenty is often quickly crossed. Standards common elsewhere become useless in this land of excitement, and all this is especially true of Lofoten and its fisheries.

The congregation of so many thousands of men from widely separated parts of the country stimulated exchange of ideas, spread new songs, and legends, promoted a feeling of unity, a spirit of co-operation among the people. Political and economic issues were discussed sometimes with heat, but generally without anger. The chief topics when our young man was at Lofoten were the question of a perpetually closed season for whales along the coast, the union between Norway and Sweden, the Russo-Japanese war, international relations, and socialism.

The fishermen were unanimous in demanding that whale-hunting should be forbidden in the Arctic Ocean because they believed the whale helped to drive herring to the coast. They favored continuance of the union with Sweden provided the Swedes would recognize that it was one of partners absolutely equal. During the war in the Far East their sympathies were with Japan. For generations Russia had been the bug-bear for the people of the north. Despite the trade between the White Sea region and Finnmark when every summer some hundreds of Russian vessels brought grain and flour to that province in exchange for fish, the suspicion was deeply rooted among the Norwegians that Russia wanted to annex northern Norway because of its numerous ice-free harbors. Stories of Russian spies popped up every year and were told and retold at Lofoten. Without exception these spies, always saw-grinders, were described as wearing shabby outer garments and fine linen shirts. Engaged in work requiring little skill, they were said to be excellent map-makers. None of the fishermen had actually met any of these mysterious strangers; they simply knew someone who had encountered the Russian saw-grinders.

The hostility between Norwegians and Russians was one of long standing. In the Viking age Norwegians had raided the regions of the White Sea, but later when Norway became weak and Russia strong the raiding had been reversed, and the people from Finnmark told tales of churches and settlements which had been razed by marauders from Archangel. At one time representatives of Norwegian kings had exacted tribute from the inhabitants of the Murmansk coast, but the boundary settlement of 1826 which fixed the frontier at Jacob's River was considered a defeat for Norway. She was thereby deprived of good fishing grounds. It was firmly believed that Russia intended to continue her westward expansion in order to secure control of the provinces of Troms and Finnmark. This question had assumed international significance in the middle years of the nineteenth century, and the treaty of November, 1855, whereby Britain and France guaranteed the territorial integrity of Norway and Sweden, gave much comfort to the inhabitants of northern Norway. Nevertheless, they watched with apprehension the building of railroads through Finland toward the borders of Norway and Sweden. The policy of oppression adopted by the tsar in Finland was viewed as a preliminary step for an attack upon Scandinavia.

The russification of Finland begun at the turn of the century with compulsory study of Russian in the schools of Finland, the drafting of Finns for service in the armed forces of Russia, and other attacks upon the autonomy of the country, sent shivers through northern Norway. The sympathy for the Finns was strong and widespread; it was voiced by the great nationalistic poet of Norway, Björnstjerne Björnson, in a moving lyric: "A moan wafts through the forest. From the Land of the Thousand Lakes. It comes from a nation in peril."

A sprinkling of Finns among the fishermen added poignancy to the discussions of the Russian danger. Russia stood for the things most abhorred by the Lofoten fishermen — economic and political oppression. The use of the knout by Russian police officers, the wretched state of her peasantry, and the horrors of Siberian concentration camps were elaborated upon and discussed with much animation. Fantastic stories were told about the inhumanity of the Russian government. In the winter of 1905 a red-headed Finn had solemnly related that naval reservists among crews of Russian vessels visiting Finnmark in the previous summer who had been convicted of wilful neglect in obeying summons to join ships of the Baltic fleet were sentenced to be burned alive. "Yes," said Nels the Finn in all seriousness, "they were burned, just think of it! What beasts those Russians are!" Not everybody believed this tale, but with great unanimity the fishermen hoped that Japan would trounce Russia.

Some of them had sailed the high seas, a few had been in

America, and many had relatives there; nearly everyone read newspapers and all were interested in what happened in the outside world. The great powers were regarded with a certain distrust. France was of course far away and her republican form of government appealed to the individualistic and democratic society of fisherfolk. But since Frenchmen were reported to be either atheists or Catholics, they were not admired. With the Germans, Norwegians had the strong bonds of kinship and religion. That Martin Luther, Paul Gerhardt, and Johann Sebastian Bach had been Germans atoned for many of the sins committed by the German merchants in Bergen. Moreover, Kaiser William II visited Norway every summer, had a cabin on one of the Lofoten mountains, and had acted with great promptitude in dispatching aid when the city of Aalesund was practically destroyed by fire. On the other hand, his bombastic sermon every New Year's Day to the German fighting forces, reports that warships of his squadron took soundings in Norwegian fjords during his summer cruises, and that he sympathized with the Swedish point of view in the dispute over separate consular and diplomatic service for Norway dampened the enthusiasm for him and his country.

About Britain feelings were curiously mixed. On the debit side were the blockade of 1807—1814, the attack upon the Boers, and the belief that Englishmen considered themselves superior to other people. Yet seafaring had created a bond of sympathy, stronger among those who didn't go to sea than among those who did. An impression existed that the English government favored the Norwegians in the disputes with Sweden, and all nourished a deeply-rooted conviction that Britain would protect Norway against Russia. Among the great powers of Europe Britain was the most favored by the fishermen.

The United States held a unique position. Everybody was awed by accounts of American speed and efficiency. Reports of the tall buildings in New York and Chicago, the speed of American trains, and the life in American mining camps aroused admiration as well as misgivings. The land seemed so strange, its society almost inhuman. It also attracted the natural curiosity of men who had travelled a good deal and listened to tales of adventures since their childhood. Indeed, few topics within the range of ordinary human experience were not discussed at the stores and in the cabins at Lofoten.

Marxian socialism was little known among the fishermen until after the turn of the century. It so happened that at the station, Kalle, where the young man worked, a number of boats hailed from the parish of Karlsöy in the province of Troms. A merchant there had for many years swindled the fishermen until they found a champion in their parish priest, Dr. Alfred Eriksen, who brought the merchant to his knees and thereby became extremely popular. Dr. Eriksen represented the unusual combination of a minister in the state church and a socialist. He was elected to the Storting (the Norwegian Parliament) by admiring fishermen, who followed his parliamentary career with the closest attention. Every boat's crew from the parish of Karlsöy contained one or more subscribers to the stenographic reports of the Storting debates; Dr. Eriksen obliged his constituents by speaking frequently. In the evenings or on days too stormy for fishing the men took turns reading aloud these speeches, and the *pros* and *cons* of every political or economic question were then discussed. The words "capitalism" and "capitalist" came into common usage. Most of the fishermen were a bit vague as to the meaning of the former; the latter was, of course, used as a label for anyone who did not agree with Dr. Eriksen. These debates stimulated discontent and superceded that older topic of general interest—religion. In cabins which formerly resounded with the singing of Lutheran hymns, men now strove to fathom the mysteries of Marxian economics.

As a class the fishermen had always been religious. Their life was full of enigmas. The origin of the majestic scenery and of the mighty forces which they fought invited questions and speculation. The good and beautiful came of course from God — the bad, ugly, and unpleasant from the devil. Aware of their own impotence, they believed that they were in the care of an all-good, omnipotent and omnipresent Divinity and so gained peace and contentment. Nearly every one of the Lofoten fishermen had had experiences which seemed inexplicable except for the guiding hand of Providence. They recalled how all of a sudden they got the inspiration to try their luck fishing at a new place where they had obtained a large catch; or when at another time they had by a miracle, it couldn't be anything else, escaped drowning. Escapes from drowning were the experiences most often cited as proof of divine guidance. A raging snowstorm and the arctic night had hidden all landmarks, none aboard knew where the channel was. Then by mere chance the lookout man had discovered a black streak, a dark ribbon between the foam of breakers. Steering for it had brought them to safety. But the next day the channel was not visible. Providence must have had a hand in steering the boat, human skill alone could not have guided it into this harbor; evidently the days of the crew "had not yet been numbered."

Trying, even soul-searing, experiences had fallen to the lot of most of them. The young man recalled the story of the drowning of his cousin, Adolph Salomonsen. Off Röst one winter day the fishing fleet was caught by a sudden storm and rushed for harbor; an unexpected breaker filled Adolph's boat, which sank immediately, the men clinging to oars and other wreckage. Half a mile behind was the boat of Adolph's younger brother, Ingvald. The man in the bow reported that a sail which he believed to be Adolph's had disappeared. They had three reefs down in the mainsail. Ingvald ordered them taken out, the brother and his crew must be saved. In a few minutes Ingvald reached the scene; his lookout shouted that he saw men floating on oars. His crew lined the gunwhale. With sails lowered he steered close, but his men bungled. Letting the tiller go for a second Ingvald grabbed two of the men in the water; with superhuman effort he jerked them both to safety. But Adolph had gone down; the brother was lost. Quickly Ingvald seized the helm anew, for the boat was amid reefs over which broke thunderous waves. He brought it safely to harbor and then collapsed. Yes, Cousin Ingvald was a fine sailor. One day early in April, 1903, a terrible storm had broken while a large part of the fleet was still on the grounds. The fishing covered so wide an area that the one life-saving smack could not possibly survey it all. The fishermen who had reached harbor gathered to select boat and crew to man a second life-boat. By popular acclamation Ingvald was chosen to be the skipper. He had gone out and saved many lives. And now this fine young cousin was fighting a losing fight against tuberculosis, another great enemy of the fisherfolk.

Such experiences at sea had made the fishermen religious, and their religiousness generally found outlet in song. They liked to sing lyrics, ballads, and especially the great Lutheran hymns. One Sunday the young man had attended service at the parish church in Vaagan, Lofoten. The bishop of the diocese preached the sermon that day and the big church was filled to overflowing. Men sat everywhere, in the aisles, on the altar railing, in places generally closed to the congregation; the fishermen simply took possession of the church. Though Bishop Boekman, dignified with flowing blond beard and a large gold cross hung from a chain about his neck, spoke eloquently of life and death, faith and salvation, somehow the impression of the sermon had vanished while that of the singing remained. Two thousand powerful male voices had sung "A Mighty Fortress is Our God"; they sang with conviction; their singing dominated the service and drowned the great organ. Equally memorable and moving was an Easter service at the meeting house at Kalle. Conducted by an ordained minister but in a place not consecrated as a church, the service was extremely simple, a prayer, a sermon, and hymns. Here there were about 700 men present, and the hymns were songs of joy, of victory, victory over death, the enemy which faced them daily. Whole-heartedly they sang, these men who lived bravely and walked humbly before God.

Such were the young man's impressions of Lofoten, the cod

fisheries, and the men who plied their dangerous trade in the Arctic Ocean. He knew they would stay with him wherever he went, "Be it East, Be it West," be it across the wide Atlantic.

Chapter 4

Church and School

RELIGION AND THE CHURCH had played a very important rôle in the life of the young Norwegian. Both parents, Mother especially, were deeply religious with strong pietistic leanings. Early in the nineteenth century a lay preacher of southern Norway, Hans Nielsen Hauge, had led a revival against the dead formalism then prevailing in the state church. He ran afoul of legislation against unlicensed preachers and was imprisoned. Released after a few years, he never resumed preaching, but his earlier activities had started a movement which exerted a quickening influence upon the religious life of the country. Shortly after Norway gained self-government in 1814, the law forbidding lay preachers was repealed and soon men imbued with the zeal of Hauge traversed the length and breadth of the land.

In its early days the Haugeaner movement had been influenced by the German pietists, and Mother had often talked of Spener, Francke, and others of that school. From her the young man had learned of Count Zinzendorf, the Moravian Brethren, and the school for girls at Herrnhut. Mother was keenly interested in this pioneer effort in women's education; she resented the injustice of excluding her sex from educational opportunities. From her side of the family had come books of sermons which were read aloud on the Sundays when services were not held in the church close by home. In these collections were the sermons of the German, Ludwig Harms, and the Swedes, Rosenius and Lars Linderot, the latter a hell-fire preacher unpopular with the children. Late in the nineties these were replaced in his home with sermons written by Norwegian churchmen whose ideas were more easily understood by the younger generation.

Eldest Brother Astrup was "converted" as a young man, and to the family library he added the books of the Englishman, Charles Haddon Spurgeon, and the American, William Vaughn Moody. In lay circles the influence of England and America replaced that of Germany, a change due in part to the missionary activities of American Methodists. Mother and Brother Astrup's interest had made the home a center for religious meetings. Among the young man's earliest recollections was that of speeding around the neighborhood announcing that lay preacher so-and-so had arrived, and soon the living room of his home would be tightly packed with people sitting on benches rigged up for the occasion. Father who was a deacon in the church had once been reprimanded by the rector for opening his house to traveling lay preachers. Father's sharp reply that none could dictate to him what sort of meeting could be held in his house, as long as the preachers were orthodox Lutherans and everything was done quietly and in a proper manner, had left a deep impression on his youngest son. Father was evidently not afraid of anybody.

Although it was Father who led the singing and read the sermons in devotions at home, Mother talked more about religion, especially during passion week. The gloom which prevailed in the house on Good Friday was so heavy that the children looked forward to Easter Sunday almost as eagerly as to Christmas. From an old book Mother had learned the expression "die Stille im Lande" which had been applied to the German pietists, and she liked to think of herself as one of them.

At five the youth had learned to read, and Mother often urged him to read the Bible aloud to relatives and friends who came to visit. He had plowed through the Old Testament, stumbling over the strange names, puzzling over the meaning of the word "begot," and wondering at the longevity of the patriarchal "begetters." He had been intrigued by the Old Testament stories and confused by the morals of their heroes. That David, the shepherd boy, became king was exciting, but his later conduct seemed hardly befitting of a man of God. Reading of the miracles performed by Jesus, the boy had often wished something like that would happen to cure his eczema. It was hard to be house-bound with the burning, itching rash while other children were out playing.

With such a home background the church quite naturally assumed an important place in the youth's imagination. It seemed very mysterious and filled him with awe. Stories told on winter evenings, stories about gatherings of the spirits of the dead in the old parish church and about tolling of church bells in the night intensified this feeling. The church was the largest building on the island. Erected on a prominent spot, it had a slate-covered roof and a coppered steeple whose spire towered so high it was almost lost in the clouds. And its bells were something wonderful when they were rung by the sexton; to be able to climb up where they were hung and to watch them being rung had long been the boy's ambition.

He recalled the first time Mother took him to a church service. With wonder he had looked upon the throng of people, the immense auditorium, the altar which, he was told, was an especially holy spot, and the minister in his white surplice. Memories of church attendance were a curious combination of how cold the auditorium had been in the winter and of the large number of children baptized at Whitsuntide. Because the church was unheated and because most of the fathers were away at Lofoten in the winter, baptisms were postponed until the first fine Sunday in the spring. Then what a spate of families congregated for the sacrament!

Completed in 1886, the church near his home had been considered quite grand, but it could not compare with the main church of the parish on the other side of the fjord on the road to Bodö. The true age of the parish church was unknown — the date usually given was the thirteenth century, a time so remote that a child's mind could not grasp it.

Around the old church, which had once served as parish church for an area of hundreds of square miles, centered many legends of the district. Nearby had stood the residences of the secular officials for the entire province. The parish priests had almost always been men of outstanding ability. All his brothers and sisters had been baptized and confirmed in the old church. Here Father and Mother had worshipped until quite recently; it had been the holy place for ancestors during many, many generations, and in the surrounding churchyard they all were buried. The parish church of Bodin had therefore assumed great significance; it seemed a place even more sacred than the church which he saw every day.

When he was six, Sister Julianne was confirmed, an event of deep significance in the lives of all country children. Preparation for this rite included a five weeks' course of religious instruction given by the parish priest. The classes were held in the parish church every day of the week except Sunday so Sister had to get lodging close by and be away from home for the first time in her life. This was, of course, of keen interest to the youngest brother. He learned that occasionally a candidate for confirmation failed to meet the standards of knowledge about the history of religion and the dogmas of the church, a failure which proved an indelible disgrace. He learned, too, that on confirmation Sunday all the candidates were lined up in order of their rating in the subjects studied. To be among the highest was the ambition of all the ablest candidates; to be number one was a badge of distinction worn throughout life. But in discussions about this grading of confirmation candidates he discovered that not only ability but the social standing of the parents were determining factors in the children's rating, a custom which puzzled him — it did not seem fair. Deeply concerned about his sister's welfare, he joined with the rest of the family in hoping that Julianne would achieve a high rank. His relief was great when he found she had succeeded.

Confirmation was still held only in the parish church. The religious aspects, the renewal of the baptismal vows and the participation in holy communion had no meaning for the little boy. The exciting thing was that he with Brother John, Mother, Father, and Sister Julianne would have lodgings close by the church the weekend of confirmation Sunday. This involved many "firsts" — crossing the fjord for the first time, nights away from home, a view of the old parsonage and the mansions of important people, and, above all, a first visit to the far-famed parish church. Mother took him to visit her mother's grave, that of the almost mythical Katherine Arnsberg. Graves of other ancestors seemed to have been forgotten; no markers had been placed on them; he knew only that his ancestors rested somewhere in this plot which had been used as a graveyard for more than 600 years. With solemn respect he read inscriptions on monuments denoting the burial places of sheriffs, judges, merchants, big landowners, and other prominent persons. Inscriptions on the outside walls of the church aroused special interest, and he was told that some people had even been buried under the floor of the church itself. A real marvel was a glimpse of the windows of a room in the parsonage known as the "chamber of the Prince." Here, he was told, had lived a real prince who later became King Louis Philippe of France. That a French prince had actually lived in this very place and walked these same paths seemed like a fairy tale.

The climax of this wonderful trip came on Sunday when he entered the old church about which he had heard so many stories. It had box pews some of which were reserved for the leading families of the parish. The child was fascinated as he watched them enter; in the church at home all pews were open. On the walls and on the panelled pulpit were pictures of the apostles. The dim light in the choir gave this part of the church an air of oppressive solemnity; it was indeed a holy place. He sat very still, overcome with awe. Then all of a sudden the organ burst forth. He had never heard anything like that before! At home there was no organ. A teacher led the singing and occasionally a man in the front, wanting to attract attention to himself, would sing much louder than the rest. But in the parish church the organ dominated; it was truly marvellous. The service, however, proved too long for the little worshipper. In addition to the usual hymns, prayers, and sermon, there was the catechization of the confirmation candidates. Mother and Father listened eagerly and critically both to the preacher's questions and to the children's answers. Did this class show the same mastery of Bible history and Lutheran dogma as had those of bygone years? To his parents this was the most important part of the entire service. Not so to the boys. They were bored, and finally he and Brother John were allowed to leave the church. Once outside John, who was of an exploring turn of mind, decided to investigate the loft above the auditorium. This he did and returned to report that he had seen many strange images. Doubtless they were the effigies of saints whom people had worshipped in days of long ago when all were Catholics. The boys had been told that Catholicism was a heathenish practise, and the youngest brother was glad that he had not seen the old idols.

Yes, that initial visit to the ancient parish church was an event of first-rate importance. Four years later the main part of the building was torn down. Although the church was rebuilt, the interior was modernized, and the box pews were eliminated, the private ones with all the rest. Through this remodelling the church seemed to have lost much of its sanctity. The cemetery around it was abandoned, and a road now passed through those grounds. Human bones uncovered in the digging had been lumped together in a deep pit. Bicycles, wagons, and carriages traversed the former burial ground. To shorten the road a few rods in a place where no one was ever in a hurry, the cemetery had been desecrated. His parents like all others of the older generation had bemoaned this act.

As he recalled the discussion about the road and the old grave-yard, the young man realized that his own attitude toward burial grounds had changed. When he was a child he had been afraid of them; people said that ghosts roamed among the graves. His eldest brother had died when the boy was eight years old. Brother Astrup had always been very kind; it was he who had given the boy the first pennies he ever possessed. At the funeral the whole family had gathered around the grave as the minister intoned, "ashes to ashes, dust to dust;" they had listened to the awful 'thump,' 'thump' as shovelsful of dirt fell upon the wooden casket. The words and that sound of falling earth had haunted the boy for years; he had heard them in his dreams. Often he had fancied that the funeral was only a nightmare, that Brother Astrup was not really dead, that he had just gone away on a trip. It had been a soul-searing experience. The cemetery with the brother's grave was visible from the hilltop; he could see the rowan planted there. But now the old pain was gone, only regret and wonder lingered, wonder at what life would have been like for the family had Astrup not died when he was thirty-one.

Sunday church services gave the people of the parish an opportunity to come together. Many of them lived on lonely farmsteads, separated from their neighbors by mountains or sea. In their toilsome lives weekdays could not be spared for visits to friends and relatives, but at church they all could meet. Those who lived farthest away usually came first; an hour or more before the service began a crowd had collected outside the church. There was much handshaking and many inquiries about health, prospects for crops and fishing, and reports of recent events. The Sundays when the men had just returned from fishing stations or from trips to sell the cured fish were rich in conversation. Full accounts were given of storms, accidents, the winds on particularly hazardous ocean stretches, of failures or successes. Although in true Norwegian fashion the tone of conversation was always subdued, the general scene was one of animation, friendly smiles, cheerful greetings. Here swains met maidens, old men and women exchanged reminiscences, and craftsmen took orders or delivered products. The deeply religious and highly respected Arnoldus Torstensen was here delivering to customers the excellent drills made by hand in the smithy on his farm. Here, too, was the frivolous Constance Field inquiring about the best dressmaker or making special efforts to attract attention to her new hat. Poor Constance! A buxom lass, she had the broad hips and general build of girls who work in field and barn, climb mountains, herd sheep, or pull an oar for father and brother on fishing grounds. Unlike most of her class she was exceedingly unhappy about her figure. In a fashion magazine she had seen pictures of girls with wasp waists. Longing to be like them, she bought a corset with stout stays. Too tight to be worn during the week when she was working, it was donned only with holiday attire. She pulled and tugged to make her waist-line small, and one Sunday as a result of these efforts she fainted in church. After that Constance Field was a much talked-about girl.

As soon as the minister was sighted down the road, the church bell rang. As he drew near, the crowd parted, hats flew off, and he passed through the lane of parishioners. They were in no hurry to follow him into the church for parts of the service such as burials or the confession affected only a few. The rest remained outside until the ringing of both church bells announced that the minister would soon mount the pulpit. Then all entered, quietly and reverently they took their seats, the men to the right and the women to the left. A few newly married couples or some very old people might break the convention that husband and wife should separate in church. For couples to sit together was a recent innovation, as was the wearing of rubbers and overcoats or women's hats. The sermon over, the majority of the congregation left the church to resume their visiting outside. Only a handful remained for the baptismal and communion services and the occasional wedding, all of which took place after the sermon.

Perhaps these men and women were a bit casual in their worship, but religious and even pious they were in their own way. Stirred by reports of conditions among the heathen of Africa and Asia, they contributed liberally out of their limited means. Many a widow's mite went toward the maintenance of missions in China, India, Natal, and Madagascar. Visits by missionaries from these fields always attracted large crowds who felt deep concern for the benighted heathen. Most of the work for foreign missions was carried on through ladies' aid societies which met at the various farm houses. While the president read aloud from the *Journal of Foreign Missions* the other members sewed on articles to be auctioned off once a year. These mission auctions held on Sunday afternoons in schools or private homes supplied another form of semi-religious diversion where people met and discussed mundane as well as spiritual matters.

Mother was a devoted supporter of foreign missions. The young man recalled with a tinge of regret that she had made him return a toy sailboat costing all of thirty öre which he had bought from a comrade. He had so much wished to own the boat, and the money had been his, earned by selling blueberries he'd picked, but Mother had said the pennies ought to be given to the mission, so with a heavy heart the boy returned the boat and put the money into the mission chest. When one of the missionaries, Nielsen-Lund who had made a great name for himself with his work among the Sakalavs of Madagascar, came to the parish he stayed at the youth's home. While he was there he urged the boy to train for the mission field, but for that work he felt no special "call."

In recent years interest in the total abstinence movement vied for attention with the various missionary enterprises. The organizational meeting of the abstinence society was held at his home when he was ten years old. A young school teacher initiated the project, and in what the boy had considered a very moving speech she depicted the evils of drink and urged her audience to take the pledge. He and Brother John, feeling extremely virtuous and brave, had signed up. John later found that pledge a real help to him. As a sailor before the mast he visited many of the world's largest seaports. Going ashore after the long voyage the crew usually indulged in the proverbial spree. Moderate drinkers found themselves in trouble, but when John told his comrades that he had been a total abstainer since childhood, he was left alone. Among sailors there was no half-way mark.

Before the total abstinence society was organized there had been quite a lot of drinking among the fishermen; afterwards, one rarely saw a man drunk. The youth knew of only two or three who were alcoholics, and one of these, Hammond Dinesen, had left the parish. Another, Jörgen Johansen, had gained possession of a large fishing boat and celebrated by getting drunk. In his drunken state he set out to recruit a crew. With great solemnity he assured prospective crewmen that he would be a careful skipper. "If a wind comes up," said Jörgen, "I'll furl all the sails." This unseamanlike promise made him forever the laughing-stock of the area.

The third weak and thirsty soul was Norman Hansen who alternated whiskey with spiritual jags. After sinning came repentance and abject confession. But the state of grace never lasted long; he would soon backslide and start the round afresh. During his periods of "conversion" Norman gained the sympathy of the island's more respectable people who rejoiced at the return of a prodigal. They never ceased to hope that the conversion would prove lasting. This fleeting prominence gave Norman his greatest satisfaction in life; his own family was the poorest of the poor, intellectually weak and totally undistinguished.

The community as a whole had experienced few of the religious "awakenings" common in southwestern districts of Norway. The ministers of the state church who frowned upon these spiritual eruptions wielded much influence among the fishermen, so most lay revivalists turned their attention to more promising sections of the country. Only one notable "conversion," that of Johan Olufsen, had occurred within the youth's memory. Johan who had been considered very wild, had gained notoriety as the author of ribald songs about episodes from the Bible, the best known of which was a ditty on King David and Bathsheba. Johan's conversion had been genuine. He became a lay preacher and planned to train for missionary work in Africa, but his life was cut short one stormy day at Lofoten.

Occasionally the abstinence societies and the various missionary organizations had a district convention. This was known as the Big Meeting; it was attended by representatives from neighboring parishes and addressed by celebrities of more than local reputation. The promoters of missions had a Big Meeting almost every year, a particularly active group being the one which supported work within Norway. This "home" or domestic mission competed for contributions with the societies which financed missions to the heathen. The latter were actively aided by the pastors of the state church who not only belittled the need for lay preachers in Norway but looked upon them as rivals who might become leaders of dissenting movements. The preaching laymen on their part accused the pastors of lack of spiritual insight and fervor, insinuated that many of them were not converted, and charged that they failed to set proper standards for a true Christian life. Gatherings addressed by lay preachers were held in private homes or in school houses; only on rare occasions when a duly ordained minister was present were the Big Meetings held in the church. The youth recalled that one time when the crowd was too large for any other building his father had assumed the authority to allow use of the church by a lay preacher, a man known for his strict orthodox Lutheran views. But this was a bold and unusual action.

Dissenters such as Methodists were few and found only in the towns. Although free to worship as they pleased, they were considered queer and irreverent people who held heretical doctrines altogether foreign to the country. Somehow Lutheranism had become identified with Norwegian nationalism, and the youth had been shocked when he learned that in Trondheim the Catholics actually had a small church dedicated to the old patron saint of Norway, the martyred King Olav Haraldson.

Every other year religious education was inspected by the

dean or the bishop, the dignitaries alternating their visits. On such occasions school children over twelve and the members of the two last years' confirmation classes were questioned orally in the church. Those still of school age were examined first by their respective teachers and then catechized as a group by the bishop or dean. The young people who had been confirmed were tested by church officials only. As in the case of confirmation, the examinations covered Bible history and phases of Christian doctrines as interpreted by Lutheran ecclesiastics. Teachers, rated on the performance of their charges, were careful to question the brighter pupils most often. None of the children really grasped the meaning of difficult scholastic terms like "regeneration," "justification," and "sanctification," but a verbatim recital of the answers found in the appropriate Lutheran "epitome" was deemed satisfactory.

The catechization was followed by a pastoral sermon in which the dean or bishop addressed himself principally to the youth, their parents, and teachers. These visits often left a deep mark. Although political considerations occasionally influenced the choice of bishops, the men selected were generally of outstanding ability. The young man thought of the dignified Bishop Boekman and his eloquent admonitions in his pastoral sermon on the text, "Be thou faithful unto death, and I will give thee a crown of life." Deans seemed less imposing perhaps because the rectors of the parish of Bodin were also as a rule deans. Well known locally, they created little stir on their special visits. However, the present one, Dean Diedrichson who was rector at Bodö, had the special distinction of having been born far away in Wisconsin, U.S.A., where his father had ministered to the spiritual needs of Norwegian immigrants. On Dean Diedrichson's last visit he had spoken with fervor on a verse from the Psalms, "I was glad when they said unto me, Let us go into the house of the Lord." This sermon gave new significance to the white church at home, for the young mind had been profoundly moved by the comparison of this simple, wooden church with the gorgeous temple on Mount Zion, and with the emphasis placed on the theme "the kingdom of God is within you."

After each of these visits by bishop or dean a special meeting of deacons, teachers, and other parishioners interested in the moral and religious life of the people was held in the parish church. The high ecclesiastic then inquired into the conduct of all parishioners, the church attendance, the observance of the ten commandments (among which those dealing with blasphemy and adultery always seemed the most difficult to obey), and discussed other matters of importance to a Christian congregation.

These periodic visitations and consultations emphasized the religious aspects of life and strengthened belief in the dogmas of the state church. They also gave children a chance to distinguish themselves in public. Lacking self-confidence, our youth was filled with apprehension during the catechizations and never did so well in them as did Brother John whose mental reactions were quicker, and who had less fear of making mistakes.

Although sometimes aloof and a bit snobbish, the parish clergy were closer to the people than were the other state officials. Old men and women still called the priest "Father," a custom traceable both to the practice of Catholic times and to the fact that the pastor had often protected his flock against dishonest secular officials and rapacious storekeepers. The officials had greatly improved since 1814, but the storekeepers still were often guilty of sharp dealing with poor and trusting customers. Then the clergy would come to the aid of parishioners.

Moreover, there was the tradition that in emergencies the clergyman would help to protect his people against marauders. In the winter when all able-bodied men were at Lofoten lonely farmsteads were sometimes terrorized by roving Lapps or other lawless persons. This had occurred in the neighboring parish of Skjerstad when Mother was a young girl. A band of Lapps came to the isolated settlement of Alnes where there were only two farms. At first they behaved like ordinary beggars, but on seeing that the only male inhabitants were a very old man and two boys of thirteen the unwelcome visitors took possession of the place, raiding the storehouses and feasting to their hearts' content. The boys were able to sneak away and, crossing the fjord, they went to the rector for help. The Reverend Mr. Sandberg immediately buckled on an old sabre, returned with the boys to their home, and cowed the outlaws. They were tied up, and until other aid came and took the band off to the Bodö jail, the rector with drawn sabre stood guard over them. Mother had seen them as the sheriff took them to jail, and the story of this episode had been told and retold on many winter evenings. Such events belonged to a past which now seemed very remote. Peace and security had long prevailed in the land.

With the introduction of the telegraph, news of drownings at Lofoten or elsewhere was generally sent to the parish pastor who then bore the sad tidings to the bereaved family. For two winters in succession tragedies had befallen fishermen from the island. In each case all the crew had been lost and the pastor had to call at five separate homes. These episodes bound him closer to his parishioners. But except for such visits and an occasional call to administer holy communion to a dying person, the clergyman seldom entered the home of the average family.

Many laymen refused to accept in humble submission all the views of the pastor. A reliance on the validity of private judgment and a belief in the equality of all men before God was deeply ingrained in these quiet, independent folk. Lay preachers, despite the fact they had little or no formal education, were often thoroughly familiar with the Bible and the writings of Martin Luther and the church fathers. They frequently argued with the minister on questions concerning infant baptism, absolution, free-will, and predestination. These discussions stimulated thought, broke down social barriers, and helped to create a certain amount of mutual respect.

Because school and church were administered by the same governmental department, and because so much time at school was devoted to religious instruction, the two institutions were closely linked in the minds of the people. Though Norway had had compulsory education for a long time, educational progress had been slow at first because the country was very poor and sparsely populated, especially in the northern provinces. Not until the early nineties had the parish of Bodin secured separate schoolhouses; the one on the island was completed the year the youth began his education there. Before then classes had been held in the living room of one of the cottars' houses or in an upstairs room in the teacher's residence.

Father and Mother were much interested in education. In their childhood the teachers in the country schools were often men unfit for the strenuous work of farmers and fishermen; not infrequently these teachers were indigents who had picked up the merest smattering of elementary learning. Lame Daniel had been Mother's teacher. Poor fellow, he knew only enough to be able to drill the children in the rudiments of religious education, but luckily many of the country folk considered this the only education worth having. They felt that though people must learn to read in order to know the road to salvation, all other education was pernicious or at any rate useless. The compulsory education law was denounced by some as legislation which inflicted hardship on the poor, and sometimes this was true. Cottars had been fined because their children were kept out of school so they could work for the family.

He recalled incidents from his years in the island's one-room school-house, and he wondered if fate would permit him to attend school in America. He had enjoyed school. The teacher, a graduate of one of the state normal schools, had been an able and conscientious man and a strict disciplinarian. Woe to the boy who caused any disturbance and to any pupil who had not mastered the day's lessons. Frequently ears were boxed and knuckles rapped. The dunce's corner was filled almost constantly.

There were three divisions of children in their school district with each class never exceeding twenty-five pupils. The program for each division consisted of three four-week terms with an interval of eight weeks between every term. This arrangement brought children of about the same age and level of achievement into the school together. The youth began school when he was seven years old, and from then until his sixteenth year he attended classes there for an annual total of twelve weeks. Much was learned for the stern schoolmaster, Ole Beck, not only assigned a great deal of home work during term, he outlined lessons to be completed between terms as well. Called at eight in the morning, school lasted till two-thirty in the afternoon, with only half an hour for lunch and a fifteen minute recess forenoon and afternoon. The six-day school week was crowded with studies, and dull pupils had tough going.

In the winter, school meant trudging across the half mile of windswept marsh while it was still pitch dark, on the return the daylight had faded. One and sometimes two periods a day were devoted to religious instruction. Other subjects taught daily were reading, writing, and arithmetic. The history of Norway, geography, natural history, drawing, and singing came only on alternate days. Most of the religious instruction consisted in memorizing questions and answers from an epitome of Lutheran doctrines. In other subjects texts were also learned by heart, and with an occasional bit of discussion interjected, were recited back to the teacher. History had been a favorite subject and, allowed to work independently of the rest of the class, he had read widely especially in the history of Greece and Rome. This study had given him pleasure, and it had come in handy in discussions with older people who always showed the greatest respect for factual knowledge.

The walls of the schoolhouse were lined with maps. Before school opened in the morning the children tested each other on names of oceans, islands, promontories, and mountain peaks. Jawbreaking foreign names such as Cape Chelyuskin, the strait of Bab-el-Mandeb, or Mount Kilimanjaro held special fascination. Names of Norwegian towns, fjords, rivers, and mountains were memorized with an avidity befitting sons and daughters of sea-farers.

During his boyhood, circumstances had combined to arouse a special interest in history and geography. Shortly after he entered school the out-break of the Sino-Japanese war of 1894-1895 stimulated speculation as to whether the modern David, Japan, could defeat the giant, China. A few years later Greece and Turkey were at war. By that time he had read about the Persian wars and Leonidas' defense of Thermopylae. He and Brother John had discussed with becoming gravity the possible outcome of this struggle between Greeks and Turks. The sympathies of the boys were, of course, with the Greeks, and they were much disappointed when the newspapers reported that Thermopylae could not be defended as of old. The Spanish-American war, the Boer war, and the Russo-Japanese war were similarly followed with the closest attention by young and old alike in this remote corner of Norway. Newspapers had carried accounts of Spanish excesses in Cuba. The natural tendency of Norwegians was to be hostile to all oppressors, and with interest in the United States always very great the cry "avenge the *Maine*" was loudly echoed in Norway. It was popular to root for Uncle Sam. "Yes," said old Jakob Morrisen, who never read even a newspaper, "the American will lick the Spaniard, there can be no doubt about that." At the turn of the century everybody had sympathized with the Boers and hoped against hope that somehow a miracle might save them. As for the Russo-Japanese conflict, it was felt that the Russians, whom the Norwegians hated and feared, deserved their ill luck.

A small lending library was a gold mine. Books of travel, biography, and history the young man liked best. He had read with amazement about the seals at the Pribilof Islands, Stanley's accounts of Darkest Africa, stories of the American Civil War, and of the Commune of Paris. The last left him completely bewildered, and so had Zola's *Debacle* and Dickens' *Oliver Twist* because they described conditions utterly unlike anything he had ever known. Dumas' *The Count of Monte Cristo* had been much more interesting. All this miscellaneous information was of no practical value to a salmon fisherman, but somehow it gave a certain satisfaction.

In reviewing what little education he had, he found himself repeatedly thinking of his training for confirmation. Perhaps because it was the last class before he took over a parish in southern Norway, the Reverend Mr. Holter seemed to have made a special effort to influence the fifty-eight boys, all of whom were about fifteen and preparing for admission to the church. The familiar tenets of theology, Old Testament stories, and New Testament parables gained added significance when explained by this learned man. He talked to the boys as if they were men, explaining and elucidating points frequently discussed by their elders. The youth remembered with special clearness how the scholarly, grayhaired pastor had posed the question: "Why do we Christians rest on Sunday instead of on Saturday?" He then pointed out that the resurrection of Christ with victory of life over death marked a new dispensation. When he had finished his discussion all the boys agreed that sects like the Seventh Day Adventists were surely heretical. The drill in the fundamentals of dogma made them more earnest and orthodox Lutherans. But this was not all. As father of five sons the pastor knew a great deal about adolescent boys. To them he explained some of life's most intimate problems, and gave advice which they all knew would be of lasting benefit to them.

The young man appreciated that he had got something out of the little schooling he had had, something of real and permanent value. Five years had passed since he left school. Plans for further education had been discussed and discarded because of the one insurmountable obstacle — lack of money. An inexpensive way might have been to attend one of the schools which trained non-commissioned officers for the army.

But as most of the time at these schools was devoted to military exercises, the academic education offered was rather superficial and was not worth the three years spent in acquiring it. Another possibility was to win one of the scholarships offered at the Tromsö normal school to students who were willing to study either the Finnish or Lappish language so they could later teach in the remote districts of Finnmark where a knowledge of one of these languages was considered necessary. Though such teaching posts were deemed the least desirable in all Norway, he had decided to apply for such a scholarship. But upon inquiry he learned that the Finns and Lapps' progress in Norwegian had been so rapid of late that bilingual teachers were no longer necessary. The scholarships were to be discontinued that year. Thus the last way to obtain a higher education was closed to him. America might offer educational opportunities not found in his native land.

Chapter 5

People and Institutions

FOR ALL HIS TWENTY YEARS
the young man had lived in the same district. He knew the
people of the island well; he had been a partner in the
common enterprises of the small community, a sharer of the
joys and sorrows which had befallen its inhabitants. But he
was also conscious of membership in the larger units, the
parish, the province, and the nation. He felt that the years of
his life had been crowded with events of country-wide significance, that he had witnessed a great upsurge of Norwegian
national consciousness. Discussions on manhood suffrage, a
Norwegian national flag without the jack which indicated the
union with Sweden, separate consular service for Norway, and
now the dissolution of the union with Sweden constantly
came to mind. The school teacher had belonged to the Left or
liberal party, and he had preached the gospel of a strong
nationalism with emphasis upon the dignity of the language
spoken by the common man as a language more truly Norwegian than the written idiom with its many traces of Danish
influence. This language controversy, Landsmaal versus Riks-
maal, was still hotly debated. The achievements of Norsemen
both in olden times and more recently had been stressed in
school and in the press. Youthful hearts had swelled with
pride when the sagas of the Vikings were read and explained,
and when attention was called to the accomplishments of the
Norwegian painters Dahl, Gude, and Tiedeman, the mathe-

maticians Abel and Lie, the musicians Bull and Grieg, the poets and dramatists Wergeland, Björnson, and Ibsen, the explorers Nansen and Sverdrup. The young man knew that he had participated in a national renaissance, a quickening of the spirit of the north. Farmers, sailors and fishermen now walked with a firmer step, possessed a greater sense of inborn human dignity than had their ancestors but one generation before.

From his parents he had heard numerous tales of the proud and overbearing attitude of officials and merchants in olden times. Nearly all members of these classes had stood apart from the majority of the people not only by virtue of education and wealth, but because their ancestral trees were rooted in foreign soil. During the 400 years of Norway's political union with Denmark the royal house of the dual monarchy had been German, and German, too, were the members of the council of state and government officials both lay and clerical. These foreigners were often corrupt and incompetent. In northern Norway they were nearly always birds of passage anticipating the day when they would get posts in places nearer the centers of civilization or retire on the plunder they had gathered in the north. Fattening on the land, they felt infinitely superior to those who supplied the provender.

After Norway became self-governing the influx of foreign officials ceased, and by intermarriage with Norwegians the remaining members of the bureaucracy had become more closely identified with the interests of the country. Of late scions of these "official" families had entered business and the professions; older firms in Bodö bore names such as Fische, Holst, Jakhelln, and Koch, reminders that the forbears of their owners had come from Germany. A still greater change had swept the land since Father and Mother were young. Then a claim to foreign ancestry was a badge of social superiority, but now people of the parish who could trace their genealogy to the Benkestoks, a noble family of the northland, maintained that they were the true blue bloods.

In government and business names like Dahl, Egge, Larsen, Olsen, and Amundsen were supplanting the foreign ones.

By slow degrees Norwegians became accustomed to political independence, gained confidence in themselves, and acquired pride of race and nationality. The people whose ancestors had dwelt along the shores of this fjord for centuries before the merchants of the Hanseatic League and the Dano-Norwegian kings of the Oldenburg dynasty laid their blight upon the land no longer considered themselves members of an inferior race. These were men and women with an allodial right to the soil, lawful masters of their country's destiny, the equals of the representatives of any other nationality. This new national consciousness had created a strong sense of solidarity in the country and of kinship among its people. The young dreamer on the hilltop was identified with these fishermen and farmers; he was close to them all. For him the uprooting of emigration would be a lacerating ordeal.

As if viewing a crowd from afar, he picked out of the mass of people certain types which represented the past or reflected characteristics peculiar to the inhabitants of the island and district. There was the Bodö merchant who had chosen the lad as a walking companion one morning as the latter brought his fish to town. The merchant, Otto Koch, was the son of a judge and the proprietor of the largest store in Bodö; he owned a spacious town house and a charming country villa. His name revealed his foreign origin, he felt himself to be a real patrician, and he treated those who bore Norwegian names with polite condescension. Acting on a sudden impulse he spoke to the youth whom he doubtless had noticed before as one of the salmon fishermen from the other side of the fjord. The conversation had been a monologue by the merchant on the folly of the universal manhood suffrage recently introduced in Norway. "It stands to reason," opined Herr Koch, "that men of property, education, and a tradition of public service are the only ones who are fit to carry on the government of parish and nation. To equalize the votes of such men with those of the rabble will lead to ruin." Though the lad listened silently and respectfully, he had been heart and soul in favor of the reform; in politics all members of his family belonged to the Left, the party responsible for the extension of the franchise. Herr Koch's arguments were familiar, in fact they were hackneyed, for they had been repeated over and over again in the debates on the new franchise bill. The young fisherman had not argued with him. In truth he had thought less about the old gentleman's tirade than that this arch-conservative seemed so foreign despite the fact that he was born and reared in the parish. Upholding a lost cause, Mr. Koch in no way fitted into the new scheme of things.

He was totally different from the storekeeper on the island who had been the magnate in the community during the eighties and early nineties. Portly and blustering was Johan Andreassen, a mighty man in his day. The son of a fisherman whose log hut stood on a bare knoll without sufficient land to keep even a goat, Andreassen had by sheer ability and force of character risen to become master of one of the vessels which carried fish to Bergen. This was no mean feat because the competition for such a post was keen, and in those early days a young man without money and social standing had little chance to become a ship's master. Despite family opposition he had wooed and married the squire's daughter, and with the wealth she brought he purchased an island farm with twenty cottars, started a store which for thirty years did a thriving business, and became the owner of several warehouses, fishing boats, seines, and small vessels used in coastwise shipping. How proud the cottars had been of the fact that their manorial lord had originally belonged to their own class! How eager he was to show that now he could bestow boons and largesse. To Mrs. Andreassen came widows in distress and wives whose husbands had gone fishing leaving behind an empty larder. An order from her to the store meant bags and baskets would be filled. Andreassen's charity may have been ostentatious, perhaps more an exhibition of vanity and a bid for popularity than love for his fellows, but he understood and never lost touch with the humble folk. Unlike Herr Koch, Andreassen had no fear of entrusting the ballot to them. When he died the whole district mourned.

It was Johan Andreassen who had given the youth half a dozen peppermints, the first candy he had ever had. A very small boy then, he had brought the treasure home to show to his mother before he even tasted it. What a busy spot Andreassen's place had been at that time! Crowds of people were all about, boats coming and going, the store jammed. All this had changed. Andreassen, childless and intestate, had died nine years ago. A Bodö lawyer became administrator of the property and somehow everything, seines, boats, ships, warehouses, and farm, had come into his possession. The imposing main building, 200 years old said tradition, was now at Sulitjelma serving as a barracks for miners. Warehouses had been moved to Bodö to be used for a herring oil factory, and the farm was divided up and sold to the more prosperous of the cottars. Perhaps this was a portent. The cottar class was disappearing. Herring, no longer a staple of the people's diet, rendered up its fat for machine oils, and its other parts for cattle fodder. The world was changing.

In reviewing the people of the parish the youth realized that it was not the officials, merchants, skippers, and landowners who would linger longest in memory. The most interesting individuals were found among the fishermen. Poor though they were, from their ranks came many amusing and unusual personages. They were a picturesque lot, healthy and vigorous despite their way of life. They rarely ate meat, eggs, or vegetables except potatoes; their chief food was fish, fresh in the summer, salted the greater part of the year. Perhaps the large quantities of fresh boiled pollack and the fish's liver which the people consumed during the summer months explained their vigor, their large families, the low rate of infant mortality, and the absence of "the English disease," rickets.

That the cottars had both strength and endurance was demonstrated when they fished in the tide current. During the runs they were active day and night, a week or two at a stretch. When the tide was flowing they fished with line and troll; as it changed they used small seines. This fishing season was generally short; when the pollack was running, halibut and redsnapper were also moving into their grounds, and since these fish were even more valuable than pollack, they must be caught too. Fishing in waters near home alternated with cod and herring fishing farther afield. How well he knew these Oles, Hanses, Johans, and Jenses, their boats, habits, and peculiarities. In the past the supply of baptismal names had been rather limited, but of late some parents, usually those in the poorest families, had tried to gain distinction by naming their sons after families of national fame. One little chap was loaded with the pompous array of Shöning Tiedeman Nordahl, and his parents hoped that some day one of these would replace their commonplace patronym of Hansen.

If fishing failed both at home and at Lofoten, the cottar-fishermen were in a sad plight. There had been such a disaster a few years earlier. Father had been called upon to distribute a small relief fund collected by Norwegian-Americans, and to the youth had fallen the task of carrying the news to various cottages that sums ranging from one to five dollars were available as gifts. The profuse gratitude showered upon the messenger showed him how near destitution were many of these families though they all had been too proud to ask for aid from the parish relief fund.

Judged by almost any standard most of the cottars were humble folk; to the outsider they seemed quite un-distinguished. But nearly all of them, men as well as women, were experts in some branch of work connected with their calling. This one was especially keen in detecting when the pollack run was on or particularly skillful in handling his boat amidst whirlpools; another excelled in catching the fish, or was quickest in cleaning and splitting it. As at Lofoten, the really prominent ones were those who were most proficient in handling a boat, in adjusting the ballast and sail so that their boats were fleet, in judging winds, waves, and breakers. But distinctions were not limited to occupations connected with the sea. The cottars could match their skill at farmwork with that of the landowners and their sons. A man of little use aboard a boat might plow a straighter furrow, or be more effective with a scythe than his companions. Similarly, a girl might outstrip rivals in milking, knitting, spinning, or at any other of the numerous tasks reckoned as woman's work. Since opportunities to surpass one's fellow man were numerous, few lacked some mark of distinction, distinction which satisfied the universal human craving for applause and admiration and gave these people a sense of personal worth. Lucky it was for them that this was so for none among the cottars could find comfort in that last refuge of the incompetent, pride of ancestry.

Musing over the ways individuals had gained local fame, the young man recalled two who had been friends in life and now rested side by side in the potters' field — Ole Rörvik and Jens Arntsen. Ole, whom the children nicknamed the "queer one" ("raring"), was a son of the very poor. None seemed to know anything about his relatives. He had been "on the parish" as a child and there he stayed for sixty years until he died and was buried in a pauper's grave. Small and weak, lacking skill and courage as sailor or fisherman, Ole never counted for much in an assemblage of men. His thin, swarthy face with its dark, sunken eyes always wore a haunted expression. He looked half-starved, and when school-boys, cruel and vigorous, encountered Ole they shouted in unison, "Ole, Ole, Queer One." But this they did only as a gang; alone they stood in awe of this man who shunned the company of his fellows and roamed over hill and moor during the light summer nights. He was always by himself then, moving swiftly and noiselessly with a curious gliding gait, his eyes fixed on the ground. When he came within earshot of others he mumbled as if he were conversing with an invisible companion. Children scurried off as quickly as possible, certain that Ole was communicating with gnomes or "hill-folk." Indeed, someone had heard of someone who had seen Ole with a man dressed all in blue, the uniform of the hill people. Grown-ups laughed at these stories and ignored Ole Rörvik, the no-good, but children eyed him with fascination and respect. Thus the poor devil stood apart as "somebody" and in a small measure won the renown which his soul craved.

Ole Rörvik's only friend and confidante had been Jens Arntsen, one of the many Jenses on the island. This particular Jens, however, differed from others of that name in that he was smaller than the rest, he spoke with a lisp, he slobbered, and at every third step he kicked his right foot against his left ankle. What fun he had given the boys! "Hey," the gang would shout, "here comes Jens. One, two, kick, one, two, kick," and for ten or fifteen minutes a platoon of boys might march along like Jens Arntsen. But Jens had other claims to distinction. He loved to talk both when alone and in company; a sociable chap, he was full of strange stories. The most credible of them were accounts of gathering hundreds of redsnappers along the shore of the tide current on November or December mornings after a blizzardy night with the wind from the northwest, for on such nights redsnappers were often thrown ashore. More thrilling were Jens Arntsen's tales of meetings held by the fish in the deep of the fjord. "Oh, yes," said Jens, who incorporated this exclamation in every sentence, "thus said the halibut to the pollack," and then followed a marvellous account of disputations and arguments among the fish. But because the fishes' conversational powers and vocabulary were somewhat limited, the stories tended to be repetitious. Though Jens was vague as to his source of information for these debates of the fish, it was considered unfair to pin him down on this matter. By some kind of inspiration he felt absolutely sure of his ground. "Oh yes, the fish gather and talk things over, exactly like you and me," he often said. Among his queer bits of information was the fact that the halibut was immoral and suffered from venereal infection. "Oh yes," said Jens, "the halibut has the French disease I know." And this unique knowledge gave him a claim of expert in the field.

Thus had Ole and Jens courted recognition and tried to gain fame. A few years ago their struggle to keep body and soul together had ended. Now they slept in nameless graves; their resting place like their fruitless toil would soon be blotted out, and, forgotten by the children whom they had frightened or mystified, their mouldering bones would become one with the earth in a windswept God's acre.

Separated from the graveyard by a deep ravine stood the cottage of Ingeborg Zakariassen. Ingeborg's lot in life had been hard. Her husband drowned in the tide current many years ago leaving her destitute and with four small children. The yield from her two acres of ground and the supplies distributed free from Andreassen's store and Mrs. Andreassen's kitchen had, however, kept the family going and saved Ingeborg from the humiliation of having to seek aid from the parish. When the supply of fuel ran very low she had often come to Father and asked permission to rustle juniper and twigs on his land. Ingeborg's husband had been a Norwegian; she was a Lapp. Since Norwegians considered Lapps an inferior race, the social intercourse she had had with other cottars ceased upon her husband's death. Her own people who herded reindeer far away on the mountains near the Swedish frontier had apparently disowned her; at least none of her kin had ever been seen on the island. One of her children died in infancy, a second drowned when he broke through the ice, the third died at the age of thirty so Ingeborg was left with only one son, Aksel, who at times behaved queerly.

Though Ingeborg Zakariassen trusted in the Christian God, she entertained many superstitions tinged with the animistic worship peculiar to her race. Her ghost stories resembled those of her Norwegian neighbors, the very old of whom might also share her belief in goblins, but she stood alone in her conviction that every rock or tussock housed a spirit of some kind. Consequently if a person fell on one of them the sure cure for a bruise or twisted ankle, according to Ingeborg, was to beat the offending object. Years earlier when Brother Julius was herding cattle he had seen poor Ingeborg banging away at a tussock with her rolling pin. Superstitious or not, Ingeborg was a devout Christian, and Mother and Father had long befriended her. They knew that throughout her many years of loneliness, sorrow, and poverty she had been sustained by a faith in God's goodness, a faith as simple as it was abiding.

To the young man the Lapps, especially those who were still nomads, had always seemed strange and phantom-like. With their herds of reindeer they flitted hither and yon over the mountains and coastal areas. With no fixed abode they were in the country yet not of the country. Although Lapps may have preceded Norsemen as inhabitants of northern Norway, until quite recently they had never settled anywhere as tillers of the soil or as fishermen. Their real home was the mountainous upland of the north; this was their realm. Small and lithe, clad in brownish-grey homespun or in the fur of the reindeer, they blended with the landscape like the lemming, the ptarmigan, or the reindeer itself. Since their abode, a rude temporary structure built of rocks and turf was almost invisible, the Lapps would appear as if from nowhere. At the trapsite on the mainland was a scree of gigantic boulders; hidden away between these rocks were several crudely made coffins, which by the action of rain and frost had been split open exposing the skeletons within. The interments had doubtless taken place long ago, but since even then the parish church was not far away from the scree, it was evident that the people who had hidden their dead in this secluded spot had not considered burial in consecrated ground desirable or necessary. They must have been heathen Lapps among whom effective missionary work was not begun until the seventeenth century. As the youth kept watch at the salmon trap and looked at the "Scree of the Dead" across the bay, he had often wondered what weird rites these shores had witnessed when the coffins were stowed away among the boulders. The Lapps were a highly emotional people; he had seen them in outbursts of joy or grief so extreme as to be unthinkable for a Norwegian. As far as he knew they lacked songs of their own, but when they were deeply stirred they burst into a sort of yodeling which resembled a primitive chant. The steep mountainsides above the scree and around the bay had probably echoed and re-echoed to this type of dirge as bereaved Lapp families hid their dead.

The 300 years of not very systematic missionary work among the Lapps had failed to uproot all their traditional beliefs and practices. Far away on lonely mountains they had sacred places dedicated to gods or spirits who must be propitiated. In Swedish Lapland there was a mountain, Jokmok, by some Lapps considered holy, by others a mountain inhabited by evil spirits; to all it was a place of special significance. The suspicion that many Lapps were still half-heathen made them objects of curiosity or even fear. Sensing this, they sought to profit by it and at times threatened to use their evil magic if they were refused handouts by the farmers. Some Norwegians believed themselves to be victims of spells cast by Lapps. Indeed, Father had known two old spinsters crippled by arthritis who were certain their affliction was caused by Lapp magic, magic from Jokmok.

The most widely known of the stories about Lapp sorcerers came from the neighboring parish of Beiarn. Here, so ran the legend, had roamed a Lapp named Snerrn. He was a loafer who had never owned a single reindeer nor ever worked as a herder. He just tramped from place to place carrying on his back an old gunny sack filled with bones filched from many graveyards. If people gave him what he demanded, all went well, but "God help the person upon whom Snerrn threw his evil spell." Misfortune of the most dire and diverse kind would be the lot of the one who treated Snerrn badly. Crops would fail, nets and lines would be forever empty, farm animals would die, and members of the family would waste away from strange diseases which no doctor could diagnose. So Snerrn always was given food and shelter. But retribution came one dismal and fearful night as he lay on his deathbed; then the spirits of all whose graves he had desecrated sought revenge. They filled the room and drove him frantic with fear. He shouted and writhed, prayed and cursed; the house shook and bolts of lightning clove the sky as the magician departed this life and devils came to fetch his soul. Superstition among the Lapps kept alive superstition among Norwegians.

In the past poverty had made beggars and sometimes marauders of the Lapps. But by the turn of the century their condition had improved. The extermination of wolves, better regulations of the Lapps' right of pasturage, and an outside market for the meat, hide, and horns of the reindeer had wrought marvels. Many Lapps were now considered wealthy; very rarely did one come begging. Some of them had even taken to fishing and farming. Yet whatever their means of livelihood, the Lapps retained their nomadic traits and racial peculiarities. They were restless, they had to move their cottages every little while or change the doors and windows in them, and a fishing boat manned by Lapps could be recognized from far off because they rowed with quick choppy strokes. They were always noisy and excited.

Though some became farmers or fishermen the majority of the Lapps continued as owners and herders of reindeer. Their realm was a vaguely defined region embracing sections of Norway, Sweden, Finland, and Russia; these countries had agreed on regulations governing migrations and pasturage rights of the Lapps. It was difficult to ascertain to which country they owed allegiance, and of this, too, they sometimes took advantage. With remarkable tenacity they clung to their language, habits, and customs. The reindeer which supplied them with food and clothing also pulled their curiously shaped sled, the pulkha, at an astonishing speed over the snowy wastes of Lapland. From earliest childhood the young man had been fascinated by the Lapps. They seemed relics of an age reaching back to the glacial epoch, an oddity in the present-day world. Small though their number was in the region bordering Saltenfjord, their customs and way of life provided interest and contrast for the district.

Though the nomadic Lapps were wards of the national government, obeying laws and regulations framed for them, the resident population, Lapp and Norwegian alike, had full control over the affairs of the parish. In grandfather's day it had been different. During the union with Denmark and for several years after Norway had gained political autonomy, appointed officials, sheriffs, and judges had lorded it over the people. Habits engendered by this system died hard, so for a long time after the introduction of elective parish councils, nationally appointed officials were usually chosen chairmen. This was perhaps more true of the northern than the southern part of the kingdom, for the people of the north were poorer and more distrustful of their own ability to fathom the mysteries of government than were the well-to-do farmers of the south.

The first to break with the tradition in Bodin parish was Carl Lökke, farmer and skipper. A peppery little man was Lökke, a man with considerable ability, much energy, and a vocabulary rich in profanity. He held the leadership of the parish council for several years. After he retired he visited Bodö every day and held forth on street corners about the state of the world, nation, or local parish to all who cared to listen. And many did, since by the time our youth began to bring salmon to Bodö Lökke had become almost legendary, a grizzly bantam who in his younger days had led the fight against officialdom. The present chairman of the parish council was, like Lökke, a farmer, a quiet man who without bluster simply took it for granted that management of local affairs was not beyond the intelligence of the native-born people — he was a living symbol of a silent political and social revolution.

The parish was the unit of secular government; its council stood high in the estimation of the people. Elections which were often bitterly contested, centered almost wholly on local personalities and issues. As the population was only about

5,000 the unit was small and the actions of the council were subjected to close and continuous scrutiny. Records of the voting were often published in the Bodö newspapers, and the minutes were open to inspection by the voters. Electors did not hesitate to demand explanations from councillors who had been overly generous with the public money or had discriminated against a section of the parish; every third year the councillors faced the test of a new election with vote by secret ballot. The local government had proved an excellent training school for democracy, and chairmen who had shown special aptitude for public business were often put forward as the logical candidates for the national parliament, the Storting.

The parish council was mainly a legislative body; commissions or boards handled the administration of education, poor relief, and the assessment and collection of taxes. Father and the older brothers had served on these bodies and their problems had often been discussed at home. For many years Father had been on the commission which administered poor relief, and among the young man's earliest recollections was that of Father's futile efforts to convince members of a notoriously lazy cottar family that they should abandon their shiftless habits and become self-supporting. Father, like most of the people in this community, had been thrifty and hard-working all his life, and the cottars' argument that Father and others on the island were obligated to support all indigent families even though they were able-bodied made him furious. But no persuasion availed against the family; its head and the younger son were absolute geniuses at inventing dodges and subterfuges. The son, Jens Hansen, was a liar *par excellence*. Born into a different social stratum, he might have won fame as a swindler or raconteur. Because he was no good as a sailor and his travels were limited, his tales were tall within very narrow limits and his swindling dealt with only petty projects. Neither Jens nor his relatives deceived Father with their stories, they only wearied him, and he looked longingly toward his sixtieth birthday, that milestone beyond which none could be compelled to serve the parish.

In the early nineties it was still customary to send paupers on "rounds" to live from one to four weeks at the home of farmers. The last to make such "rounds" on the island had been Old Daniel and Johanna-with-the-limp. Old Daniel, who had been at the home of the youth when the latter was a boy of six, created radical changes there. For some mysterious reason Old Daniel considered himself a guest around whom the household should be organized. A fussy fellow, the pauper insisted that his bed be set up in the living room. From that vantage post he annoyed everybody, especially the youngest child who during the roundsman's stay hardly dared to move. The family was much relieved when Daniel hobbled on to his next host. Not until many years later did the boy discover why Old Daniel considered himself so important. Fifty years earlier he had gained a reputation as the best scytheman in the parish, and for half a century Old Daniel had nursed the memory of that day when he had bested seventeen competitors in a hay-cutting contest at the glebe.

A hip injury suffered in childhood had given Johanna-with-the-limp her sobriquet. She was of a later vintage than Old Daniel, and she stayed only at the larger farms, a fact of which she was immensely proud. Children liked to talk with her partly because she was a simple-minded person who said foolish things, but chiefly because she always confused weights and measures. The metric system, introduced into Norway after she had reached middle age, was too complicated for Johanna's limited intelligence. Terribly funny it seemed to hear her talk about a "meter" of milk and a "liter" of cloth. One winter day when the blast from the Blue Man's Glacier was particularly penetrating she came limping up to the youth's home feeling especially important because she bore the astounding news that the thermometer at the store, the only thermometer on the island, registered "fifteen meters below freezing."

The men and women on the "rounds" were not unhappy with their lot; the farmers who housed and clothed them were kind, and the paupers enjoyed peddling gossip. But the system had been abandoned in the late nineties, and indigents were now boarded out for a fixed sum paid by the parish. Of late the possibility of establishing a poor farm had been discussed, but opposition came from both taxpayers and paupers. Some of the farmers feared that a poor farm would prove expensive, and the paupers objected because such institutions savored of the prison or insane asylum.

The parish school board was, like the commission on poor relief, chosen by the council. This board had charge of the building and maintenance of school houses, hiring of teachers, selection of textbooks, and, subject to the supervision of dioscesan and national authorities, the parish school board had general control of the content and character of elementary education. Its chairman was generally a teacher, and the schoolmasters and schoolma'ms held a secure and honored position in the community. All male teachers first had to have a good elementary education and then three years of training in academic subjects in one of the nation's normal schools. Women teachers had had a one year's training course in addition to their elementary work. For women, teaching had not yet become the profession it was for the men. The youth had had only one teacher, a man, but of late women teachers had been engaged for the primary classes in all the schools of the parish. They were paid less, and, it was believed, they were more successful than men in handling young children.

Each member of the parish board of education was chairman of the elected school committee for his local district. This committee nominated candidates for vacant teaching positions, exercised supervision over the school and playground, assisted the teacher with the more serious disciplinary problems, and was present at the annual review of the work covered during the school year. Meetings of all the voters in the school district were well attended and discussions of educational standards and of texts often waxed warm. Though the teacher might be criticized, he enjoyed the prestige of a good education and security of tenure. He was quite independent, and it was with considerable regret that the young man had abandoned hope of entering this profession. All services connected with education conferred distinction upon the performer; membership on the parish board of education rated only a shade below that of the parish council.

Less desirable was the work of assessing and collecting the local income tax. The rate was high, about 10 per cent of estimated income after the deduction of fifty kroner for each child, and neither depreciation of implements nor taxes paid could be subtracted from the taxable income. The tax was paid by every householder and all able-bodied persons over sixteen; even maids and unmarried daughters living at home had to pay. This tax was a heavy burden upon the people in a community where the cash income was always very small, and complaints about the high taxes came from all classes. To assess and collect them was a thankless task.

The assessors, one for each school district, were chosen by the parish council. These then went around to farmers and fishermen collecting data on the farm animals, field crops, wages, and proceeds from fishing. The young man recalled the struggle Brother Bernt had had with a farmer, Ole Pedersen, who could not remember how many sheep he had or how many barrels of barley and potatoes he had harvested from his small fields. At least three times Ole had called at the family home to make corrections, the figures getting lower at each visit, and Bernt finally settled matters by striking an average. With all the information in hand the parish assessors met in sessions lasting ten days or two weeks. Each person's income was discussed, and new information generally was turned up since the assessors knew a good bit about each other's districts. The completed tax list was then made available for public inspection and the taxpayer had the right to complain both if he was over-assessed and if his neighbor's income was set too low. Chances of concealing income were thus reduced to a minimum. In common with all local officials, the assessors served without pay and had to defray costs of board and room during their meetings; they also often had to take abuse from irate and unreasonable taxpayers.

The taxes were due in the spring or early summer right after the men returned from the Lofoten fisheries. No bond was required from the collectors who for about a week walked from house to house getting the money and then turned it over to the treasurer of the parish. By autumn the list of delinquents was placed in the hands of the sheriff who soon made his rounds attaching possessions to be sold for taxes. Implements, farm animals, boats, gear, watches, jewelry might be so designated; they remained, however, in the possession of the owner until the time of a public auction. Though very few articles were actually sold at these tax auctions, it was still a melancholy business, and the announcements of tax sales shouted by a crier on the church steps after Sunday service had distressed the young man even when he was a child. Haakon, the ex-sailor and story teller, had had the crier's job for several years. It gave him a chance to be seen and heard, a rôle he thoroughly enjoyed for he was one of the few exhibitionists of the island. Father had always criticized the announcing of tax auctions at church as a remnant of barbarism. Did America have anything like that? It was said that taxes were practically unknown in that enchanted land.

Other governmental institutions of special local interest were the boards of conciliation and the jury. The boards of conciliation consisted of three of the most respected men in the parish, chosen by the council, whose duty it was to effect settlements in minor civil disputes. The jury system was used in the provincial court, and members were drawn from panels carefully chosen by the various parish councils. To serve on a jury was considered a real honor; the young man's teacher had often been drawn for jury service. But when the teacher served it caused his pupils much vexation for the days school was closed in the winter had to made up during the summer vacation.

The quickening of the national consciousness and the active participation in local and national politics were only a few of the many changes the young man had witnessed in his own lifetime. Customs and habits had altered in many ways. Girls wore hats instead of kerchiefs, people carried umbrellas at times, and it was no longer only skippers and officials who owned fur caps and overcoats. Stoves had been put in the church, and a newly installed organ drowned out bald-headed Johan Hansen, who had formerly been heard over all other voices singing the hymns.

Some of the changes indicated a rise in the standard of living, others were signs of sophistication and a tendency to ape customs of other lands. The youth remembered that in his boyhood a common greeting used by older people upon entering a house was "peace" ("fred") which implied "God's Peace be with you." And as they met in the road they would say "a good meeting" ("godt mot"). But these expressions had gone out of use entirely. Only now and then would a caller who found the family at table say as he entered "May God bless your food" ("signe"). To knock on the door before entering a house was another recent custom. In olden times one simply entered, and many did this even now. Since stealing from a house was unknown, doors were left unlocked night and day. Occasionally pilferers might take an oar or gear from the boathouse, but this happened so rarely that it created a real sensation when it did occur.

This summer, however, these little matters seemed of no consequence, and even mission festivals and the customary Big Meeting were of slight importance. National events had overshadowed all others. On June 7 the whole country had been electrified by the news that the Storting had declared that the king, Oscar II, whom Norway shared with Sweden, having failed to find ministers willing to assume the responsibility of governing the country, had ceased to be king of Norway and *ipso facto* the union with Sweden had come to an end. Although startling, the action was not wholly unexpected. For ninety years the Norwegians had striven to secure Swedish recognition of the fact that the union of the two kingdoms was one of equals. Many points had been gained by the Norwegians, but a crucial one, that of a separate consular service for Norway, the king and his Swedish advisors had not conceded. There had been so much bickering between the two kingdoms that the announcement of the separation, though it aroused some apprehension of war with Sweden, also brought a feeling of relief. For ninety years Norway had been at peace; all agreed that war was barbarous, a relic of bygone times. Wars might seem natural in the Balkans, in Africa, and in Asia, but in Scandinavia such a calamity had become unthinkable.

Though the young man had relegated the possibility of a war with Sweden to the realm of the irrational, Mother had been much disturbed by the rattling of sabres on the other side of the boundary. But the youth had assured her that there would be no war, and since she greatly wished to believe his statement, she accepted it as true. In his meditations on the hilltop he tried to analyze why he felt so certain that there would be no armed conflict. Perhaps the conviction that war was barbarous was no valid ground for his optimism. It was said that in Sweden the liberals and the socialists were opposed to war, and many liked to believe that the old king himself would help to find a peaceful solution of the Norwegian-Swedish problem. Still others felt sure that Britain would not permit a war in Scandinavia; this was perhaps the most decisive factor in the widespread confidence in Norway that somehow peace would be preserved.

As the young man gazed at the calm fjord and the homes

which dotted its shores, he hoped that the tranquility of the land would never be disturbed. The conviction that peace would be maintained was a comforting thought which made planning for the future possible. He would emigrate to America next spring.

Chapter 6

Stories and Legends

ON THE ISLAND
and along the shores of the fjord were many cairns, burial
places of people long dead. Artifacts found at old building
sites and in refuse heaps bore testimony to the antiquity of
Norse settlements in this region. Several hundred years before the Christian era the tall, fair-haired Håleygr tribe had
moved into the arctic circle area which eventually became
known as Hålogaland. Here the sea teemed with fish, the
forested land abounded in game, and the coastal climate was
mild. In the latter part of the ninth century when Norway
was united, the "jarls" of Hålogaland were among the
strongest chieftains of the kingdom.

It was a source of pride to the inhabitants of Knaplundöy
and Straumöy that these islands of Saltenfjord had been the
home of a tenth century chieftain, Raud the Strong. He was
among those who offered armed resistance to the efforts of
the heroic king, Olav Tryggvason, to Christianize that part
of the kingdom. Raud, defeated in a naval battle, fled to his
home where he was sought out and tortured to death when
he scornfully refused to accept baptism. His hall was fired,
and his grand dragon-ship, the *Serpent,* sailed out of Saltenfjord with King Olav at the helm. This ship, the pride of
the northland, served as a model for the most famous war
vessel of the Viking era, Olav Tryggvason's *Long Serpent.*
Raud the obstinate heathen had become a local hero, and

96

even now the location of his hall and his burial place often sparked animated disputes.

Although in modern times no enemy had attacked the district from the sea, the settlements at the head of the fjord had occasionally been raided by Finns. Father told the story of one of the invasions when the Finns compelled a Lapp to serve as guide in the rough terrain of Sulitjelma. The intended victims of the raid were friends of the Lapp, and he hastily devised a scheme to save them. He explained to the invaders that surprise could be effected only under cover of a snowstorm and that he knew the paths so well they need not fear getting lost. Near the settlement the mountain plateau first sloped gently and then ended in a precipice, a sheer drop of more than 1,000 feet to the waters of the fjord. One night as the snow fell thickly, the Lapp guide said the moment had come to attack. But instead of leading the Finns down the valley to the settlement, he guided them toward the precipice. All were on skiis. With the wind at their backs they sped down the slope. "Follow me!" shouted the Lapp, throwing his lantern over the edge of the precipice and ducking quickly under a juniper bush. The marauders plunged to their doom, and from then on the spot was called "Finn Precipice."

One of the few events of the Saltenfjord area which attracted more than local attention was the "Bodö Affair." The elders often related the local version of the episode that had occurred a scant dozen years before Father was born. It was an important item of parish history, and even as a boy the young man had been filled with indignation over the injury and injustice inflicted on Norway. Because his grandfather knew the local officials connected with the case it had been much discussed at home.

The bare facts of the affair were that in 1818 Norwegian customs officials had attached a British vessel engaged in smuggling and had lodged its crew in jail at Bodö. The prisoners who were weakly guarded broke out, recovered their ship and part of its cargo, and sailed home. Using perjured testimony the owners, Peter Pole and Company of London, secured the help of the British foreign office. The result was that Norway was compelled to pay an indemnity of £18,000, a very large sum in those days, for alleged injuries inflicted on British subjects by the Bodö authorities. The Swedish foreign minister whose duty it was to protect Norwegian interests showed an amazing ineptness, and the king, Charles John, supported the British side. The Bodö affair became a *cause célèbre,* and in 1904 and 1905 it was a strong factor in creating a demand for an independent Norwegian foreign service.

Before Bodö became a town the secular officials of the province lived on farms along the northern shore of the fjord. All of these were visible from the young man's lookout. During the union with Denmark most of the officials were of Danish or German origin and disdainful of the natives. One of the worst of the officials was Sören Randulf the "Silver Sheriff" ("Sölvfuten"). This rapacious person had amassed a silver hoard that filled a barrel, and had buried his treasure in a secluded glen called the Peaceful Valley (Den Stille Dal). Warned that the district governor was coming to investigate his doings, the sheriff hurriedly prepared to leave. His last act was to exhume his hoard. On a dark night he went to the glen, but the ground was covered with snow. All landmarks were hidden. Frantically he searched and dug, but in vain. The treasure could not be found. In despair he hung himself on the limb of a birch tree, and when the corpse was found the head was severed from the body.

From that time on the Peaceful Valley was haunted. The road along the shore from Bodö passed through this glen. Farmers returning from town claimed they had seen the headless Silver Sheriff moving restlessly to and fro between the birches; with a shudder they whipped up their horses and fled the glen as quickly as possible. Indeed, in olden times only dire necessity would induce a man to enter the Peaceful Valley after sundown. Even in the daytime travellers were silent and carefully examined all the surroundings as they passed the haunt of the Silver Sheriff. To the relief of many, a new road built about 1900 skirted the ill-omened glen.

Among the ancient superstitions fast disappearing were that spirits roamed the earth on the eve of St. Lucia's day, that running water possessed special healing qualities on Christmas night, that horses and cattle knelt before their mangers at mid-night, and that a fearsome male banshee or sea sprite sailing recklessly on a vessel split in two would appear in the wake of a doomed fishing boat.

One story which persisted and always commanded respectful attention was that of a blessed island near Röst known as Outer (Ut) Röst. Only people with "second sight" could see the island. It was rumored that Uncle Salomon had seen it, but when his nephew inquired about this, Uncle Salomon was mysterious and evasive. The tradition was that when a heavy iron ring in the red, north door of the Bodin parish church had worn through, Utröst would appear out of the sea and become clearly visible to everybody. By the early 1890's the ring was very thin so hopes ran high. But to the people's disappointment the church was remodeled in 1895, and door and ring disappeared.

In local tradition Utröst was also associated with the famous Erik Gerhard Schytte, rector of Bodö from 1776 to 1808. In common with many rural pastors of his time, Schytte's advice was sought on business matters and legal problems, so he was not surprised when a stranger appeared in his study one day and asked counsel on a difficult question. The parish was so large that the minister could not know all members of his flock. He asked his caller where he came from. "Utröst," was the reply. "Then," said the pastor, "I must consider this case very carefully." "Ponder in vain," said the stranger, "Utröst will not appear out of the ocean till the Day of Judgment." With this remark he vanished, and the hope that Utröst would emerge from the northern mist was destroyed.

Schytte, a truly remakable man, was honored by the government with the title *professor˙ theologiae extraordinarius* at the University of Copenhagen. His parishioners always referred to him as "the Old Professor." Theologian, philologist, and physician, he built the first hospital in Nordland. Among the distinguished travellers who enjoyed his hospitality at the parsonage was Louis Philippe of Orleans, king of the French, 1830—1848.

"The Old Professor" so stirred the imagination of his parishioners that, as they customarily did with prominent ecclesiastics, they assigned him occult powers. A robber bent on breaking into a parsonage building would be fixed to the spot. One wintry morning the Reverend Schytte sent for the farm foreman to come to his study. When the foreman arrived he was ordered to release the man at the storehouse, for, said the rector, "He has been standing there for hours and is chilled to the bone." At the storehouse the foreman found to his astonishment a man standing on the steps with an ax raised for a blow at the door. There he had stood since midnight petrified by the supernatural power of the Reverend Mr. Schytte.

It was said of "the Old Professor" that he cast no shadow, and Father many times related how the shadow had been lost. As a reward for occult information, the students of theology at Wittenberg University, that mecca of Lutherans where Martin Luther had taught, each year made a bargain with the Devil that he should have the last one to leave the main building after graduation. The victim was chosen by lot, and the year of Schytte's graduation the lot fell to him. An exceptionally shrewd person, he arranged it so that the student body left the building facing the sun. When the Devil came to claim Schytte, he said, "You cannot take me, you must take him who walks behind me." And so the rector tricked Old Nick, but he had to walk without a shadow forever after. These and many other stories about the popular pastor were tributes to him, tokens of esteem and reverence.

The most popular among the ministers who had served northern Norway since the Reformation was Petter Dass, rector of the parish of Alstahaug. Gifted and versatile, Herr Petter left an indelible impression upon the people of the entire province. In Father's youth books were scarce and expensive, but at Lofoten songs and stories were exchanged by fishermen from all over the north. Thus legends about Petter Dass, his feats in tricking the Devil, his rhymed Biblical stories, and his descriptions of life in the Nordland province became widely known and made him a hero of the region. His cheerful hymns and songs set to easy lilting melodies were sung by the women at their spinning wheels and by herring fishermen drifting with their nets on the fjord in the autumn gloaming.

The son of a Scottish political refugee and a Norwegian mother, Petter Dass was born in Nordland. He lived there all his life, and he loved the region and its people. In an age when a majority of the officials in the north were birds of passage Herr Petter proclaimed, "Here I was born and swaddled, Here I have lived and toiled." An earnest and conscientious man, his life was a strenuous one. The parish was very large; more than a dozen clergymen now served the district once covered by the Reverend Dass and his two vicars. By boat and on foot he travelled thousands of miles, preaching and administering the Lord's Supper to the old, infirm, or dying parishioners. But he took it all in his stride, without murmur or complaint. "Such is the character of this land," he wrote, "that the servant of God must endure many hardships and much suffering. But he must not like Jonah shirk his duty. Should he perchance find rest in a watery grave it matters little. His resting place like that of Moses will be known to God."

To people prone to be melancholy and dejected, Petter Dass preached cheerfulness and courage. The hard-bitten fisher folk whom he loved responded with a rich measure of devotion. For 150 years after his death the sailors of the north carried a square of black cloth sewn into the mainsail of their ships in memory of a man who had brought them messages of joy and hope.

The fishermen liked to sing, and in the period when Father was at Lofoten songs written by a Swedish bishop, Esaias

Tegnér, vied in popularity with those of Petter Dass. Tegnér's songs were written around the saga of an eighth century Norse Viking, Fridtjof the Bold. In these poems were mingled tales of love and tragedy, gay feasts at the chieftain's hall, and grim struggles on land and sea. They caught the fancy of the men and women of the north for they called to mind that heroic age when the peoples of western Europe prayed, "From the fury of the Norsemen good God deliver us." Recently the songs of Petter Dass and those from the Fridtjof Saga were being supplanted by lyrics and patriotic anthems of Henrik Wergeland and Björnstjerne Björnson. These were in harmony with the strong upsurge of Norwegian nationalism at the turn of the century.

Story-telling, like music, was an antidote for boredom and discouragement. Accounts of actual experiences on land and sea were mingled with legends and fairy tales. When the supply of these ran low, as well they might since dark evenings were many and the winters long, someone would let his fancy roam. Then tales were spun which, even though everybody knew they were pure invention, were listened to and enjoyed. Occasionally two raconteurs would have a contest. Very soberly and with a perfectly straight face one would relate something he had allegedly heard or experienced. The competitor would listen intently, expressing confidence in the authenticity of every detail in his rival's story which, however, would remind him of another filled with even more marvellous episodes. Thus they would keep it up for hours on end to the delight of an appreciative audience. Sometimes a fabrication would prove so popular that it was appropriated by the community, fresh details being added from time to time. Such a saga was that of the wonder ship, *The Great Multiplicity, ("Den Store Mangfoldighed")*, a ship which grew to such a size that large farms were found on its spars, and the young cabin boy sent aloft would return to the deck an old graybeard.

Thus did these simple folk add spice and variety to their lives. To the outsider they might appear uninteresting and undistinguished. They had little formal education; judged by conventional standards their cultural inheritance was slight. But in heart and mind they possessed resources of no mean proportion. Their songs, stories, and legends constituted a rich heritage, one that stimulated thought and imagination. Hard and drab lives were given color and richness from inner spiritual resources. Only a person who had lived in their midst, shared their work and play, joy and sorrow could appreciate these qualities; only he could realize that by cutting the outward bonds between these people and himself the emigrant would sunder connections of the deepest, most intimate kind.

Chapter 7

Home and Family

To live in unfamiliar places, to be with people of a different background with strange customs and traditions, to be unable to understand their language — all this would make for profound loneliness. In a foreign country an immigrant would be like an uprooted tree or a ship loosed from its moorings. Strong and intimate were the ties that bound him to his own land, the most enduring of which were those with home and family. His throat tightened and his heart ached as he contemplated the final leave-taking.

Although for sailors, fishermen, and their families leave-taking was part of life's routine, as inevitable as the seasons of the year, it was something to which Mother and Father never grew accustomed. They dreaded saying farewell to their sons; in their hearts they rebelled against a fate which decreed that the family must always be divided. On the road to the boathouse lived Jakob Morrissen and his two sons. These sons never went farther away than Lofoten for the winter fishing. Time and again Father had said: "Jakob Morrissen is fortunate, he has his sons with him nearly the whole year — mine are gone most of the time."

It had been hard every time the brothers left to fish herring or to sail to Lofoten, Finnmark, or Christiansund. The flag was kept flying on the staff at home until long after the brothers' ship had disappeared from view. Particularly bitter was the parting when Brother John left to sail the high seas. And now the youngest was to leave for America. Both Mother and Father had borne up bravely when he broached his plan to them. They had grieved because they could not afford to send him away to a secondary school, and they felt that perhaps for him the opportunities to get ahead might be better in America than in his native Norway. Their outward calm was bolstered by the hope that something might occur within the year before he was to leave which would keep their son at home.

He shrank from the thought of saying goodbye. He preferred to review his life in the sod-roofed house beneath the hill which had been his home for twenty years, to recall activities and episodes in his associations with parents, brothers and sisters in this home, to engrave on his mind the likenesses and characteristics of those who were dearest to him.

The dwelling house as well as the outbuildings had been erected by his parents, built when the eldest children were small and Father had earned the family income by fishing for cod off Röst, where he battled Arctic storms and the raging ocean. Truly, the home had been founded on the toil and sacrifice of both Mother and Father. Life had been strenuous for Father, but no less toilsome for Mother, who for a large part of the year had borne alone the burdens of operating the little farm, tending the house, and caring for the children.

The main building was a two-story log house thatched in the customary fashion with birch bark on the roofboards and on top of the bark turf weighted down with rocks. Since the house stood on a slight eminence affording sweeping vistas of fjord and mountains, it was exposed to all the winds of heaven and had to be solidly built. The rocks on the roof were a real necessity. Badly constructed and insufficiently weighted roofs were often carried away by the fierce sou'westers of the autumn. On the outside the house was faced with boards laid vertically with overlapping edges, the boards securely nailed to laths fastened to the logs. The inside of the living room was panelled so skillfully that the children, however hard they looked, could never find the joints of the boards.

The family had been snug inside those walls. Neither poor nor rich, they belonged to that large class of Norwegians which earned just enough for frugal living. The small farm had been tilled diligently with implements little different from those in the time of Raud the Strong. True, the small plow pulled by the farm's one horse was of steel and the harrow of iron, but the grass was still cut with the scythe and the grain with the sickle; the potatoes were dug with the hoe, a slow and back-breaking job exceedingly unpopular with the younger generation. Potatoes, the only cash crop grown on the farm, brought in about thirty kroner in good years when as many as ten bags would be sold.

As a young boy the would-be emigrant had disliked haying because he had to work hard packing hay in the barn loft. It was a strenuous job since the space was limited and the gathering of hay must be done swiftly between showers. In most summers, hay curing presented many difficulties because of the gray and rainy weather. Spread thin on the ground, the grass when half-dry was cocked and again spread once or twice before it was dry enough for the mow. Since all the raking was done by hand, this drying process was often tedious. Of late hay was cured on racks constructed with poles and wire. Though rack building required time and labor, farmers by hanging the grass on the racks were spared further handling of the hay until it was ready for the hayloft.

Hay and barley straw constituted the feed for the barn animals during the eight or nine months when they were kept indoors. They were tended with great care and kept warm and clean; their water was carried to them from a nearby burn. But if the snow came in mid-September and stayed on the ground till June, the supply of fodder would have to be augmented with seaweed and boiled cod's heads. The family was very fond of all farm animals, and butchering time in the autumn was a period of semi-mourning. Not even the prospect of fresh meat and the delicious sausages prepared by Mother and the sisters could disperse the gloom. As a boy he had hidden on the day when a favorite ewe or heifer was slaughtered. Father, usually quiet and kind, was brusque and irritable on these occasions. Killing was a hateful business. Even hunting was disliked; Father never wanted any of his boys to hunt.

In the youth's early childhood all threshing was done by flail; then appeared some very crude home-made wooden threshing machines. In 1890 when Father bought a metal one which had a revolving iron cylinder with pegs to whip out the grain, neighbors had made fun of the contraption and predicted that it could not possibly do the work of the flail and that it would be a killing job to run it by hand power. Father was not worried; he had made careful inquiries before he bought the machine and he reckoned that his six sons would be able to run it. Before long neighbors came and begged to buy a share in the machine.

But the machine only threshed the grain out of the ear; to separate grain from straw and chaff was still done mainly by hand. The winnowing whereby the dust and lighter particles were thrown off was accomplished by primitive wooden machines operated by two men. The various kinds of sieves used were all hand-made, most of them from wood or skins.

The yield of grain was always small, and many years the barley was just ripe enough for use as seed or cattle fodder; it was not good enough to be ground for flour. The years it ripened enough to be ground it was first dried on a sail in the sun before being taken to the mill. Father and one of the brothers would take the grain to one of the mills which were run by water power and there they tended it themselves during the milling operation. Only once had he accompanied Father on such an expedition. It had seemed quite romantic. The foaming waterfall, the wooden millrace and wheel, and the heavy millstones took him back to a remote antiquity. Of late the grain was generally taken to Christiansund by the vessels which carried the dry cod to market, and there the grain was ground in modern steel mills. This homegrown meal was used for porridge and to make the thin barley bread ("flatbröd"). Unbleached and coarse, it was dark in color, but the bread and porridge made from it tasted better than did that from boughten barley flour.

The farm animals were treated as family pets. The horse was especially valued since he lightened human burdens. When running loose on the farm he would often come to the house begging for potatoes or a piece of bread. Each cow, and sometimes even the sheep, had a name and would come when called. At critical calving and lambing periods the animals received almost human care. Mother would give them warm drinks and keep watch throughout the night till the young were born. Despite this care the cows did not yield much milk compared with those the youth had read about in farm journals. He thought it must be because the hay and straw they were fed was of poor quality. One year he had taken the trouble to weigh the milk from each cow every fifth day and found that the annual yield per cow was about 1500 quarts. Just now the dairy experts advocated developing a type of small, black and white hornless cattle called the "Nordland" cow, which they asserted was indigenous to the province. The young man recalled with pride that three of the cows on his Father's farm conformed to the standards of this breed.

From time immemorial cream had been extracted from the milk by pouring it into shallow wooden or earthenware bowls placed on shelves nailed to the ceiling beams of the farmer's living room. This cream was good and thick, but it was apt to be mixed with dust and other less desirable ingredients. In the late eighties Mother had introduced milk cans which could be hung in a well in summer and a tub of water in the winter. The covered cans kept the cream clean, but some objected that the skimmed milk tasted of tin. At about the turn of the century Father bought the first cream separator used on the island. Neighbors who had criticized the replacement of the milk bowls with milk cans were even more critical of this separator. Some conceded that what they called "nature's way" of producing cream was perhaps neither sanitary nor efficient, but this new machine-method they considered a violation of a natural law; they felt sure that the skimmed milk produced by the separator would increase the incidence of tuberculosis. Thus they talked for a while, but soon all of them had purchased cream separators.

Sheep were considered very valuable farm animals. They required little care, the island had excellent summer pasture for them, and the mutton, tallow, and wool were essential to the economy of the people. The animals were small and short-wooled. Sheared twice a year, in the spring when they were let out of the barn and in the autumn when stabled anew, each clipping might yield two or three pounds of wool per animal. Years ago Father had obtained a cheviot ram to improve the breed, but this purchase had aroused much opposition. Big and powerful, the ram was rough with rivals, and he butted humans too — the youth recalled how scared he had been of this beast. So the ram was butchered while yet young and the scrubs prevailed among the sheep. Efforts to mend matters by organizing a sheep-breeding association with pure-blooded rams had not yet succeeded on the island. Most of the local farmers and cottars were a conservative lot. It was Andreas Furre, farmer and store-keeper on Straumöy, who had come from a farming region farther south in the neighborhood of Namsos who introduced racks for drying hay, pitchforks, and threshing machines in this northern area. The newly established agricultural college and experiment station near Bodö was the greatest stimulus to better farming, but the cost of machines and the barriers of established usage were difficult hurdles to clear.

During the summer and early autumn, farm work and fishing kept everybody busy. But from late September till Christmas farm operations except threshing and care of the farm animals almost ceased. In most households the animals were reckoned to be the women's responsibility, but at the youth's home he had helped with the barn chores most of the time. In families where the men fished at Lofoten, gear was readied during the stormy months of the late autumn. The long lines now used by most of the fishermen on the island required much less time to put into shape for the season's work than had the nets of earlier years. Until 1893 when Brother Malfred took Astrup's place as skipper of the little vessel owned by the family and used in its business of buying and curing fish, he had always fished with nets. Then there had been much activity in the house during the autumn months making new nets and repairing old ones, stretching them to tighten knots, and fixing the gear in various other ways; but lately the living room had not been cluttered with the big nets. Father continued to make small ones for catching herring when it came close to shore, a task which brought back memories of his active days, and it was more of a pastime for him than a real business. Curiously enough, he never wanted to instruct the youngest son in the skills of fishermen. Though Father had been on the sea since early youth he had not loved his calling, and secretly he hoped that his youngest would not have to become a sailor or fisherman.

Brothers Julius and Malfred were often away working with herring crews in the autumn, but the periods when they were ashore were days of leisure for them. Not so for Mother and Sister Constance, who were always home. Besides the usual household activities and the tending of cattle, they did an enormous amount of spinning, knitting, and weaving. Socks, mittens, and underwear, a goodly supply of which were needed for the many boys, were all home-made. The youth who often had carded wool had never tried his hand at spinning. This work Mother loved, for it was a cheerful occupation. Mother's voice was sweet, she knew by heart many hymns, and she nearly always sang when she spun. Songs written by Petter Dass were among her favorites; they were more tuneful than the Lutheran chorals, and Herr Petter's song about the numbers in Holy Writ seemed particularly well suited for the rhythm of the spinning wheel.

Mother liked to read, but only when she knitted could she find time for this luxury. She handled her knitting needles quite automatically, devoting her whole attention to the *Missionary Times* or books of devotions in which she was deeply interested. The autobiography of the missionary Lars Skrefsrud who with a Dane, Börresen, had founded a mission to the Santals in India, was read, re-read, and discussed in the family circle. From it the youth had acquired his first knowledge of the peoples and religions of the East.

Sister Constance was the weaver and seamstress of the family. She delighted in making things, inventing new patterns for weaving, and trying her hand at designing women's clothes somewhat different from the local styles. She wove not only homespun for every sort of garment, but also made bedspreads, table linen, and curtains. In these operations her youngest brother had been a handy assistant, winding bobbins and setting up the loom.

Among the pictures which he would carry with him from the old home was that of the living room on a bright day late in March. The sun was pouring in through the big south window. On one side of a table by that window sat Father deftly weaving the meshes of a herring net, and opposite him was Mother with a book in front of her while she knitted a sock for one of her sons. In the northeast corner was the loom, steadily clacking away as Sister Constance operated it; on the rag rug in the center of the room a small kitten leaped and rolled, playing with Brother Malfred's bloodhound. The dog was a poor sailor and preferred to remain on the farm when his master was at sea. It was such a quiet, peaceful scene, a scene to linger long in his memory.

The fall butchering and the preparation of various kinds of sausages for the winter was an especially busy period for the women; so were the days devoted to the baking of "flatbröd," and the two weeks immediately before Christmas when cookies and other delicacies were made for the holiday season. The baking season was a jolly one. Although ordinary leavened bread was now used every day, the old type of unleavened "flatbröd" continued to be popular. Rye and barley flour were mixed, small dabs of dough were rolled out with grooved rolling pins until they were about eighteen inches in diameter and thin as paper, then these large wafers were baked crisp on an iron griddle. To get the flatbröd thin without breaking it required many turnings and sprinklings with dry flour, and a steady hand. Since three or four women worked at the same time at a long table, there was a certain amount of competition in this work. Father always officiated at the griddle and saw to it that each wafer was evenly baked. After baking, the bread was stacked till it was completely cooled off, and if kept in a dry place, the bread would not deteriorate. Ordinarily a year's supply was prepared at the fall baking. It was stored in barrels, and the brothers would take a barrel with them when they went sailing.

The famine time in the early years of the nineteenth century had left its mark on Mother and Father. They were always anxious to have at least a year's supply of flour on hand. In October or November when Brothers Julius and Malfred returned from fishing they often brought two or three barrels of salted herring to add to the other staples. It was also customary to buy each summer a year's supply of firewood — the island was so windswept that the trees were always stunted and of little value.

Candle-making, too, had been a cheerful affair. The supply of tallow was small, and the task was generally finished in one day. The children had enjoyed watching the candles grow; when they were very young they believed that the more frequent the dipping the faster the candles would thicken, but the lesson that the candles had to cool between dippings was soon learned. In olden times tallow candles or the feeble light of a wick in a shallow pan of fish oil had been the only illumination save what came from the open fireplace during the long dark season. Although kerosene was introduced while his parents were quite young, even after they had passed middle age the kerosene lamp because of the expense involved was reserved for festive occasions. By now the fish oil lamp had disappeared completely, and the tallow candle was fast going out of use. Very few kitchens still had hearths; stoves for heating and cooking had replaced the picturesque though wasteful fireplaces. In the youth's home this change was made when Father built the dwelling house. In the parents' childhood only the officials and the well-to-do had iron stoves. Then not even the lucifer match lightened the task of housekeeping. "Borrowing fire" from neighbors on cold, dark winter mornings had been among the duties Father had told about.

Christmas held a special place among the great events of the year. Large quantities of various kinds of cookies, coffee bread, and other delicacies were prepared well in advance, sausages and cold meats were got ready, and the house cleaned from attic to cellar. Father was busy in the woodshed sawing and splitting birchwood for the stoves, providing a supply that would make such work unnecessary between Christmas and New Year. Preparations and anticipation as well as the actual enjoyment of the festivities had been a welcome break in the daily routine during the time of the year when the days were very short and dark and the weather often stormy. In this part of the world long before the inhabitants ever heard the message "peace on earth, good will towards men," their joy at the passing of the winter solstice and the prospect that the sun would reappear in another month incited them to celebrate in an elaborate fashion. When the heathen and the Christian festivals were combined there was a double reason for rejoicing, and the Yuletide had long held preëminence among all the holiday seasons.

One ancient custom was to have halibut and a custard made from cow's beestings as special Christmas treats. If the menfolk failed to provide halibut the hired man was transported to the roof of the boathouse, and if the milkmaid could not supply the beestings for the custard she was hoisted onto the roof of the barn. But this, as well as other forms of Christmas escapades, had gone out of fashion. Indeed, Mother and Father had always disapproved of horseplay at any time, and to have it part of a Christian festival seemed sacrilegious.

Although there had been no Christmas tree and few Christmas gifts exchanged at his home, this season had been such a happy one that its memories would be cherished till life's last day. Weather mattered not at all. Christmas eve had been a period of joyous anticipation. A quiet yet exhilirating atmosphere prevailed in the home, and everyone was in a holiday mood. Even the animals received extra attention and added rations. At five o'clock in the evening when the church bells began to ring and chime for an hour, the family was ready to welcome the greatest festival of the year. Dressed in their Sunday clothes, they all gathered for an early supper, not of the usual barley meal porridge with milk but of rice pudding served with sugar and cinnamon and a dab of butter. Special Christmas candles were on the table, and the cheer was intensified rather than dampened by Father's reading of a chapter from the Bible. In the young man's earliest recollection, Father's hair was still jet black and his dark brown beard only sprinkled with gray. At that time all the children except Sister Katherine were gathered at home for Christmas. When Katherine was a little girl of seven, Aunt Ellen had begged to have the child come to live with her, and Mother in a weak moment had yielded to the entreaties of her unhappily married youngest sister. But Katherine was always missed, particularly so at Christmas, when it seemed as if a place were vacant.

The picture of the family table in those early days was ineffaceably etched on the boy's mind. The long table was placed with an end against the south window. On one side sat Father, Mother, Sister Constance and Sister Julianne. Facing Father sat Astrup, the eldest son, then Malfred, Julius, and Bernt in the order of their age; at the end were Brother John and himself. After the meal, gifts were distributed to Mother, the two youngest children, and the sisters, all presents from the grown-up sons. During the evening both parents would relate stories of olden times. The youngest usually fell asleep on the floor, and it was a source of never-ending wonder to him that he wakened in his own bed the next morning, that no matter how he hurried to dress, the table was always set when he entered the living room. Years later he discovered that Mother and the sisters set the breakfast table for Christmas morning before they retired.

Christmas day breakfast was the most sumptuous of the year. The table was loaded with cheeses, cold meats, and various kinds of bread. A real feast it had seemed to youthful eyes. But before anyone partook of the food Father conducted a brief religious service. The singing of a hymn which proclaimed that "Christ is born in Bethlehem" was followed by the reading of the Christmas story from the gospel of St. Luke. Youthful imagination had been stirred with the account of the event when "God became flesh and dwelt amongst us." The scenes in the stable, in the field under starry skies, and the adoration of the shepherds were reconstructed on the basis of familiar experiences and surroundings. Before a curate was appointed for the church near home, church services were celebrated only on the day after Christmas, so on Christmas day Father would hold family devotions and read a sermon to the family at the usual time for church service. Since 1902 a resident curate had conducted services in the church on the island, and no matter how inclement the weather might be the church was filled on Christmas day.

One old Christmas custom was that everyone, or nearly everyone, should wear something new to church even though it was only a cap, a scarf, or a coat. Sad it was, and a sign of utter poverty, if one appeared in his usual attire. Another custom was that Christmas afternoon and evening were spent at home; it was on the "Second-day Christmas," a holiday throughout Norway, that a round of visits, parties, and bazaars to raise money for missions began. These festivities lasted till New Years or even until January 6, when, according to an old saying, "Knut came and hauled Christmas away."

Though Easter and Whitsuntide were great festivals with two holidays for each, neither ranked nearly so high as Christmas in solemnity and importance. Would next Christmas be his last in the old home, he wondered.

Since the youth's family was large it had been self-contained in many ways. This was particularly true in matters of amusements. His parent's religiosity meant that dancing was taboo. Moreover, the death of the eldest brother and financial reverses which came soon thereafter had depressed the household when the youth was young. Nevertheless, there had been many moments of gaiety and laughter under the turf-thatched roof. Nearly all members of the family had been great readers. Brother Malfred had subscribed to a monthly magazine which distributed a large illustrated history of Norway, and when the first installments of this work arrived Malfred read them aloud to the family on winter evenings. The sagas had made a deep impression, especially that of a ferocious and gifted Viking named Eigil Skallagrimson, whose father left Norway and settled in Iceland because he would not submit to restrictions which the first king of united Norway imposed on his subjects. Eigil's courage and skill as a fighter were tremendously appreciated, as were his defiance and rebellious attitude toward the gods. This defiance was immortalized in a poem composed by him in commemoration of his son's drowning. A small boy of nine who was still resentful against Providence for the loss of a beloved and admired older brother sympathized with the Viking of long ago.

These deep and solem thoughts mingled with dreams that cannot die. Everything centered about the home. A clear-cut picture of his parents was deliberately engraved on "the fleshy tables of the heart." Father in height was middle-sized, broad shouldered and thin-flanked; he had deep-set, keen eyes. His hair had been black and curly; now it was snow white, thin on top, wavy at the temples. His nose was well-shaped, and his chin was hidden by a square-cut full beard. He had the ruddy complexion of a man whose life has been spent in the open air. About twenty years ago he had abandoned the sea as a regular vocation. In the summer he would occasionally visit the salmon traps, and despite his seventy-three years he worked vigorously during haying. However, a goodly share of his days were now spent walking over marsh, hill, and moor, inspecting the struggling birch, rowan, and aspen growing in sheltered vales. They had to be guarded, trimmed, and pruned. Heather and juniper were cleared away lest they should rob the birch saplings of the little nourishment a poor and wind-swept land could give.

Father had been a sailor and fisherman since his boyhood. He had had the reputation of being fearless and skillful aboard ship, but he had never loved the sea. In common with many of his compatriots who had to win most of their living from the sea, he considered it an enemy. He sailed and fished only because economic necessity compelled him to do so. Given a choice he would have preferred to devote his time to the tilling of the soil. A hard-working man all his life, his arms and hands bore the marks of heavy toil. But his eyes were still clear, and he walked erect with firm steps. For more than three score and ten years he had pursued "the noiseless tenor" of his way. By precept and example he had impressed upon his children the importance of the three cardinal virtues — fortitude, honesty, and loyalty.

When the youth reflected upon his mother, what she had given and what she was, emotions surged; he felt infinitely soft and tender. She was somewhat bent, her face wrinkled yet very kind. Involuntarily he addressed her as if she were present, spoke to her words which the taciturn, reserved Norwegian would never utter to any audience. "Mother mine, a life of ease was not your lot. Fatherless in infancy, you were looked upon by your successive stepfathers as a valuable servant who should set the pace and lead in all the tasks considered women's work in a large household. As a wife you have been a true helpmeet, as a mother you have given without stint. Throughout many winters when Father fished off Röst you were without news from him from the day of his departure early in January till his return in May. As the wind shook the house and the snow whirled madly over the frozen earth you often kept lonely vigil by the bedside of a sick child, worrying over the feverish little one who tossed restlessly in uneasy sleep, worrying also over the fate of husband and father who perchance was battling the elements this stormy night and matching the wit and skill of puny man against the awful powers of the Arctic sea. Life's pain did not pass you by; childbearing and hard toil have left their mark upon you. Eleven children you bore without the aid of even a midwife. Of late you have seemed extremely weary; I know that at times your soul is heavy within you. You long to rest beside your first-born under the rowan tree in yonder graveyard. But throughout life's struggles, sorrow, and anxiety, you have shown an indomitable will, you have revealed a spirit that never flinches. You have not noticed how keenly I, your youngest, have watched you during the last few days since I disclosed my plans to you. You bore the news bravely; I have been haunted by a line from Ibsen's *Brand,* 'only the lost is yours forever.' You have given everything, strength, energy, your very lifeblood. Yes, Mother mine, you will live, the memory of you will be enshrined in my heart till life's last day."

For more than two hours the youth had surveyed the world about him, dwelt in the past, reflected on the mysteries of life's rhythm, indulged in a reverie of introspection. Suddenly a gust of cold breeze brought him out of the dreams back to the world of action. By now the sun had completed its brief sojourn behind the mountains which lined the north side of the fjord. Just east of north a golden glow was spreading over jagged peaks. Soon a few bright rays appeared, then a purple sun arc, and finally the life-giving ball flooded mountain and sea with crimson light. In the birch grove on the hillside birds were stirring with a slight flutter of wings and isolated chirps like musicians tuning their instruments. All of a sudden a full-throated chorus burst forth. From its nest somewhere in the heather a skylark swung heavenward pouring forth its blithe spirit in a song to the glory of the morning.

The land breeze from the Blue Man's Ice broke the glassy surface of the fjord. The idle sails of the little vessel ceased flapping and began to bulge, the helmsman came to life, and the ship headed for the open sea.

Again the young man observed the sunlit spaciousness of a landscape as changeless and everlasting as anything found on the sub-lunar sphere. Again he drank it all in — sights, sounds, smells. Yesterday was gone; soon the new day would join its fellows, but this picture of sea and mountains, though a year hence he would be far away, would remain with him wherever he went "Be it east, Be it west."

As he slowly descended the hill he felt that the past night formed a dividing line between youth and manhood. With grim resolve he was cutting loose from the past, closing a chapter of his life. Yesterday seemed so far behind. Like the ship on the fjord he had cast off, broken the mooring; leaving a snug harbor he was hoisting sail and heading for the trackless sea.

KRISTINE ANDREASSEN JOHNSEN KNAPLUND

1905

MARTINUS JOHNSEN KNAPLUND

KNAPLUNDOY

PAUL KNAPLUND, 1907

HANS CHRIST FARM

Part II

New Moorings

TO

KATHERINE BARBARA AND PAUL WILLIAM

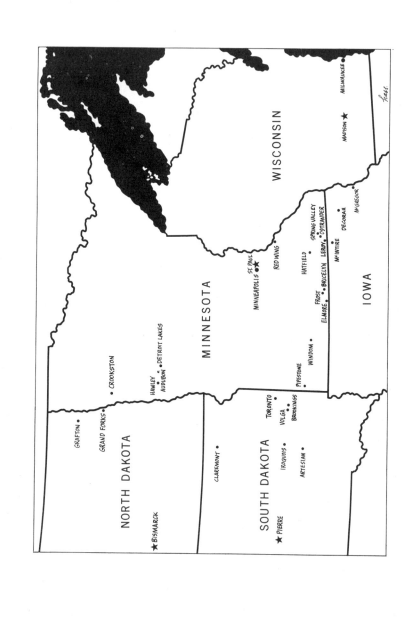

Chapter 8

A Spring Evening

IT WAS MID-APRIL
in the year 1936. Spring had come at last to the upper
Mississippi Valley. The winter had been long and severe. For
weeks on end the thermometer had registered zero or below.
Blizzards had swept over the land burying the countryside
deep in snow, blocking roads and city streets. A weary people
joyfully greeted the first signs of spring.

Among those who longed for the winter to relax its grip
was a middle-aged university professor. At the end of January
he had taken his family to Florida. Returning to his professional duties he had lived alone in a home that seemed
indescribably empty with the loved ones gone. Every room
and corner of the modest little house spoke of wife and
children. Yet the silence of the house was oppressive and he
counted the weeks and days until he could go and fetch them.
An early spring might enable them to come home in March.
But no! The cold was too stubborn. He had to wait and wait.

From his study window in an ivy-covered hall on the crest
of a hill he had watched for the first signs of the new season.
Below his window the hill sloped gently toward south and
west, its sides planted with shrubs and trees. Beyond were
other university buildings, city homes, and a church in the
background. To the west was a wide horizon. From his window he viewed a rolling countryside, trees, fields, meadows,
and farmsteads. Beyond these there were, he knew, more hills
and dales, limitless plains, mighty rivers. In years gone by

he had roamed over large stretches of this fertile western land and in memory he could visualize it all till the view was blocked by majestic mountains a thousand miles away.

The time was late afternoon of a cloudless day. Classes were over, offices closed, the building empty save for the man sitting idly day-dreaming by the window. He felt relaxed, at peace; the lonely vigil would soon be over. Tomorrow he would start south to bring the family home. No longer would he return evenings to an empty house. Again he would have a home filled with life and bustle, wife and children to greet him, to blow kisses and wave goodbye as he left in the mornings. Home was all-important to this serious, silent man. For twenty years he had had none. He had been a wanderer in a strange land. People had been exceedingly kind to him. Doors had stood hospitably open for him. Often he had felt that he was a welcome guest, but, after all, only a guest or a lodger. Nowhere had he really belonged. At no place did his leaving create an empty room. Hence, when the moment came that a beloved young woman linked her fate with his, when in time a house was acquired and children arrived, a home of his own was created at last. For him that home so long yearned for became a shrine, a holy place. With the loved ones gone, it was but a shell. Soon, very soon, it again would become a reality.

During long winter evenings before the fire he had often reminisced about events and experiences of the past years. In the spring of 1906 he had landed in New York. The money for the passage had been borrowed. The land was absolutely strange to him. American law required that all immigrants have an address for their destination. His was that of an old woman, his father's cousin, a cripple who nearly forty years earlier had left Norway in a huff because the niece with whom she stayed had not measured up to the aunt's standards in housekeeping. In 1906 this woman was in her middle eighties. No help was anticipated from her. He had good health but no special skill and no education beyond that from his Norwegian country school. Not a word of English did he

know except "yes" and "no," and those he couldn't use
because he was unable to tell which one might be the correct
answer.

That was thirty years ago. Thirteen years after his landing
he had secured the Ph.D. degree from a renowned department at a university internationally famous. Lately he had
been chairman of that department. He felt very grateful for
the opportunities America had given him. He had spent
thirty years of his life in this land which seemed so incredibly strange to him when he first landed here. Thirty
years form a large portion of the average person's lifetime;
when they are the span from twenty-one to fifty-one, they
constitute an important segment of anyone's working life.

Exactly thirty years ago on a sad spring evening he had
said goodbye to his parents and two sisters and left for far-off
America. Again it was spring. Now this country was his,
largely because it was the land of his wife and children. Old
roots had decayed, new ones had grown for the immigrant.
He was in this land; he was of it; his roots were now firmly
embedded here. In 1916 when he had returned to visit Norway he knew that he had become a stranger in the land of his
birth. For many years after he had come to America he went
home every night in his dreams. Over wide prairies and a
wider ocean, in the darkness of night his mind had rushed
back to the familiar scenes, the loved ones of childhood and
youth. But in 1933 when once more he visited Norway his
mind at night galloped in the opposite direction, to the little
white house which sheltered those who were really his own.
There he was anchored.

Visions came to him this April evening. As on the Norwegian hillside before he left for America shadows grew
longer, picture after picture flashed on the screen of memory.
The departure from home, the long ocean voyage, the landing
in New York and all the excitement connected therewith, the
train journey to the Minnesota farm of Hans Christ where
he spent the first sixteen months in America, winters at school
and summers earning the wherewithal to go to school, and

then the years in purely academic surroundings climbing the academic ladder. As he reviewed these years it seemed as if he were looking at a stranger long departed. The immigrant boy, farmhand, agent for aluminum cooking utensils, the student who had struggled with the elements of English grammar and the intricacies of English syntax — those individuals were gone. Events he remembered very clearly, yet the time and place seemed far away. It was as if he were looking at pictures through a stereopticon. Each was very distinct for a short moment, then it was pushed aside and another came into view.

As scene followed scene in rapid succession daylight faded. The pale blue of the cupola on yonder church turned dark. A lone star hovered above its steeple. Dimly the noise from the street below reached the ear of the watcher. The large building, teeming with life by day, was now silent. All seemed so quiet. This was fitting. The man by the window was weaving a cloth from the warp and weft of life's countless moments. The bitter and hard experiences were mostly forgotten. A kind dispensation permits commonplace events to acquire grace through memory. Wrinkled faces and gnarled hands gain beauty and enchantment when associated with pleasant words, kind deeds, friendly handclasps. It was fitting, too, that the dreamer about past events should be by himself. He who travels memory's road perforce journeys alone.

Chapter 9

Weigh Anchor

ON HIS WAY
to America the immigrant of 1906 had stayed for a week at
the Scandinavian Sailors' home in Liverpool. In the reading
room he found a paper which contained poems appropriate
for sailors. One of these entitled "Embark" seemed so apt for
his own case that he cut it out. This clipping he had carried
in his pocket for thirty years. The unknown poet's decla-
mation still held appeal for an emigrant:

> Weigh anchor! — from the snug harbor
> The ship glides out to sea
> Weigh anchor! Thus ties are broken
> There is no return.
> Gone is childhood's peace
> You are facing manhood's battles.

This stanza described very accurately his emotions at that
time. On a Sunday morning in April he had stood on the deck
of a small Norwegian fjord steamer waving goodbye to Father,
Mother, and Sisters Constance and Katherine assembled outside the family home where they were silhouetted against the
eastern sky. The propeller churned and the ship swung from
the tide current and headed westward toward the mouth of
the fjord and the town of Bodö where the emigrant would
catch the coastal express steamer for Trondheim on the first
leg of the long journey to America. He watched the little
family group until it broke up. Slowly, very slowly, each
turned and walked into the house. Their hearts were heavy

within them. And so was the heart of the traveller. He had caused the dear ones sorrow. Almost he regretted his decision to leave home, family, the country of his fathers, for the distant unknown land where none would know him or care what his fate might be.

The resolve to emigrate had been very hard to make. There had been no attraction for him in the glowing advertisements of steamship companies about the great opportunities awaiting emigrants in western Canada. Free for the taking would be 160 acres of fertile prairie land, the ads proclaimed, land which did not require ditching, the cutting of tussocks, or even fertilizing. A farmer needed only to plow, sow, and reap the golden grain. Not poor, half-filled kernels of barley, but wheat, the best bread-grain in the world, and oats, such oats as never could grow in the fields of Norway. Certainly not in arctic Norway where oats, and poor oats at that, ripened only in a few specially favored spots.

Many years ago Brother Julius had been gripped with the "America fever." A close friend of his was leaving and had offered to stake him with the price of the ticket. Mother had begged Julius not to go. Regretfully he had heeded her appeal, and when the friend returned home to die of tuberculosis, Mother felt vindicated. Toward the end of the nineties, Brother Bernt was tempted by offers of free passage to Queensland, Australia. He had sent for literature. Masses came with pictures showing a lush country of marvellous fertility and with perfect climate. No raging storms, no long, dark, awesome winters like those of arctic Norway. Queensland was described as a genial land with sunshine, warm climate, rich soil — everything that Norway lacked. As Bernt read and talked about this great southland his youngest brother grew cold with fear. Would Brother Bernt really leave; would he be lost to the family like so many of those from the parish who had gone to foreign lands never to come back except for the few who returned to die? Fortunately Bernt was offered a good business opportunity in Norway. His brother was much relieved.

And now he, the baby of the family of eleven brothers and sisters, was actually taking the step he had feared his brothers would take. He had been something of a misfit in a community where all able-bodied young males were amphibious. He liked farming, but the soil was poor and ill requited the back breaking toil spent thereon. To watch the sea in its shifting moods was fascinating, but to get a living from it as sailor or fisherman demanded skills for which he had little aptitude. He loved books but the road to learning was closed to those who had no money. Thus it had seemed that his only chance to earn a living for himself and aid his aging parents would be to enroll in a government training school for non-commissioned officers.

In the summer of 1905 as he weighed plans for his future, fate appeared in the guise of a beautiful young woman. She was a visitor in the parish. In common with other youths he admired the stranger. A whirlwind courtship had ended in secret betrothal to this lovely girl five years his senior. The situation called for desperate action. Only America could offer a solution, and he resolved to emigrate. The object of his adoration had gone into nurses' training in a Bergen hospital. Unused to hard work, she was unhappy and the young man was spurred to act quickly. The prospect of meeting her somewhat eased the pain of parting from his family. Yet, he had many misgivings. Perhaps he had acted too selfishly.

Torn with emotion he had a last glimpse of the old home as the steamer rounded a promontory and headed for Bodö harbor. There was no one whom he knew on the quay in Bodö when he boarded the coastal steamer for Trondheim. He was rather glad to be spared a second leave-taking. Dazed from the strain of the parting from parents and sisters, lost and bewildered, he was passively being carried on by fate. Chart and compass were gone. He was alone.

The trip to Trondheim took forty hours. As a third-class passenger he had neither stateroom nor berth; there was not even a place to sit down except on boxes or barrels of cargo.

This did not bother him much for he had travelled in this manner every time he had gone to Lofoten. As on those trips he carried some food along. Since he had had to borrow money for his ticket, expenses must be kept to the absolute minimum. Not even a cup of coffee was bought aboard.

By degrees he shook off the numbness of mind which had gripped him at the parting. For the first time he was travelling from Bodö to Trondheim, a route often discussed by his father and brothers. A map was posted on deck by the bridge. With its help he tried to identify fjords, promontories, islands, and harbors frequently mentioned in accounts of trips to Christiansund, Aalesund, and Trondheim but these only added to his nostalgia for they conjured up memories of cosy winter evenings at home. The exercise in geography had to be abandoned.

Before long he discovered that several other third-class passengers were bound for America. The common destination drew them together. Among these emigrants were a baker and a shoemaker from Bodö. The latter had spent one year in America, and his knowledge of the country was truly astonishing. To be sure, he had not been outside New York City, but there seemed to be something magical about setting foot on American soil. Having done that the shoemaker had become an authority on life, customs, and conditions everywhere in that vast land. And his command of English was simply marvellous. In fact it was so good that his mother tongue was almost forgotten. English words, or what passed for such, were mixed with the narrator's Norwegian to convey the true atmosphere of events related. It was a bit bewildering for Paul. But perhaps it was all due to his own stupidity — the baker seemed to understand everything the shoemaker said. Those two talked incessantly and laid numerous plans. They were certain that many golden opportunities awaited them on the other side of the Atlantic. They were so confident and hopeful that the farm boy listened in silence. His only certainty was that he knew nothing about this wonderland. He was ashamed to ask questions, and he had no confidence in his ability to conquer the unknown. He envied those who knew so much and seemed to be so sure of themselves. Years later he discovered that people who talked the way the baker and the shoemaker did were sorely plagued by self-doubt and lack of staying power, were in fact often defeated at the first obstacle.

Forty hours spent in listening and in pacing the deck proved wearisome even for a youth of twenty-one. He was glad when the ancient city of Trondheim hove into view. On the quay a band of agents from the various trans-Atlantic steamship companies pounced on the small flock of emigrants. Paul had already settled on the Cunard Line because of its long safety record, and he soon found the Cunard man. Both in Trondheim and throughout the journey to America the emigrant felt that he was either just carrion for others to batten on or a sheep to be herded and pushed into the proper enclosure.

Since he had more than a day to spend in Trondheim he found lodging and went sight-seeing. Trondheim with a population of 30,000 seemed a metropolis to the country boy. An ancient city, once the capital of Norway and the shrine of the country's patron saint, St. Olav, it had a long history which he knew fairly well. Its founder, that splendid Viking, King Olav Tryggvason, had been the hero of his childhood. Of the marvels of the cathedral he had heard much, for Father who had visited Trondheim had described its sights many a time. The emigrant, prepared to admire this historic place, found that impressions were registered only vaguely. His visit was not a pleasure trip; it was a leave-taking. His spirit was bruised. Even the prospect of meeting his fiancée in Bergen failed to heal the wound caused by the departure from home.

With a group of other emigrants he went to the Trondheim police station where records were kept of those who left the country. An officious-looking individual demanded curtly the reason why he was emigrating. Paul replied, "Economic reasons," an answer which evoked no comment. Among those assembled at the police station was a sprinkling of people who had been in America. All were anxious to spread information about that great land. Of the many tales told the most marvellous was recounted by a seedy-looking drunk who related that he had once walked into an American store and let it be known that he needed both a suit of clothes and a dinner. The proprietor then produced a live sheep and replied, "Both will come from this animal." And in an incredibly short time a dinner of mutton chops and a suit of clothes were ready. "That," said the drunk," is an example of American efficiency."

In Trondheim the emigrants boarded the *Tasso,* an English ship of the Wilson line, which would take them to Hull. The third-class accomodations consisted of two large rooms, one for men, the other for women; each had a thick layer of sawdust on the floor and bunks overhead. The sawdust was a puzzle at first, but as the ship crossed the North Sea its utility was demonstrated. The bunks were partitioned, each section accomodating four persons. None had a mattress, springs, or sheets, but they were liberally supplied with blankets recently returned from a steam laundry. Though all were clean, carcasses indicated that recently they had been well populated with vermin. Each passenger was supplied with a plate and other necessary equipment for food which was ladled out from huge containers. It was plain, quite well-cooked food, and youthful appetite is seldom critical.

The *Tasso,* an old tub on which even the second and first-class quarters seemed far from palatial, was larger than any other ship on which Paul had travelled. Furthermore, the ship's crew spoke English and this in itself was quite intriguing. The language sounded so strange that he began to doubt whether he could ever master this foreign tongue.

Bergen was thirty-six hours sail from Trondheim, with stops at the intervening ports of Christiansund and Aalesund. But neither these two cities nor the passage of Stadt, famous western promontory of Norway, aroused much interest. He was torn by two conflicting emotions: grief over the departure

from home and family, and joy over the prospect of reaching
Bergen and spending a day with the woman he loved. Early
Friday morning the *Tasso* was to arrive in Bergen. One of its
passengers did not sleep the preceding night. At dawn he rose
and found a quiet nook where he could shave and clean up.
He was on deck when the ship entered the harbor of the
famous city. Father had often talked about the olden days
when he was a member of the crew in the box-like square-
sailed vessels which carried dried cod to Bergen. The ships,
sailing as a fleet, would enter the harbor where the merchants were lined up to receive the harvest of the Lofoten
cod fishery. Those Bergen merchants had the fishermen
coming and going, they set the price of the fish bought and
of the goods sold. Harbor regulations forbade cooking aboard
the boats from the north while at anchor in Bergen, so any
warm meals had to be bought ashore.

The recollections of what Father had described, and the
treatment of humble fishermen by purse-proud merchants,
were vivid in the mind of the young passenger aboard the
Tasso. He recalled what he had read about stirring episodes
in the history of Bergen and of the humiliations suffered by
its citizens while the city's trade was controlled by the Hanseatic League. He sighted the high-gabled German warehouses at the quay, the famous hall of King Haakon the Old,
dating from the thirteenth century, and the city's fortifica-
tions. All this was absorbingly interesting. Moreover, contrary
to Bergen's reputation for rain, the morning was sunny and
bright. Spring had arrived. But the eager youth was anxious
to get on with his personal errand.

The day was still young when the first passenger went
ashore. Realizing that it was too early to make a call even at
a hospital, he walked around a bit, always edging closer to
the place where he was to visit. At last he thought the time
had come. From a porter he learned where the student nurse
might be. Soon the eager swain found her in the hall, but,
alas, he received only a formal handshake. Yes, she had expected him; unfortunately she was very busy. Would she

have an hour free later in the day or in the evening? No, that was impossible. She was sorry; no meeting could be arranged.

As he left the hospital the sun was shining brightly, but the day seemed black to the dejected youth. Slowly he made his way back to the quay and to the ship. By then all the other passengers had gone ashore. The third-class quarters were deserted. The bunk was dark. That was well.

Late that evening the *Tasso* left Bergen for Stavanger. Passengers began to flock aboard well ahead of the departure time. In contrast to his deep gloom they all seemed to be in a festive mood. On deck and below every nook and corner was crowded with leave-takers. Liquor was plentiful. Innumerable toasts were drunk. The clinking of glasses, the shouting of "skaal," the singing of songs, produced a hubbub and excitement far beyond anything the youth had ever experienced. Everyone seemed to have a host of friends, all were jolly and certain of finding at least one gold mine in America. As the ship glided from the quay pledges of eternal love and friendship rang across the water. Only he seemed utterly alone.

Aboard the *Tasso* the celebration continued until Stavanger was reached early Saturday morning. Paul went ashore to mail farewell letters, and then took a place in the bow as the ship steered to the west. In a moment it passed beyond the sheltering islands and into the North Sea, which this day lived up to its ancient reputation for turbulence. It was in an angry mood. Poor old *Tasso* pitched and rolled and was tossed about in a most discourteous fashion. Few people were on deck, but one lonely emigrant found that stormy day on the North Sea exhilarating. He welcomed the gale and the salt spray. For him it was a new and exciting experience to be out of sight of land. Below deck everything was in turmoil. On deck he felt free, almost defiant. Next Monday he would join Brother John in Liverpool; no longer would he be alone. John and he had stood together in many a childhood skirmish, and together they would cross the Atlantic to make their way in America.

Sunday dawned cloudless with a smooth and almost glassy sea. Everybody was on deck, but many had changed greatly since Friday night. Debauchery and sea sickness had deflated both courage and self-confidence. The loudest talkers thirty-six hours ago were now the most dejected. Their bravado gone they had swung to the opposite extreme, timorously fretting about the ocean voyage and their future in America.

Sunday afternoon *Tasso's* passengers began to scan the western horizon for signs of England. Those who had never been away from Norway were excited over the prospect of landing on foreign soil. England was the gateway to America. Expectantly, almost fearfully, they wondered what the great and powerful England would be like. Perchance Norway would seem mean and shabby in comparison with this famous land, but instinctively they rallied in defense of their fatherland. Of course, everyone knew that in scenic beauty Norway was superior to England.

Finally the coast was sighted — low and unimpressive it was. No towering mountains or rushing waterfalls met the eye. Mighty England was as flat and uninteresting as Norway south of Stavanger. The travellers grew boastful of their native land. Their ego rose. Soon they found other points of comparison in Norway's favor. The sea off the coast and the water in the Humber were muddy and yellow in contrast to the clear, cool green and blue waters of Norwegian fjords and rivers. Even passengers travelling in the squalid third-class quarters of the *Tasso* grew cocky. After all, Norway was better then England. Hadn't Norwegian Vikings triumphantly sailed up the Humber in days of long ago! The land the emigrants saw had once been ruled by a king from Norway — Eirik Bloodax. They waxed proud at the thought. The deeds of that cruel tyrant, dead for 950 years, seemed to bring them glory, inflated their self-esteem. It was dark as the *Tasso* crept into the harbor of Hull. On a hard bunk aboard a foreign ship in a foreign harbor at least one young man slept soundly, dreaming of home and family now so far away.

Early Monday morning *Tasso's* passengers were all eager to

go ashore. The checking of the passenger list took some time, but customs inspection was a mere formality for these were aliens in transit. They were treated as a herd, shepherded from the docks and piled into huge horse-drawn vans which hauled them to the railroad station. The citizens of Hull stared at the emigrants as if they were a load of circus animals. But the Norwegians did not mind that; in a strange land they expected the people to act strangely.

Several times since that spring morning in 1906 the graying man at his study window had visited England and other foreign countries. But no landing, not even the return to Norway after ten years absence, had created sensations comparable to those which stirred him during those morning hours in Hull. The ground he stepped on felt the same as at home, neither grass nor trees seemed unfamiliar; yet he had a queer feeling of a strangeness which he could not explain. Perhaps it was the sight of the heavy horses with big fetlocks, the large wagons, the drivers' shouts in an unfamiliar tongue, the street signs, and the foreign-looking houses which made everything seem so alien. The youth from farm and fishing boat of arctic Norway knew he was a stranger in England.

For the first time in his life he rode on a railroad. Experiences so decidedly new have a flavor all their own. The train compartment was far more comfortable than quarters on the Norwegian coastal steamer. The journey from Hull to Liverpool took the greater part of the day, a goodly share of which was taken up with switching back and forth at several junctions. No lunch was served, but the emigrants did not mind. Everything they saw was new and absorbingly interesting. Coming from a country with few industries the passengers thought the pall of smoke over English cities dreadful; the countryside, on the other hand, was green and altogether charming. The patterns made by hedges attracted special attention, for Norway had nothing like it.

In the late afternoon the emigrant train rolled into the Liverpool station. Again all was hustle and bustle. Men wearing caps with the insignia of the various transatlantic lines were on hand to look after their charges. Paul, with the trusting confidence of the innocent abroad, had turned his trunk over to the representative of the Cunard Line in Trondheim and accepted his assurance that it would be taken care of. Now with only light hand luggage to carry he had ample time to look for Brother John. Yes, there he was on the platform eagerly scanning the crowd. Good old John — everything would be all right. There would be two of them to face the unknown. John had left his ship a fortnight earlier and was staying at the Liverpool Scandinavian Sailors' Home to await the arrival of his younger brother. Together they rode in the van taking emigrants to the Cunard line hotel.

On the way John broached a plan he had hatched since he left his ship. John had always been a bit mercurial in temperament, had always looked for new and exciting ventures. At the Sailors' Home he had met a man of Norwegian birth who for many years had been a resident of Valparaiso. This man had learned that Chilean waters were teeming with fish. Recently a company had been organized to exploit those fisheries; the Norse-Chilean had come to England to buy a trawler and was going to Norway to hire a crew. It was planned that the company should operate from Juan Fernandez, the Robinson Crusoe Island. Prospects for profit had been described as excellent, it seemed alluring to be stationed at this famous island, and John had agreed to join in the new venture. Would Paul go along? No, Paul would not. He had never been fond of fishing, and he lacked John's gambling spirit. He felt he must carry out his original plan even though it meant that he would have to go alone to America.

Since the brothers were to take separate ways and not meet again for perhaps many years, John proposed that they should spend a week together in Liverpool. To this Paul readily agreed provided his ticket could be changed. With this settled they went to their separate hostels. The emigrants who had not eaten since breakfast, were, upon arriving at the Cunard line hotel, ushered into a bare looking dining-room with long tables and benches. The plate on which Paul was served his food was gray. He moved his finger over the edge of the plate and the finger turned black. The dirt was too much for even a hungry lad of twenty-one. He left the table, picked up his bags, and walked over to the Sailors' Home. Yes, the Swedish manager could put him up. At this place the brothers spent their week together.

In the world's leading seaports hostels for sailors were operated on a reciprocal basis by the seamen's missions of the Scandinavian countries. In one port Danes would be in charge, in another Norwegians, in still another Swedes, and natives of the three countries were welcomed in all these hostels. Since the people were overwhelmingly Lutheran and their languages mutually understood, similar arrangements were applied to the churches maintained by the seamen's missions. In 1906 both the hostel and the church in Liverpool were operated under the auspices of the Swedish mission. Swedish-speaking Finnish sailors had the same privileges as the other Scandinavians.

John, who had sailed the high seas since 1901 and had visited many world ports, had a close acquaintanceship with these sailors' hostels. He was at home in them and on the best of terms with the staff. As John's brother Paul was a welcome guest. For him the week in Liverpool and the association with sailors proved absorbingly interesting.

With so much that was new and strange for him to see, the heartsoreness eased for a time. Like all who have been brought up by the sea, he was fascinated by the stories of seafaring men and awed when he heard a bearded, ruddy-faced sailor state in a matter-of-fact way that he had been in every famous seaport in the world except Pensacola. The younger of two Swedish sailor brothers spoke freely about their experiences on their last voyage when their ship, a bark of which the older brother was the master, had met with so many storms on a trip from Sweden to America that provisions ran short. When a passing Atlantic liner refused to supply the bark with food, its crew hoisted a signal begging to be taken off. To prevent the ship from becoming a derelict and a menace to navigation, the master ordered it scuttled. But the crew had to leave in such a hurry that the job was not finished, and the abandoned ship was later salvaged. The owner of the bark blamed its master for the disaster, his license was taken away and the two Swedes were now uncertain about what the future held for them. A couple of Finns at the hostel stood out from the rest of the sailors because of their expensive clothes and unusually fine luggage. They belonged to the upper strata of Finnish society. Some years earlier they had been sent on a grand tour to western Europe; bored with sight-seeing they had shipped on Norwegian vessels to see the world. The seamy side of a sailor's life was demonstrated the first evening at the hostel when a Danish sailor celebrated his release from a hospital by getting drunk and attempting to kill a Finn of whom he was jealous. The Knaplund brothers who came to the aid of the manager in quelling the riot were known thereafter as the policemen of the hostel.

Even more interesting than the people at the Sailors' Home was Liverpool itself. For the first time in his life the emigrant was in a big city. Though he had read about art galleries, museums, and parks, he had never seen any. Those in Liverpool seemed really marvellous. Here he found Egyptian mummies like those described in Brother Bernt's *World History*. That a lock of Napoleon's hair should be kept as a valuable treasure in an English museum amazed him. The nude Greek statuary at first shocked the young puritan. St. George's Hall he viewed with awed admiration. He was surprised to learn that what seemed to him a large expanse of meadow was a public park. Altogether the country boy was much impressed with Liverpool.

The Sailors' Home was near the hotels operated by the great trans-Atlantic steamship companies. In 1906 emigrants to America passed by the thousands through Liverpool every week. These were considered legitimate prey for a swarm of hawkers, money-changers, and panderers. The men of these professions were a filthy, sorry-looking lot. The last evening in Liverpool a group from the Sailors' Home went out to bait the birds of prey. But somehow they were wary of trying their tricks on sailors and except for a few noisy arguments nothing exciting happened.

Originally the brothers had planned to go to Boston and there buy the railroad tickets to the place in Minnesota where they intended to seek work. Because of John's new plans Paul had to alter sailing date and ship, and to buy his ticket to Minnesota by way of New York. This was done the first day he arrived in Liverpool. But what would happen to Paul's trunk which had been checked through to Boston? The reply was that it would be routed to New York and be on the pier when he landed.

On Tuesday, May 8, 1906, the emigrant sailed on the *Caronia* for New York. The leave-taking from John, though less heartrending than bidding parents and sisters farewell, was not easy. John stood on the pier and waved until the mist and smoke of Liverpool hid him from view. As the tender approached the *Caronia,* the ship looked huge compared with the steamers the emigrant had seen in Norway. Aboard confusion prevailed everywhere. Fortunately, the younger of the Swedish brothers and the two Finnish sailors were also going to New York, so the four from the Home obtained a cabin together. However, the Finns found the quarters cramped; by tipping a room steward they secured an outside cabin for two. The emigrant and the Swedish sailor then plotted to keep the four-berth cabin to themselves. Fearing that Irishmen might be put in with them when the *Caronia* called at Queenstown, they unscrewed the doorknob and carried it around in their pockets until the ship was well out in the Atlantic.

The year 1906 was one of heavy emigration from Poland and from the Jewish Pale in Russia. The *Caronia* had a steerage section in addition to her other three classes; the majority of the passengers from Eastern Europe travelled steerage in one large room with berths along all four sides. Here pandemonium reigned the evening *Caronia* left Liverpool. Everybody was talking and gesticulating. The third-class passengers had no peace until after midnight when ship's officers with interpreters succeeded in quieting the din. The passengers on the deck above were worried lest the racket in the steerage resume the next morning and continue throughout the voyage, but the *Caronia* ran into a storm upon leaving Queenstown. Then only muffled groans were heard from below. By the time the storm abated the steerage people seemed to have settled their differences, or else their high spirits had vanished. They caused no further disturbance.

The large steamer was a whole world in miniature with every sort and condition of people aboard. No ship was sighted on the entire voyage. Nothing to see but water. For one who had always been within the sight of land the emptiness and vastness of the ocean was enthralling. Equally fascinating was the realization that the Cunarder's passengers were a microcosm of Europe with its babel of tongues and its class distinctions. The third-class passengers who divided into national groups never mingled with either those from the steerage or those from second. One day the Swedish sailor tried to converse in his own language with a group of Irish girls because, as he explained to his cabin-mate, Swedish was just as good a language as English, but the conversation could hardly have been called fruitful.

Paul spent many hours pacing the deck with one of the young Finns, who had gone abroad when he finished the gymnasium. After some travelling he shipped as an apprentice seaman on a Norwegian sailing vessel bound for Australia with the understanding that he would not be ordered to do any of the disagreeable tasks required of apprentices nor receive any wages. In time he became an able seaman, and during 1905–1906 he had served on a New Zealand costal steamer. Since his Swedish was quite fluent, he and the Norwegian conversed without difficulty. The Finn spoke freely about life at sea, the lands he had visited, and the Norwegian authors he had read, but he was loath to discuss his native country. When asked if he didn't intend to return to the home he had left nearly four years previously, he glumly replied, "If Finland revolts against the Tsar, I shall go back." Although thirty years had passed since these walks and talks, the Norwegian still had a clear mental picture of the dark, strongly-built, melancholy Finn who had given his name as Waldemar Kaupinen, but who in the one letter which he later wrote to his fellow passenger had asked to be addressed as Harry von Gessler. There seemed to be something mysterious about that young Finn.

The shipboard routine was broken by boat drills, checking the passenger list, and vaccination for smallpox. Steerage passengers evidently dreaded the last. The young girls screamed and ran to hide with sailors in pursuit. Perhaps the fear was simulated. At least onlookers got the impression that the sailors' chase of pretty Jewish girls gave pleasure to both the hunted and the hunters.

As on the Norwegian coastal steamer, the passengers who had been in America were much in demand for advice and information. One who had thirty years of residence to his credit was venerated as a sage, but it was a man who had been in the United States only two years who was most generous with information and advice. Indeed, it seemed generally true that the amount a person thought he knew about America was in inverse ratio to the length of time he had spent in the country.

At last on Wednesday, May 16, the Statue of Liberty and New York City were sighted. Expectancy and hope, admiration and awe were perhaps the prevailing emotions. Some shouted and talked excitedly, others just stared in silence. By nature taciturn, the emigrant from arctic Norway was always very quiet when faced with the strange and unusual. To him the New York skyline was less awesome than to many of the other passengers for the sublimity of the natural scenery in his homeland made man's greatest efforts seem puny when compared with the Alps of Lofoten. But the strangeness of what he saw roused apprehensions. After all, he knew not a word of the language spoken in this land. Not a soul therein cared about what might happen to him. Never before had he been homeless. Now he was. To be sure, he had written to a Miss Hannah Elstad, the elderly cousin of his father. The letter had been answered in an unsteady hand by a bachelor farmer who signed himself Hans Christ, Ostrander P. O., Fillimore C. O. Minnesota. The emigrant had tried to find out what the P. O., and the C. O. meant. In Norway none could tell him, though the agent for the Cunard Line in Bodö had said that C. O. obviously meant "company." The elderly Norwegian—American aboard the *Caronia,* however, interpreted C. O. to mean county and P. O. post office, but since he had never been in Minnesota, he could not answer the question of where in the state these obscure places might be. So the immigrant remained in the dark about his destination. This uncertainty had a depressing effect.

The stream of immigrants was so heavy that the *Caronia* had to wait in New York harbor from Wednesday afternoon until Friday morning before she could land her passengers, except those who were American citizens. The intervening day was May 17, the Norwegian independence day. Some Norwegians attempted to celebrate on a small scale, but the national anthem "Ja, vi elsker dette landet" (Yes, we love this country) sounded strange and unnatural aboard an English ship in New York harbor. It recalled the Biblical story of the displaced Jews who were asked to sing about Zion by the rivers of Babylon. Somehow that feeling remained throughout the years. The Norwegian songs which rang so true when sung in Norway sounded hollow in America.

At last came the morning of the disembarkation. Everybody rose early. The excitement was greater than at the landing in Hull. America was after all magical and unique. Moses viewing the burning bush had been ordered to remove his shoes; the immigrants felt an urge to do likewise as they first stepped on American soil. As it happened there was no stepping on any soil, only on planks until Ellis Island was reached.

In New York the herding of the immigrants was done more efficiently than in Hull and Liverpool. Soon most of them were at the Ellis Island immigrant station. That, too, had a certain fascination. Thousands of people of all ages and nationalities were gathered in one large room. From the concourse fenced aisles with gates led to desks where inspectors examined the eyes of the immigrants, studied their papers, and inquired how much money they had and what their destination was. Several tragic scenes were witnessed. A Norwegian mother with a crippled child who had travelled to America to join her husband was taken to a separate room for further examination. Her sister who had come along to help was refused admittance to the room. This young woman had been gay, carefree, and self-reliant aboard the *Caronia;* now she wept bitterly. The elderly Norwegian-American had brought with him from Norway a young nephew. The uncle was not permitted to accompany his nephew to Ellis Island and when he finally succeeded in getting there in a chartered launch, the nephew was nowhere to be found. The uncle was frantic.

The long waiting in line provided an opportunity to observe the attitude of Americans toward the immigrants. The newcomers were pushed around a good deal, perhaps an inevitable result of their being so numerous and unfamiliar with the language of the officials. Somehow Paul had the feeling that he was not being treated as a human being but as a commodity to be processed. On the gallery running along one side of the concourse he spied a Negro charwoman watching the milling mass of humanity below. Her face expressed utter disdain. Ever afterwards when he was treated condescendingly because of his foreign origin, he saw behind the face of the disdainful person the contemptuous expression on the countenance of the unknown Negress at Ellis Island.

Looking at his fellow immigrants he was struck by their docility. Bewildered and apprehensive, they moved about like sheep. The majority ranged in age from eighteen to twenty-five. Most looked healthy. In no way could they be classed as the dregs of Europe. On the contrary, many of them appeared to belong to the European middle classes.

Each had cost his parents and his country of origin thousands of dollars before he reached manhood. By thus exporting her youth Europe was contributing billions of dollars annually towards stregthening the productive capacity of America. This idea which had first occured to him while waiting in line at Ellis Island had stayed with him these many years. Frequently he had felt that the United States failed to appreciate the full extent to which she was indebted to Europe for her economic prosperity.

Representatives of various religious denominations and a strange assortment of peddlers mingled with the crowd. Among the former was a Danish Lutheran pastor who urged the young Norwegian to buy a Bible. This he did; he had kept it ever since. A man wearing some sort of uniform asked to see the immigrant's money. Thinking this was one of the numerous inspectors, he produced some dollar bills. The stranger grabbed one of them and thrust a parcel into the youth's hand. To his chagrin he found he had been tricked into buying a package of food.

At last he reached the final barrier where a number of officials were seated around a table. One of them flicked the upper eyelids of the immigrant. Another asked how much money he had, but did not check the amount. As he left the immigrant station he was given a tag and from then on until he reached Ostrander, he always wore a tag of some sort. In company with several other passengers from the *Caronia* he was escorted to a railroad station and put on a train for Chicago. Throughout this whole procedure he simply followed a guide, paying no attention to the route of travel by water or land. Later when he tried to recall what had happened from the time he left Ellis Island until he was seated in the railroad coach he found that his mind was a complete blank. The impressions had been so numerous that they cancelled one another.

The train to Chicago made up of coaches filled with immigrants left New York about five-thirty Friday evening and did not reach its destination until nine Sunday morning. It jolted along making numerous stops and was often shunted to sidings while faster trains passed. Fortunately many of the *Caronia* passengers got together in the same coach. The old exchange of views and surmises was resumed. Since the train had no diner the food package proved a good investment after all. The day of embarkation had been so exciting and exhausting that despite the crowded conditions and uncomfortable seats most of the immigrants slept the first night. The following morning found them in Buffalo. The omniscient young Norwegian-American who had spent two years in Michigan was in Paul's company. Discovering that the train would stay in Buffalo for some time the two went in search of breakfast, and the newcomer had his first meal of bacon and eggs. When the waitress learned that he came from Norway and could neither understand nor speak a word of English she looked at him with wonder and pity. A kindly person, quite different from the charwoman on Ellis Island, she gave him a friendly smile which with the good breakfast made the morning seem pleasant. Perhaps he would like America.

The railroad crew was in no hurry to get them to Chicago. A delay of about three hours in Buffalo was followed by several other shorter ones. The day was spent in looking at the countryside and commenting on what was observed. Railroad stations and the houses nearby seemed surprisingly dingy for this wealthy land. Perhaps America, too, had her poor. This was a disquieting thought for immigrants who all expected to make a fortune. Though the young man from Michigan could not explain the unequal distribution of wealth in America, he pontificated on many other topics. His assertion that one would never see a straight telephone pole in the whole United States somehow stuck in Paul's memory, and for years the sight of telephone poles would recall the ridiculous statement.

When Chicago was reached the immigrants were bundled into taxicabs and sent to various stations. At the new station Paul tried to find a map but was rushed on to a train before he succeeded. The group from *Caronia* had now dwindled to four. The day was bright and warm; the contrast between the Illinois and Iowa countryside with that of Norway was duly noted. At one of the stations a former *Caronia* passenger got a bag of popcorn which was appreciated since the food package bought at Ellis Island was now gone. As the train stopped at the various stations Paul observed that a trainman would collect the slips put above the seats of the passengers before they left. This happened to the *Caronia* group who departed one by one. Toward evening the man bound for Ostrander was alone. Finally he picked up his slip and showed it to the conductor who immediately burst into excited talk of which the immigrant understood not a word. However, he gathered that he was to get off the train. Soon he stood with his bags on the platform while the conductor scurried around hunting for an interpreter.

As luck would have it, a man on the platform could speak Norwegian. Soon matters were straightened out. The station was Hayfield, Minnesota, but passengers for Ostrander should have left the train at McIntire, Iowa, a station which had been passed an hour earlier. The interpreter was a carpenter working on a construction job in McIntire. At 11 P.M. he would board a train for that junction and, good Samaritan that he was, he volunteered to shepherd the lost immigrant, now provided with a large tag which explained what had happened, as far as McIntire. It was still some four or five hours before the southbound train arrived, so the carpenter took his ward to a restaurant and ordered dinner for two. When the train finally came it was equipped with reclining seats — the height of luxury.

McIntire was reached at midnight. The carpenter ascertained that a way-freight with a passenger coach would leave for Ostrander at five o'clock Monday morning and that the regular passenger train would leave at six. He then asked his charge whether he wanted to come along to the hotel or remain in the station five hours. The immigrant chose to stay in the station. As his guide left he said, "Look after your watch." Those parting words called to mind stories read about American robberies and other hair-raising events. The immigrant decided not to sleep.

About 3 A.M. a train came thundering in. Soon he heard an excited feminine voice inquire in Norwegian, "Is this Ostrander?" The depot agent who did not understand Norwegian brought the newly-arrived passenger to the lone occupant of the waiting room. Now he could give information, he could be the guide. Though the new arrival had been on the *Caronia,* the two had not met on the ship. She was bound for Ostrander where a married sister lived. She also had two brothers in that vicinity. At last the phantom Ostrander P. O. began to seem a reality.

At five o'clock Monday morning the two passengers boarded the coach attached to the way-freight. It was early when they arrived at their journey's end, so early that the girl's sister was not at the station. However, an old Norwegian on the platform could give directions, and the sister soon put in an appearance. But the new informant was not certain where Hannah Elstad lived. A friend helped him out. Then in a curious language which the informant thought was Norwegian but which in reality consisted mostly of English words with Norwegian endings he explained that Hannah Elstad stayed at the farm of Hans Christ one-half mile south and three miles west of Ostrander, and that Hans Christ's house was the second one on the right hand side of the road.

Leaving his bags at the office of the Ostrander lumberyard the immigrant set out to find his father's cousin. It was a warm, sunny morning, the meadows were green, and the birds were singing. Though he had had but two meals since Friday morning and very little sleep, he felt neither hungry nor tired. The overwhelming sensation was that of being a foreigner in a strange land. The conversation in Ostrander with Ole Heimsness, who knew the names of two of the immigrant's maternal uncles famous in northern Norway as herring kings, had given him some confidence. Still, it seemed queer that the earth he trod was not that of his own land. New to him were the black hogs; new also the Lombardy poplars on both sides of the road, which reminded him of pictures of soldiers lined up for inspection. The birds were not like those of Norway either in appearance or in their song. Only the cattle and the grass seemed at all familiar. A little uncertain as to how Ole Heimsness had counted the houses to the right of the road the newcomer stopped at a farm to inquire about Hans Christ's home. But the woman who answered his knock on the kitchen door could not understand Norwegian; she appeared almost frightened at the sight of the stranger. So he continued to trudge along hoping he would strike the right farm.

Finally he reached a place with trees planted to form a square around the buildings. He entered a short driveway to a yard with a small dwelling house and many low sheds thatched with straw. A young girl came from one of the sheds carrying milk pails. When she saw the stranger she shouted in Norwegian: "Hans, Paul has arrived!"

Chapter 10

Hans Christ

In answer
to the girl's shout an elderly man appeared from behind the
sheds. He wore an old battered hat, rough working clothes,
and half-boots. His beard was trimmed Uncle Sam fashion
and his heavily lined, weather-beaten face was wreathed in
smiles as he greeted Paul. The girl introduced herself as
Matilde Pedersen, a grand-niece of Hannah Elstad; she had
arrived from Norway the year before. Hannah was in the
house. The man with the beard was Hans Christ, for whom
Paul worked from May, 1906, until September, 1907. From
Hans he received his first instruction in the mysteries of
American life and customs.

The events of that May morning, 1906, were still vivid; the
mental pictures of the farm of Hans Christ in Bennington
township, Mower county, and of the people of that place were
as clear as they had been thirty years earlier. From the road
Paul had had only a glimpse of the dwelling house. The
buildings and the yard were hidden among trees, all planted
by Hans Christ. The drive from the road to the house was
lined with blue spruce on the left, hard maples on the right.
In front of the house were beautiful Norway pines, healthy,
vigorous-looking trees, so different from the stunted aspen
and birches on the old home island.

Though he admired the trees, the appearance of the farm
buildings surprised and shocked him. He had imagined an
American farm would resemble in buildings and equipment

the country homes of Norwegian merchants and professional men. But instead of large barns and a spacious dwelling, he saw dilapidated sheds thatched with rotting straw and a small frame house painted white. Entering the house he found that its one large room downstairs served as living-room, dining-room, and kitchen as well as bedroom for Old Hannah. In after years he saw even meaner-looking farmsteads in the richest agricultural region of America. But the first sight of such a one was sharply disillusioning.

Upon entering he was greeted warmly as a kinsman by Old Hannah. In true Norwegian fashion she immediately began asking questions about relatives and friends. Despite her crippled condition and her eighty-six years she moved about with amazing agility and was mentally very alert. She evidently had had plenty of spunk in her youth.

Had Paul had breakfast? No, that he hadn't. The first meal on Hans Christ's farm was unforgettable. Strangely enough, though more than twelve hours had passed since he had eaten he did not feel hungry as he sat down to the bread, butter, honey, and apple sauce.

The meal finished, the next question was, had Paul slept? Very little since Thursday night. Old Hannah was shocked. Then she recalled the travel conditions for immigrants when she had arrived in America about forty years earlier. Of course he had to go to bed. But sleep refused to come; he was too keyed up. The hundreds of new impressions of the last four or five days, which had set the mind racing, and the realization that he was 5,000 miles from home drove sleep away.

The newcomer — thus he was designated for more than a year — had to explore his new surroundings. The blood relationship with two members of Hans Christ's household and the fact that they spoke only Norwegian made the immigrant feel almost at home on the day of his arrival. He found that Hans expected him to work as a farmhand. Since he knew nobody in the land, this arrangement was entirely satisfactory. He also learned that as he was inexperienced he would not get the going wage for hired men — that rate was $ 30 a month from March until November. Perhaps he would be paid $ 20 a month until the end of the hiring season. Translated into Norwegian kroner and judged by Norwegian standards this did not seem an unreasonably low wage. Furthermore, the newcomer had no choice in the matter.

Long before noon on the day of his arrival Paul had explored the farmyard and outbuildings. The run-down sheds served as barns for fifty to sixty head of cattle and eight horses. In the pig sty he counted twenty large hogs and many young pigs. He saw unfamiliar machinery, seeder, corn planter, harvesters for grain and corn; and he was told that on the 160 acre farm seventy acres were in fields. The newcomer was impressed. At the county agricultural school near Bodö he had seen a field of twenty-five acres. The whole district referred to it as "the big field," and it was the marvel of the county. Hans Christ's horses were much bigger than the old mare on Father's farm. Proudly Hans announced that his horses were nearly pure-bred percherons, far superior to those of his neighbors. The newcomer had not the faintest notion of the meaning of "percheron". Evidently it was something very grand.

As the professor reviewed the events of his first year in America it occurred to him that he then was very young for his years — a naive boy eyeing everything wonderingly and with eager curiosity. All that he saw — trees, implements, farm animals, the birds, and even the rabbits that swarmed about — differed from those he had known at his home. But to his surprise he discovered many Norwegian ways and customs. He took the Norwegian speech of the household for granted; all its members had grown up in Norway. But it had not occurred to him that anyone not born in that country would speak its language. The day after his arrival two young women came on an errand. To his amazement they addressed Matilde in the Stavanger dialect of Norway. Yet they had never seen that country. To be sure, some of the words were rather strange, but the articles, the plural of nouns, and the inflection of their speech were indubitably Norwegian. Soon he learned that many English words in common usage among Norwegian-American farmers if dressed up with the Norwegian definite articles "en" or "et" at the end of the word were considered part of Norwegian speech.

One Sunday morning a couple of weeks later Hans Christ suggested that the household, except Old Hannah who was deaf, should go to church in Ostrander. The pastor had come from the Bodö district of Norway and the newcomer was eager to meet him. In after years that acquaintanceship proved of great benefit to the homeless young man, for the minister and his wife, the Reverend and Mrs. H. J. Berg, were always very kind to him. On that first Sunday he attended church Paul saw that the small congregation stood around outside waiting for the minister, exchanging comments about the weather and crops and inquiring about the health of each others' families just as people had done back at Straumen. The church itself looked like a doll's house, everything — bell, steeple, organ, auditorium — was in miniature. And the church service was much less formal than back home. The minister wore no vestments. The cassock, surplice, and ruffled "millstone" collar of ministers in the state church of Norway were missing. This seemed quite appropriate. To hold a genuine Norwegian service in such un-Norwegian surroundings would have seemed out of place. In later years when Paul attended church services with a ritual more or less identical with that of the Norwegian church they seemed unnatural. The atmosphere of the old country could not be duplicated; he wished the imitation had not been attempted. In this as in some other matters he differed from many Norwegian immigrants who nostalgically tried to carry the homeland with them to the new world.

On the farm of Hans Christ the working day was long. Horses had to be fed and curried, seventeen cows milked by hand, calves fed, hogs swilled, manure hauled, corn planted and cultivated, and the yard tidied up. For several years Hans Christ had done all the farm work alone except during haying and harvest. The result was that the yard had acquired a weedy, run-down appearance. Because he had worked and farmed in Illinois for ten years before he came to Minnesota, Hans liked to cultivate corn. One-fourth of his farm was in corn, a larger percentage than was customary in that township. Hans took considerable pride in that fact — in the cornfield he spent nearly all of the month of June.

A multitude of chores fell to the newcomer. Besides tending cattle, horses, and hogs, fenceposts had to be sharpened, trees trimmed, and weeds dug in yard and fields. In performing these tasks, the newcomer acquired a lifelong hatred of burdock and quack grass. The latter was a recent and most noxious weed on this farm. Being of a suspicious nature Hans hinted broadly that some evil-minded neighbor had brought the quack grass to his fields. The newcomer was ordered to dig it out. Every rootlet must be removed. What a tedious job that was! In the end it proved futile — for this lack of success he was severely censured.

Four weeks after his arrival the immigrant was introduced to that interesting American institution, the poll tax. Instead of paying for the upkeep of the dirt roads which ran along every section line, the farmer, his grown sons or his hired man would work off the tax by grading the roads. Hans Christ labelled every task as difficult. He impressed upon the newcomer that to handle a road scraper pulled by two horses required a great deal of skill. Moreover, the scraper must not be filled too full, and the horses must rest frequently because the work was very hard. Obediently Paul followed instructions and was praised by Hans and the road boss for his efficiency. But a few days afterwards the newcomer came to grief when he applied the same instructions as he used the scraper in filling some holes by the hog-pen. Hans Christ became irate when he discovered that the hired man did not fill the scraper to the brim, and that he rested the horses after every other load.

Rather early the newcomer got a chance to observe the versatility of American farmers. A farmers' telephone company had been organized. Hans was a shareholder, and his hired man was sent to help build the line. In Norway such work required the supervision of trained engineers. Only they could install telephones. How great was Paul's amazement therefore when he found an ordinary farmer, Ludvig Christiansen, as foreman of the telephone crew and as installer of the telephones. Ludvig, a jack-of-all-trades, was farmer, carpenter, mason, smith, harness-maker, painter, roofer, and veterinarian. As a member of this crew the newcomer lived up to the immigrants' reputation for ineptitude. Ludvig spoke the Norwegian dialect current among the farmers of the neighborhood. For the names of the tools and the sundry tasks he used English words with Norwegian articles. To the newcomer "posten", "forken", "crowbarn", and "pickaxen" were just as foreign as "the post", "the fork", "the crowbar", and "the pickax". But this fact his fellow workers on the telephone crew did not understand; they concluded that the newcomer was just plain stupid.

The members of the crew ate their noonday meal at the home of a farmer, generally referred to by Hans Christ as "that damn Irishman." For the first time the newcomer, curious to meet people so unflatteringly described, entered a house where Norwegian was not spoken. Though the place was pretty much like any other farm, at the table the newcomer found himself in a predicament. All spoke English and the dishes were passed around only when asked for. He didn't know how to ask for anything. Fortunately, the host's elderly sister, realizing the plight of the blond, pink-cheeked Norwegian lad, waited on him assiduously. In the evening he told Hans Christ about her kindness. Hans admitted grudgingly that Miss Emlen was not so bad as her sly, grasping brothers. But, of course, they were all Catholics, and that was enough to damn anyone. Anti-Catholic the Norwegian-Americans were because of their Lutheran upbringing, and anti-Irish they had become because of experiences with Irish foremen on railroad construction crews and in lumber camps. This was, however, something the newcomer learned later and by degrees.

Hans Christ's household was not a cheerful one. Hans himself suffered from something akin to "morning sickness." At least he was out of sorts every morning, a state of affairs which he blamed on the climate. The extremes of heat and cold, he explained to his hired man, thinned the blood, hence it was necessary to take medicine to put the system in working order. Some drank intoxicating liquor, of which Hans strongly disapproved. In pharisaical fashion he was thankful for not belonging to that sinful crowd. He had a better remedy for morning sickness — he took laudanum, little knowing it was a habit-forming drug. Occasionally Hans offered the hired man this wonderful medicine, but his offer was turned down.

Hannah Elstad who had been Hans Christ's housekeeper for many years, was no longer able to do housework. Still, she resented having been replaced by the young and inexperienced Matilde. Old Hannah was convinced that her grandniece was hopelessly inefficient. That came, of course, from her mother. The father, Hannah's nephew, had been quite all right. The upshot of the dissension between the two women was that Hannah scolded and went on a sit-down strike, while Matilde who preferred working in the barn cut housework to a minimum. The result was a monotonous diet of bacon, fried potatoes, bread, butter, and coffee morning, noon and night. There was never any variation.

Hans Christ kept a daily newspaper, *The Minneapolis Journal,* a farm paper, *Farm, Stock and Home,* and a semi-weekly Norwegian language paper, *Skandinaven,* published in Chicago. The newcomer marvelled at the first, its size and its comics. His attempts at guessing the meaning of headlines were miserable failures. But Hans, who never read it, said that *The Minneapolis Journal* was the best newspaper in the state; he was proud of being a subscriber. His favorite, however, was *Farm, Stock and Home.* Not that he read that much either, but it had, said Hans, the right slant on things. It called attention to the exploitation of farmers by railroads, grain elevator companies, and Chicago packers, and it attacked the trade unions. For "lazy trade unionists," constantly demanding higher wages and a shorter working day, Hans Christ had no use. They would surely bring the country to ruin. He was certain that the number of scoundrels, thieves, and lazy bones in the world was increasing at an alarming rate. Unless they were checked and driven out of high places disaster would befall America. His one great hope was that President Theodore Roosevelt might save the country.

Except on very rainy days, Hans took no time off for reading. Though theoretically a Sabbatarian, he reserved a variety of jobs for Sunday. Among them was that of cleaning the pig sty. Not that he actually ordered his hired man to perform this delectable task on the day of rest, but very clear hints were dropped during the week. It annoyed Hans if the hired man got up early and worked hard and fast Sunday morning to finish the regular chores in time to walk the three and a half miles to Ostrander church. In the evening Hans would pointedly call attention to the fact that *he* had cleaned the hog house while his hired man had gone to church and frittered away his time with other young people. Such things could never have happened in Illinois where Hans had worked as a farmhand. But then life had been much harder than now.

The generosity of the Bergs to the immigrant was truly amazing. If they saw him in church they always invited him to their home for dinner. And this hospitality was offered even though the Reverend Berg's salary from three congregations totalled only $ 500 a year. Some fees for clerical services, and gifts in kind, chiefly feed for his horses, were his only additional income. At these Sunday dinners the newcomer met other farm youths as well as young men of the congregation who were preparing for professions. One from a farm near Ostrander was a senior law student, and another, an immigrant, was in his last year of medical school at the University of Minnesota. That these university students deigned to talk to a worker on a farm was a new experience for the immigrant. Although Norway prided itself on being democratic, her social democracy had not reached the stage where class differences between university students and farm workers had been obliterated.

The medical student interested Paul a great deal. He had been a country school teacher in Norway and had come to Ostrander about six years previously. Upon arrival he attended the graded school in the village much to the amusement of the village loafers who sat whittling in front of the drugstore. To see that big oaf of a newcomer go to school with the kids was really something to laugh at! But he had paid no attention to them, and after a course of study at a church school he had been admitted to Minnesota's medical school. Years later when Dr. Wiig had become a successful medical practitioner in a western state, the loafers at Ostrander spoke jealously about his wonderful "luck."

Two other young men whom the newcomer met at the Berg home were, like Berg and himself, from arctic Norway. These youths had come to America a few years before. Soon after their arrival they had entered a school at Red Wing, Minnesota, a school belonging to the Hauge Synod of the Norwegian Lutheran Church. They explained that at this school expenses were very low. By teaching in the summer in parochial schools, instructing children in religion and in Norwegian, and working on the farms during the harvest and threshing seasons, they earned almost enough money to carry them through the whole school year. This information the newcomer filed away for future use.

From every available source he eagerly sought to learn all he could about America. At first he got this knowledge only from *Skandinaven* and Hans Christ. The newspaper was read between nine and ten at night after all the evening chores were finished. Hans was not really pleased with the reading habits of his hired man, but since the latter got up with alacrity when aroused at five each morning Hans could find no real ground for complaint.

In the years marked by bitter political conflicts between Norway and Sweden Paul, then in his teens, had become interested in politics. Now he plied Hans Christ with questions about this country's government and the men who ran it. What local officials and governmental institutions did America have? Hans Christ knew something about the sheriff, a police officer whose position resembled that of the "lensmand" in Norway, but as to the other officials and instruments of local government he could give little information. His neighbor, Mr. Roberts, had at one time been a county supervisor; what this meant Hans did not really know. He was better informed on the government of the state of Minnesota with its legislature and governor. He knew that the state had representatives in the two branches of Congress. But the question concerning the differences between American parties baffled Hans Christ. To the untutored newcomer the American party labels seemed strange indeed.

Were not all Americans both democrats and republicans? What did those party names really signify? In Norway parties were called Left and Right. The meaning of the terms seemed clear, the former wanted reforms, the latter opposed them. All that Hans could say was that he thought the Republicans favored a high protective tariff while the Democrats opposed it. More important to him was the fact that Abraham Lincoln had been a Republican and he had freed the slaves. Whenever this point was mentioned Hans never failed to add that when he reached Trondheim on his way to America he had learned that the Civil War was ended. Upon arrival in Bergen he heard that Lincoln had been murdered. The fact that he arrived in Lincoln's home state shortly after the president's untimely death created in Hans Christ a feeling of kinship with the martyred president. He was like the many people who claimed distinction because they could say "I once saw Lincoln" or "I heard Lincoln debate with Senator Douglas." Oddly enough, the fact that Hans Christ had at one time heard General Logan of Civil War fame speak, strengthened Hans' proprietary interest in the Civil War president.

All in all, Hans Christ was far from a satisfactory guide through the maze of American government and politics. He hadn't even voted in an election. For knowledge of the broad-

er aspects of American life the hired man read *Skandinaven*.
Its editor, N. A. Grevstad, later U.S. minister to Uruguay,
was an able journalist who packed an amazing amount of information into the columns of his paper. It carried news from
Norway and much about Norwegians in the various states of
the Union, and still it found room for accounts of the doings
of the president, of Congress, of American politicians, and
political parties. Since 1906 was an election year the campaign
received much attention. By November the newcomer knew
the names of more American congressmen and senators than
he did at any later period.

While still in Norway he had learned about President
Roosevelt. That energetic, hard-hitting American chief executive appealed strongly to him and his Norwegian contempora-
ries. Like them, Roosevelt was an active out-of-door man; they
believed him to be brave, honest, and forth-right, and they
loved him for those reasons. He personified their idea of a
true leader.

In 1906 President Roosevelt took up an issue which made
a strong impression upon the newcomer. One day he read in
The Minneapolis Journal that the president had used the
expression "undesirable citizens." By then he had learned the
meaning of the noun, but the adjective puzzled him. Nor
could Hans provide a satisfactory translation. Fortunately, the
next issue of *Skandinaven* explained the phrase. With care
Paul perused the paper's account of Roosevelt's blast against
divided loyalties. The newcomer felt as if that message was
aimed at foreign-born people like himself. In later years
evidence of hyphenism among Americans often disturbed him.

The routine of farm work was seldom broken by callers.
Occasionally a neighbor got stuck in the mud road which
passed by the farm and came to ask for help. The "skimmer"
called every other day or so for the cream and took it to the
co-operative creamery in Ostrander. At irregular intervals,
usually in the spring or fall, a cattle or hog buyer would make
inquiries about animals for the market. Twice every fortnight
Hans Christ would go to town to sell eggs, buy groceries, and

get a harness or other equipment repaired. Hans had much trouble with the grocerymen over the quality of their coffee. None seemed able to provide the right quality, so for that reason he boycotted the stores in Ostrander. Those at LeRoy, seven miles distant, he distrusted. More to his liking were the merchants at Spring Valley, eleven or twelve miles away. But with his heavy work horses and the lumber wagon for transport a trip to this town took the whole day. Since he owned no tools and had no skill in repairing his equipment he went quite often to Spring Valley. His excuse for not making repairs himself was that it didn't pay. He was too busy. Curiously enough, he did not reckon the value of the time he spent on the road whenever a harness needed mending.

Haying brought work with which the newcomer had some experience. It was lucky he was strong and skillful with a pitchfork because all the hay had to be stacked in the yard by the cattle sheds. Since tall stacks had proportionately less spoilage than the low ones, Hans Christ favored big stacks. This, however, created problems for the hired man who pitched the hay on to the stack. The farm was on the prairie and in the winter swept by cold winds. Hans Christ, in common with many people born in barren, treeless regions, was a lover of trees. Moreover, a windbreak was very important as shelter for the farm animals that even in mid-winter spent the greater part of the day outside. Consequently, Hans Christ had no sooner fixed on a site for the farm buildings than he began to grow trees. To the north and west of the yard he planted first fast-growing hardy willows, in the lee of those soft maples, and in the lee of the maples were evergreens. To the east were maples, evergreens, and an apple orchard. On the south side of the quadrangle he had blue spruce, pines, and hard maples. Having started the planting in the seventies and having tended the trees with great care, Hans Christ had his yard and farm buildings completely surrounded with trees by 1906. Neither winter winds nor summer breezes reached the yard where the hay was stacked. Paul's mother had supplied him with an ample stock of heavy underwear made from homespun. Anxious to pay his debt to the bank in Bodö, he felt that he could not afford to discard these clothes and buy lighter ones. With the thermometer registering well above 100 degrees he continued to wear his Norwegian clothes as he pitched heavy timothy hay on to the tall stacks. That he survived the first summer in America was something of a miracle.

Fortunately hay-loading in the field provided a respite. Here Hans did the pitching and also a great deal of talking. For years he had been much alone, and he disliked nearly all the neighbors whom he roundly abused in both Norwegian and English. By combining all the nasty words he knew in the two languages Hans Christ had a goodly supply of defamatory terms. With considerable relish he told the story about a neighbor's wife who had deserted husband and children to run off with another farmer, who similarly abandoned spouse and offspring. The lovers, who rented a farm and set up housekeeping about ten miles from their respective homes, parted after three years and rejoined their families. Another long tale had to do with a local minister whose reputation and career had been blasted by slanderous gossip. When the maligned divine attempted to win rehabilitation in the courts his chief witnesses disappeared, suborned by the slanderers. Thus the newcomer learned about the seamy side of life in rural America.

He learned also the saga of Hans Christ which though it was the account of a bitter, frustrated man, contained some epic elements as well. The adjustments of an immigrant to the conditions in a strange land, the hardships and sufferings of life on the frontier, defeats and disappointments, courage and steadfastness often provide material for heroic tales.

Hardship had been the lot of Hans Christ from early childhood. The son of a fisherman, he was born far north in arctic Norway. His father died early and his mother married a man whom Hans hated with deep fervor. Apparently the step-father's chief sin was laziness. As a youth Hans had earned his living by fishing. The storms, the surging seas, the raging blizzards, and the winter darkness of his home region had made an indelible and overpowering impression on him. Never once did he mention the Lofoten fishery without a shudder. The eerie beauty of the midnight sun had been forgotten. He felt no nostalgia for the parish of Dyröy in the county of Troms where he had spent his childhood and youth.

At the age of nineteen Hans Christ migrated to America. In those days very few left northern Norway for the United States. But shortly after the outbreak of our Civil War a well-to-do farmer and fisherman in Hans Christ's home parish sold all his possessions and left for America. Benefitting by the depreciation of the dollar and low farm prices, he bought a considerable amount of land in a settlement of Norwegian immigrants southwest of Chicago. Hans Christ always spoke of him as "the wealthy Fries." This enterprising and successful person provided a stimulus for more emigration to America from the parish of Dyröy.

In April, 1865, young Hans Christ, or Christensen as his name was at that time, secured passage on a sailing vessel from Bergen to Quebec. In common with many immigrants of that era, he had a long passage, poor food, bad drinking water, and crowded accommodations. From Quebec he reached Chicago via the St. Lawrence-Great Lakes water route. Not until July did he arrive at the settlement at Fox River, Illinois. Acclimatization proved difficult. The young fisherman clad in his Norwegian homespun was plunged into the unaccustomed labor of the harvest field in the heat of an Illinois summer. Working for an American, "a Yankee", farmer he got only three meals a day — Norwegian-Americans served at least four. With breakfast at six and supper after sundown the time between meals was long, and the physical fatigue was intensified by heavy perspiration and much water drinking. Young Hans Christ was tough. He survived, but many a healthy Norwegian immigrant succumbed. Like horses working in the field on a summer day, the immigrants knew nothing of the symptoms of oncoming heat prostration. They only knew that they needed to earn money and were expected to work hard.

When Hans Christ reached America demobilized soldiers and masses of newly-arrived immigrants created keen competition in the farm labor market. Hans was proud of the fact that he obtained employment on a farm owned by a Yankee. By working for a Mr. Bushnell Hans got an early start in learning English and acquired, he believed, a good vocabulary. This was probably true, though until the end of his life he was a bit confused in his use of Latin and Greek derivatives.

Like most immigrants, Hans Christ looked upon Americans of the older stock as members of an aristocracy. In all ages and in all lands where social cleavages have existed, laborers have found a certain satisfaction, have believed that they acquired special distinction, by toiling for the socially select. To this rule Hans was no exception. It was a feather in his cap that he was employed by Mr. Bushnell. Though Mrs. Bushnell's custom of serving the winter choreman only two meals a day created a lasting grievance, Mr. Bushnell could point obvious morals to his hired man without their being resented. Hans often related how Mr. Bushnell before going out driving with his wife would visit the barn and strike the flanks of the horses with his gloved hand. If it showed evidence of dander, Hans had to do more currying.

The Fox River Settlement of Norwegian immigrants was thirty years old when Hans Christ appeared on the scene. The early trials of a frontier immigrant community were still fresh in people's memories. Cholera had ravaged the settlement; nearly all the immigrants were poor; bank loans could be had only at exorbitant rates; and anything resembling social equality was denied the new arrivals by the native Americans. To the Norwegians, a people traditionally independent and individualistic, the last was a bitter experience. Young men and women who had arrived in America filled with high hopes and great expectations found that life in the new world meant only toil, loneliness, discouragement. Some despaired, others fought grimly on and succeeded in the end.

By the mid-eighteen sixties the Fox River community had become well established. Industry, frugality, and co-operative efforts had brought prosperity to the pioneers. The immigrants might be irritated occasionally when Yankee neighbors treated them condescendingly, but by then they had overcome the early hurt because they had held their own in the struggle for survival on the frontier. The odds had been against them, and they had won. Language and religion had at first proved the great binding forces in the immigrant community. Ultimately, however, theological dissensions rent the Norwegian-Lutheran church in America. Conflicts over religious issues which had existed in Norway were transplanted to Illinois and waxed bitter on the banks of the Fox River. Episodes in these struggles were described by Hans Christ in the summer of 1906 as he loaded hay on his farm in Minnesota.

His own life story followed the pattern common to many Norwegian immigrants of that era. After several years of work as a farmhand he had saved enough money to buy a team of horses and some implements. Then he rented land and farmed on shares. But the value of Illinois land rose quickly in price and he soon realized that he must go farther north and west if his dream of becoming a landowning farmer was to materialize.

In the autumn of 1875 Hans Christ took the trail leading to cheap land. He had three good horses. His personal belongings were loaded on the lumber wagon. With two companions he headed first for Wisconsin following the route of earlier Norwegian immigrants. The little band visited Rock and Dane counties in Wisconsin, making inquiries about quality of soil and prices of land. From Madison the trekkers took the old military road to Prairie du Chien. Here they crossed the Mississippi river. Then they headed for a Norwegian settlement in Winnishiek County, Iowa, near Decorah, the seat of Luther College, oldest among the schools founded in America by Norwegian Lutherans. But again land prices were too high and Hans Christ did not tarry long. Before the first snowfall he had reached the Hellickson farm on the Root River near the western edge of Fillmore County, Minnesota,

only a few miles north of the Iowa-Minnesota line. Here he
went into winter quarters. Some time before the small band
had broken up. Hans Christ always had had difficulties with
companions.

The Hellicksons, their relatives and friends were immigrants
from southeastern Norway. They had been farmers and
woodsmen in the old country, and they preferred to settle on
wooded land near a stream. Moreover, at the time they came
to Minnesota the belief was widely held that the soil on the
open prairie was inferior to that where trees grew. Settlers
would rather face the heavy toil of clearing land than gamble
with farming on a treeless plain. Though the settlement
around the Hellickson farm had been occupied for about
twenty years, the prairie land on its fringes had not been
taken up. Hans Christ was no woodsman but he had had
experience with the Illinois prairie. Finding 160 acres of
good prairie land for sale five miles from where he stayed, he
purchased it at $ 15 an acre, a price which seemed low to
one coming from Illinois.

In the spring of 1876 Hans Christ started as a wheat farmer
in Minnesota. He had his horses, his wagon, his ten years of
American farming experience, a knowledge of English, and
good health. His debt of about $ 1,000 did not alarm him.
He began to break up the tough prairie sod. The first year
he had twenty acres in wheat. The yield was good, the price
tolerably so. It seemed a promising start. In the autumn and
the following spring more new land was ploughed up. In 1877
he had sixty acres in wheat. Lacking machinery he rented
what was needed, and also hired help for harvesting the crop.
It cost him forty dollars that year to harvest twenty acres,
an outlay which proved a net loss because the wheat had
wilted, ruined by disease.

Then followed years of heartbreaking struggle with not the
slightest chance of success for the wheat farmer. Since wheat
had been grown in this area from the time white man first
broke the sod it seemed unthinkable that this crop would
have to be abandoned. Surely the blight was a passing af-

fliction, the farmers said, let us try again next year. But again there was failure. A change of seed grain might help. Seed was bought at fancy prices — three or four dollars a bushel. All to no avail. Then some farmers took up dairying, but Hans Christ a fisherman who had grown corn in Illinois and wheat in Minnesota was loathe to turn to cows. Moreover, he was a bachelor; milking was woman's work, and he had no woman to help him.

Reluctantly he became a woodsman, but with his curious aversion to working with a gang he never went to the lumber camps of northern Minnesota in the winter as some farmers did. An out-and-out individualist he much preferred to be alone, so he leased a piece of woodland near the town of Spring Valley only nine miles from his own farm. In the woods he built a shack and spent several winters felling, sawing and splitting oak, selling the cordwood to the townspeople. It was unaccustomed work. All was done by hand. The price on firewood was low, but ready money was scarce, and the logs brought hard cash.

Finally Hans Christ gave up wheat-farming and turned to corn and hogs. This was the type of farming carried on by Mr. Bushnell and the other Yankee farmers in Illinois, and Hans Christ felt that corn-growing bore with it a certain social prestige. He longed to become a shade better than the ordinary clod-hopper, a yearning due in part, perhaps, to the fact that he had been a seafarer. In Norway those who sailed the seas, whether as fishermen or before the mast, considered themselves superior to stay-at-home country bumpkins. Hans Christ sang as he cultivated his corn — not very melodiously, to be sure, because he could not carry a tune — but the attempt indicated a happier frame of mind than was usually the case. Guiding the cultivator drawn by two powerful horses he felt the same urge to sing which he'd had in his youth when his square-rigged fishing boat scudded before the wind over northern seas.

Hans Christ soon discovered that corn-growing in Minnesota was quite different from that in Illinois. The soil was poorer, the season shorter, and the summer was not so hot. But hard though it was, he stuck to it. Gradually he built up a herd of forty hogs. He tried to finish them off so that they would fetch a good price in the Chicago market. Just a week more and he would be ready to ship them. Then hog cholera struck and for two weeks Hans Christ spent his time burying hogs. Not one of them was sold.

Hog raising on a large scale was then abandoned. Next he turned to raising horses. He bought a percheron stallion and arranged a regular circuit for it. Again he was dogged by misfortune. Many of the neighboring farmers preferred horses mixed with western breed to the heavy percherons. The westerners were tougher, not easily overheated during the harvest, and their shoulders, unlike those of the percherons, did not need such careful attention. In the nineties prices on horses, as on everything else grown on the farm, dropped to almost nothing. Hans Christ kept his surplus horses hoping for a better market. But his fields, meadows, and pasture were fenced with barbed wire. The idle animals fought with each other or were frightened by rabbit hunters. They got tangled in the fences, were badly cut, and had to be killed. By 1906 seventeen of Hans Christ's horses had met their death that way. No profit for him in raising horses.

Most of the neighbors had come to Minnesota as family groups. They co-operated in farm operations. During hard times they practised the self-sufficient type of farming to which they had been accustomed in Norway. Hans Christ, erstwhile fisherman that he was, had no skill as a cabinet maker, carpenter, or smith. He could not even repair harnesses. He had none to spin, knit, weave, and sew for him. To be sure his family from Norway joined him for a short while but they were more of a burden than a help. They came as a surprise, mother, stepfather, a sister, and three brothers, suddenly appearing at his house which was even smaller than the one he occupied in 1906. The lazy stepfather had always been anathema to Hans Christ, and the cramped quarters made everybody's temper edgy. The young brothers and the sister refused to accept his advice. Soon the stepfather did the wisest thing he had ever done — he died. The eldest brother, the silly boy, left for a lumber camp and had not been heard from since. The younger brothers who were twins, the sister, and the mother went to northern Minnesota and took land there. The sister married, then died leaving an infant daughter. The brothers remained bachelors with their mother as housekeeper. In the opinion of Hans Christ they had gone to a cold, God-forsaken section of the state. Corn would not grow there, and for that reason the land was hardly worth working. No, the family had not benefitted from Hans' experience and superior knowledge of American farming. He continued to live and work alone. Though now and then he had had a hired man who was worth his wage, such men were rare. Most of the farm hands had been lazy, slovenly louts.

Only Hannah Elstad had managed to stay with Hans Christ for a period of years. In Illinois she had nursed him through a bout with typhoid. This care he remembered with gratitude. Only "Old Hannah" had stood by him in his emergency. But when some years later she had joined him in Minnesota to act as his housekeeper, they often quarrelled, so when she was able to get work at the hotel in LeRoy she lived there. Lately she had been with Hans on the farm. Her deafness made life more tolerable for her now. She could not hear Hans' scolding.

A curious man was Hans Christ. Thwarted, lonely and bitter, he was also indomitable — a man who greatly loved the soil and all that grew thereon, especially his trees. He had tended them with infinite care; working in the field by day he had cultivated around the young trees by moonlight. They responded to this solicitous treatment, and no farm in Mower county had a grove comparable to that on Hans Christ's farm. He had also planted a large apple orchard with many varieties of apples. In fact a considerable share of what he made on the farm had been paid out for nursery stock. Since the apple trees were never sprayed, no money was realized from this venture, but Hans had his beloved trees. And how he enjoyed eating apples! Despite his toothless state he could wolf them at a remarkable rate.

In the hayfield Hans Christ told his life story and retailed all the gossip he knew about the neighbors. This gave the newcomer a little respite from hard work. Loading after Hans Christ was not difficult. But the story-telling took time, the day had to be stretched into the night, and when Hans realized that the haying did not progress as fast as he had hoped it would, he got cross.

Harvest provided a new type of work and, in a measure, some thrills. In Norway it had been done with the sickle — a slow, laborious, back-breaking process. The self-binder which neatly tied the sheaves, and the bundle carrier which left several sheaves in a single heap were certainly great labor-saving devices. Though hard work, the shucking of the grain was a simple mechanical process and not too strenuous when the newcomer who at first raced after the harvester discovered that by allowing it to make several rounds of the field before he started shucking he could save many steps and keep pace with its progress. A dyed-in-the-wool conservative Hans Christ did not want to have his grain threshed from the field. He believed firmly that the grain would improve in quality if stacked in the yard and threshed after colder weather set in. This meant pitching in the field and from the wagon to the stack in a manner similar to haying, an operation not very difficult for the immigrant who liked to work with the pitchfork.

During the threshing the newcomer had his first chance to measure himself as a workman with native American farm-hands. He had often been told what terrific workers Americans were, a gospel sedulously preached to all immigrants. So when he found himself able to hold his own in the competition of a threshing crew, he gained a degree of self-confidence. It was customary for the farmers to co-operate during the threshing season and on the crew that autumn the newcomer represented Hans Christ. From the other men he learned that good farmhands were scarce. After that he no longer submitted meekly to his boss' temper tantrums.

Except for cornhusking the fall work on the farm — threshing and plowing — was pleasant. But as it happened husking was Hans Christ's favorite job for it brought back memories of Illinois husking bees in which he had excelled. The weather was fine those crisp October days when Hans Christ and his hired man rose early to get the seventeen cows milked and the other chores done so that they could be in the field at sunrise. The length of the working day did not bother, what caused trouble was that horny-handed Hans husked without gloves. Paul's hands were not soft, but the constant handling of dry hard ears of corn caused the skin and flesh to crack to the bone. It was a long time before the pain vanished and his hands healed.

The regular season for farmhands was eight months — from the beginning of March until November. In the slack winter months many of them worked for room and board only. But since Hans Christ had sixty head of cattle, twenty hogs and eight horses the winter chores were a steady all-day job lasting from six in the morning until eight at night. For this work the newcomer was paid the magnificent sum of $ 36 for the four month period. To his astonishment the stock was turned out every day to drink and munch straw, but the windbreak around the yard which had been a doubtful blessing in the summer, proved an excellent barrier against Minnesota's winter winds. The windbreak was a god-send both for the chore boy and for the animals.

Many of the preparations for the winter intrigued him. There was the banking of the foundation of the house with straw and tar paper, a practice which, unfortunately, provided a haven for rats, and the insertion of a sheet iron heater in the water tank which proved a necessary precaution when the temperature dropped to fifteen below zero. Since Hans Christ's apples were not of the winter varieties a barrel of New York apples made a welcome addition to the monotonous diet. Even in winter the daily menus held no surprises.

During these months when more time was taken for meals Hans Christ had further opportunity to relate details of his life's saga. He frequently chose incidents to fortify his contention that the conditions for farmhands were much harder when he came to America than they were nowadays. To prove that he at one time had been a man of fashion he produced a gray cutaway suit, tailor-made and of the same style as the clothes worn in the 1860's by Mr. Bushnell when he went to church. Hans also had an expensive coonskin fur coat which like the gray suit was carefully put away in mothballs and never worn. The smart pair of harnesses for carriage horses, which didn't fit any of the farm's percherons, were kept under the bed in Hans' own room. The reason for this precaution was that a similar pair, also never used, had been stolen from the buggy shed. Every winter their replacements were carefully oiled and then returned to their place of safety under the bed.

To the newcomer the tales of life in Minnesota before the railroad came held great interest. It was easy to imagine the landscape devoid of roads and trees and with only a shack here and there. When the Hellicksons settled by the Root River, the closest town was McGregor, Iowa, seventy miles away. Thither the wheat was hauled by oxen. The round trip took two weeks, the men sleeping under the wagons while the oxen grazed at night. To buy food for men and beasts would have taken all the money received for the wheat. The fact that the pioneers had come from southeastern Norway and had been trained from childhood in the skills required for self-sufficient farming proved a great help. Hans Christ's lack of those skills plus the fact that he was a bachelor had been his great handicap. Wives worked with their husbands in barn and fields. Children, too, did their stint. Mused Hans Christ, "If I had my life to live over I would marry and raise a family."

Perhaps the best example of what could be done despite or perhaps because of a large family was exemplified by the Ole Eastwolds. Penniless immigrants, husband and wife with two or three children had arrived at LeRoy in the late eighties. They secured land, farming first on shares, then as full owners. The family had grown to thirteen children, nine sons and four daughters. All survived infancy, a perilous period in pioneer days. Hans admitted ruefully that Ole Eastwold who had come to America much later than he and had raised a large family was a far happier man and better off financially. It was a puzzle to the bachelor. Hans was physically stronger than Ole, he had lived frugally and he believed he had worked harder than Ole Eastwold. Was it luck? Hans did not try to solve this puzzle.

Among the "new" things for Paul during his first winter in America was the sight of the sun at Christmas. Back home it vanished on November 17, not to reappear until January 25. It didn't seem Christmassy with the sun shining. Moreover, on Hans Christ's farm that day was just like every other day; there was no vestige of a holiday spirit. But the strangeness of the physical surroundings numbed Paul's senses and helped ward off homesickness during the season which had always been treated as very significant in his family. The chiming of church bells on Christmas eve, the Christmas breakfast table beautifully set by Mother and Sister Constance, the singing of a hymn, Father reading from the Gospel of St. Luke — these memories flitted before the mind of the newcomer as something which had happened during another existence, a dream of the far distant past.

Reverend Berg invited Hans Christ and his household to join the congregation at a gathering at the Hellickson farm the day after Christmas. Hans refused to go. Not a member of the congregation, he felt that he would be an intruder at such a gathering. Paul had no such scruples. Since he had been invited he naively believed that he was wanted, so he walked the five miles to the Hellickson farm. Everybody present was very kind. A homeless waif, he was treated as a special guest. All the people spoke the usual Minnesota sort of Norwegian to which he had now become accustomed, and always anxious to learn, he asked many questions about pioneer days. Hellickson who had been very young when he came to this farm with his parents had distinct recollections of those days. Now a prosperous farmer he seemed pleased with the interest which Hans Christ's hired man showed in the tales from the past. As Hellickson told his stories, friends and relations chipped in with their reminiscences. In his imagination the listener not only reconstructed the life described but lived it with the narrators, and began to feel a certain kinship with them. These men and women had made the land as he saw it. Now he had become part of this group, and from that day forward he ceased to be a complete stranger. Even Hans Christ's later reference to some members of the party as unreliable sneaks did not dispel Paul's joy in "belonging."

The days wound their monotonous way through winter into spring. Tending the animals was a constant care. If pauses occurred in the daily chores, Hans Christ would always suggest an extra cleaning of the cowshed. Though the temperature fell lower than any which the immigrant had experienced in arctic Norway, the farm's excellent windbreak made the cold less noticeable. He was surprised that he did not miss the mountains and the sea. Like so much else they belonged not only to a different land but to a past existence. In the summer the strange trees, insects, and wild life of this new country had aroused his curiosity. In the winter the appearance of the sun every day reminded him of the fact that he was far from home. During his working hours he had so many adjustments to make that the old home and the beloved ones who dwelt therein were not much in his thoughts. But at night he was always with them. On the wings of dreams he annihilated distance and joined his family and friends.

As spring progressed into the summer of 1907, Paul decided that his old yearning for education must be satisfied. A month after his arrival at Hans Christ's farm an eagerly awaited letter came from the one who had caused him to break away from the old moorings and seek new ones in America. It was short and impersonal. The engagement had been a mistake — an infatuation, a dream created by a white arctic summer. To Paul the message was a shattering blow.

He was glad at the moment that he was in a distant land where no scene or landmark could bring to mind memories of lost bliss. The disenchantment was heart-breaking, but after the first crushing blow, he realized that the cruel news had set him free. Brother John was earning good money as mate on a trawler fishing off Valparaiso, Chile; he could lend a helping hand to parents and sisters. From Reverend Berg, Paul learned that the small Lutheran school at Red Wing had a curriculum arranged to meet the needs of newcomers in America. Moreover, it was inexpensive. The earnings of 1906 had enabled Paul to pay off his debt. For the six months from March until the opening of the school year in 1907 Hans Christ's hired man was paid $ 26 per month. He calculated that this money would carry him through a year at school.

Hans was disappointed and annoyed at the prospect of losing his farmhand. To be sure, that hand was only a newcomer not accustomed to the intricacies of farm work in America. Hans had constantly assured him that it would take years before he could learn to drive the harvester and become a first-class hired man. Somehow, Hans Christ was a strong believer in apprenticeships for hired men. "But," said Hans patronizingly, "you are strong and honest, and with experience you might become a good farmer." To Hans Christ this was worthy of any man's highest ambition. Frequently he elaborated on the theme that the farmer as his own employer was a free and independent man. An analysis of his own life and experience refuted his thesis, but this was hardly worth arguing about. For a while Hans Christ maintained that the growing infirmities of Old Hannah obligated his young housekeeper, Matilde, the grand-niece of Hannah, and his hired man, her first cousin once removed, to stay and care for her. Her sudden death in July, 1907, solved that problem. Matilde then decided that she, too, would leave the farm and seek work in Chicago.

Hans Christ was sure that Matilde's plan was foolish. The big city was no place for her. Darkly he hinted at its perils.

Less was said about Paul's decision for Hans secretly regretted his own lack of education. As the summer turned into autumn, grumpy though he was, he did not whimper at the prospect of being left alone with the housework and all the chores. In fact he fancied himself a good cook who could easily manage the housework if only he had not so many cows, horses, and hogs to care for. In the end he hit upon what seemed a perfect solution. He would hire a couple who lived in Ostrander. The wife had operated a hotel of a sort, one that had not had any guests for several years, and the husband had done odd jobs. "Gunhild," said Hans, "is an excellent cook, and her husband, though not much good, is an experienced farmhand." Hans believed he stood to gain by this new arrangement.

Early in September the newcomer left for Red Wing Seminary. This event opened another new chapter in his life. After that autumn he paid only brief visits to Ostrander during Christmas holidays and occasionally in the early fall. Though he then stayed with the Bergs, he never failed to call on Hans Christ. Indeed, Hans was most eager to have the former hired man as his guest, but this was not an unmixed pleasure for Paul. Poor Hans Christ. He grew even more crotchety with the years. Whether he operated with part of his acreage rented out on shares or farmed with hired help, the result was always the same — the men were lazy and thievish, and the women demanded impossible wages. So he had decided to carry on with just help by the day; he did his own house-keeping in a fashion that made living in the house with him something of a trial.

Nothing daunted Hans. A tornado swept over the area and ruined his apple trees. He took it in his stride — the trees weren't much good to him anyway since they were never sprayed. One long winter he brought together the lumber and other materials for a big barn, built the following summer, of which he was very proud. He continued to have many milch cows but had no business sense about them, and made no distinction between profitable and unprofitable animals.

As a result he never got out of debt. Frequently and truthfully he stated that his life was nothing but hard work. Never had he had any leisure, rarely any pleasure. After 1914 farm prices were booming. It was pointed out to him that by selling his farm he could live a life of ease on the invested capital. To such advice he refused to listen. His farm was his home. He had won it from the wilderness. By living on it he was his own boss.

The last time the newcomer saw Hans Christ alive was in the autumn of 1915. In some ways he had changed very little. The fancy cutaway tailored like Mr. Bushnell's Sunday best and the coonskin coat were still carefully kept in mothballs. The splendid harnesses were stored under the bed upstairs. One concession he had made to changing times — he had acquired a set of false teeth, but old habits are not easily abandoned and he put his teeth in his pocket when he sat down to meals.

In 1916 Paul went to Norway, Returning in the autumn to resume his studies at the university, he postponed his planned visit to Ostrander. In November he received a telegram — Hans Christ was dead. As was proper and fitting, he had been alone when he died. Swiftly and painlessly an internal hemorrhage had taken him to the silent land of no return.

Paul went to the funeral. The farm seemed sadly strange without its owner. Ludvig Christiansen, still the handy man of the neighborhood, had taken charge. Wearing Hans Christ's coonskin coat he felt quite important. Hans Christ's brothers were there. One of them had donned Hans' cutaway. The fancy harnesses had disappeared, none knew where. For his last journey Hans Christ had been decked out in tails, dickey, stand-up collar, black bow tie. It seemed odd to see him thus attired. But then he probably would have approved, for Mr. Bushnell might have worn just such an outfit for that occasion.

Hans Christ was buried in the cemetery on the edge of the village of Ostrander. Here he rests in the embrace of the soil he loved so well and tilled so long — far from the barren rocks and stormy seas of his native land. His erstwhile hired man mused over the fate of Hans Christ. For fifty years he had labored in the land of his adoption. His working week was always seven days. His body was tough and sinewy. In all his habits he was abstemious. It was 1876 when he got title to his 160 acres of Minnesota prairie land. Then his debt was $ 1,000. At the time of his death forty years later he still was $ 700 in debt. His farm was then valued at $ 225 per acre, but the increment had brought no benefit to Hans. Even his heirs, two brothers and a niece, refused to sell the farm. In 1936 after years of neglect, it was sold at a sheriff's sale for $ 25 an acre. As far as Hans Christ was concerned his toil went for nought.

Peace be to the ashes of Hans Christ. He was lonely and cantankerous with little love for his fellow man, but he had courage, integrity, and steadfastness. He made the earth produce, made the prairie habitable, and added to the wealth of this land. All life brought to him was ceaseless drudgery. For him there was no rainbow at the end of the road. No stone marks his grave, nor even one of his beloved blue spruce trees. It is scorched by the summer's sun, swept by the winds of winter. The wild prairie grasses and flowers which he strove so hard to destroy spread their mantle over his last resting place. Around him lie companions in toil, the many unsung heroes who conquered the wilderness and helped make America rich and strong.

Chapter 11

School Years, 1907-1913

RED WING SEMINARY
is no more! This thought came as a shock; it gave pain like
the death of a dear friend or a close relative. An institution
which for six years had been home, school, and a means for
new contacts and experiences was now closed and would soon
be blotted from the face of the earth.

Memories welled up in the mind of this graduate of the
little school on a hill overlooking the Minnesota town from
whence its name came. It had belonged to the Hauge Synod, a
branch of the Norwegian Lutheran Church in America. But
in 1917 when the Hauge Synod united with two other Norwegian Lutheran church bodies, the theological branch of Red
Wing Seminary had amalagated with the seminaries of the
other groups in St. Paul, and the college department had been
absorbed into St. Olaf College at Northfield. For several years
more the school at Red Wing was maintained as a college
preparatory and teachers' training institution, and for a brief
period it had been a junior college, but early in the 1930's the
governing body of the church had decided to close its doors.
The classroom building and the dormitories, once teeming
with life, were now empty and silent. Windows had been
broken; through the rooms formerly thronged with eager
youth the wind whistled and bats fluttered about.

Not to this ghost but to the living institution the thoughts
of the former student returned. From the shore of memory he
reconstructed the school and the school years from September,

1907, until June, 1913; for him they had been eventful, pleasant and significant years. He recalled that September afternoon when he first climbed Seminary Hill, the initial impressions of the school, its students and faculty, the life at the Seminary, the earnest, hard-working, deeply religious men and women who had built and maintained the school.

In the late afternoon on a cloudless autumn day, Paul Knaplund, the ex-hired man on the Hans Christ farm, arrived at the Great Western station in Red Wing. The Reverend O. R. Wold, Lutheran missionary to China home on a furlough, accompanied the student who had not yet learned to speak the language of America. At Rochester where they changed trains four young men took seats close by the Reverend Wold and his ward. They guessed that the Norwegian-looking youth was headed for the Seminary. Addressing him in his native tongue they introduced themselves. Two of them, born in Norway, had arrived in the United States in 1904. A year later they had entered Red Wing. During summer vacations they taught farm children the Norwegian language and religion, and worked on farms. The other two were brothers born in America who had spent the summer on their parents' farm. All were friendly to the prospective student, and assured him that he would be happy at the school. He at once felt at ease with them.

In Red Wing the Reverend Wold delivered his charge at Sumner Hall, the smaller of the school's two dormitories. Here he was introduced to the president of the Seminary, the Reverend Martin Hanson, who was busy welcoming new and returning students and assigning them to rooms. His face radiated kindness and he showed a keen interest in each of the young men who came to his school. The ones who were Norwegian-born he addressed in their native language. By his benevolent attitude and gracious manner President Hanson won the heart of his new charge.

Paul chose a room on the top floor of Sumner Hall. With him was a farm boy, Ole Hofstad, from Eagle Bend, Minnesota. Born in America of Norwegian parents, Hofstad was bilingual. Paul, remembering that he had learned to read Norwegian by first memorizing the alphabet, asked his new room-mate to name the letters of the English alphabet. These were immediately written down in phonetics and committed to memory. Thus Paul got his first lesson in English.

Shortly afterwards a bell rang and the new students found that this meant dinner was being served in the basement dining room of Sande Hall. It was a large room with bare walls and several long deal tables and benches. The furniture would have met the severest standards for a monastic refectory. No tablecloths or napkins were in evidence. The fact that the students were all men, that the Bible was read, and grace said in unison at each meal strengthened the impression of a monastery. But the simple fare, though plentiful, probably would not have satisfied some of the more sophisticated medieval monks.

Again Paul felt lonely and strange. Returning students exchanged hearty greetings with their old friends; everyone seemed to know everyone else. His new acquaintances from the train were nowhere in sight. Then the young man at Paul's right asked his neighbor on the other side what place in Norway he came from. To Paul's great astonishment the answer was "Bodö." The man from Bodö was Conrad Andersen from the farm Mjelde in the parish of Bodin; he and Paul had been in the same confirmation class! Because the parish was large, the Mjelde farm a long distance from Knaplund, and the class of fifty-eight boys met only a few hours a day for four weeks Conrad and Paul had not become acquainted. But now, meeting like this in a foreign land, the two youths from Dean Holter's confirmation class felt as if they had known each other all their lives.

About one-fourth of the students at Red Wing had been born in Norway, and half of the remainder spoke Norwegian more readily than English, so recently-arrived immigrants could cherish the illusion that they were living in a little Norway on the banks of the Mississippi, an illusion which made the Americanization process gradual and painless. By educating immigrants who did not fit into the American graded public school system the Seminary rendered valuable services before vocational schools were established to fill that long-felt need.

The day after his arrival Paul learned the routine of the school. He registered and purchased the books required, and he explored the campus and its surroundings. The rules of the school were rigid and simple. A bell which hung atop Sande Hall gave the signal for rising and retiring and for the meals. It awakened the boys at six in the morning. At seven breakfast was served. Classes began at eight; a break with chapel service came in the middle of the forenoon. Dinner was at twelve, supper at six. Study hours were from two to four in the afternoon and seven to ten in the evening. At ten the curfew rang and fifteen minutes later the lights went out. The Hauge Synod imposed on President Hanson the duty of enforcing these rules. By this method the school authorities integrated a practical type of character building and discipline with the educational system.

Except for the students' own pictures and knick-knacks the dormitory rooms were furnished with the same Spartan simplicity as the dining-hall. Candles and flashlights were forbidden, so in the night residents of the upper storys had to grope their way to the toilets on the first floor. The only bathing facilities were in the locker room of the gymnasium in Main Hall, the classroom building. But students from farms with outdoor plumbing were not upset by these arrangements. The dormitories had hot and cold running water and central heating, comforts which made the simple living-quarters seem luxurious. Nor were the students disturbed by the lack of maid service. Uncomplainingly they made their beds and cleaned their rooms without overmuch concern about standards.

As Paul inspected his new surroundings he realized that to be registered at this school marked the fulfilment of a long-cherished dream. He was prepared to like whatever he found here. Accustomed only to a one-room log schoolhouse he was impressed with Main Hall. Across its entrance was engraved in large letters "Lys og Sandhed" ("Light and Truth"), surely an appropriate motto for a school. Main Hall stood on the edge of a high bluff commanding a magnificent view of the city, the countryside, and the river. Majestically the Mississippi flowed between steep banks. While the landscape lacked the sublime grandeur of the fjords and mountains of his childhood home, the youth from arctic Norway was entranced by the Mississippi. As a lad he had read about the Father of Waters. The very name had a fascination; it ranked with the Danube, the Rhine, the Nile, and the rivers of Babylon.

The registration of students was handled by the teachers all of whom spoke Norwegian, a help to the immigrants. For Paul the curriculum was fixed; he was to take the eighth-grade subjects with a course in Norwegian in addition. Fees, board, and room rent were very low, a great boon to a student whose entire capital was $160. Paul made this amount suffice for the first school year.

At the book store in the dormitory basement he purchased two dictionaries, one a Norwegian-English and the other a Webster. The former had been compiled by a self-taught man whose translations were inexact and his phonetic transcriptions confusing. Yet the book greatly aided the newcomer. Armed with the dictionaries he immediately went to his room to grapple with arithmetic, his favorite subject in the school at home. Within a surprisingly short time he found that arithmetic was easy; he had no trouble solving the problems. But to explain their solution posed serious difficulties. The dictionary was of little help. The fact that both teachers and students were bilingual saved the situation. Only one member of the class laughed at Paul's clumsy efforts to find English equivalents for Norwegian terms. The scoffing was somewhat troubling, but the realization that in this subject he outshone the American-born members of the class gave the immigrant a big lift.

Though he didn't know the English language Paul distinguished himself in the English grammar class. In the country school of his childhood the pupils were drilled in the rudiments of grammar, the parts of speech, and sentence construction. The text used was an eight-page pamphlet which presented the most elementary facts of the subject, facts which transferred well to English grammar. It became something of a game to classify words and to diagram sentences even though he often did not understand their meaning. His success in this subject also helped the student who for many weeks felt utterly bewildered when his comrades conversed in English. His too small store of self-confidence needed bolstering.

Other courses gave him real difficulty. At first it took a full hour and the use of his two dictionaries to read one page of the physiology lesson. Fortunately persistence and a good memory enabled him to learn by heart the pertinent facts in the text. American history came in the second semester. By then Paul had no difficulty in getting the meaning of the words, but their pronounciation and use presented formidable stumbling blocks. So, as with physiology, he memorized the assignment. After two readings the daily lesson of ten pages was learned word perfect and could be recited verbatim when he was called upon in the classroom.

In their struggles to overcome the language obstacles the foreign-born students got no help from the teacher in the English class. Selections in an elementary reader were read — after a fashion — while the teacher stared absent-mindedly into space. He was obviously bored with the whole business; the poor newcomers had to get along as best they could unless some American-born classmate came to their aid, a rescue which seldom occurred because of the pupils' deference to their teacher. Fortunately for the students this teacher lasted only one year at Red Wing.

The first year at the Seminary marked a turning point in Paul's life. In June, 1908, the newcomer who had been so helpless and ignorant the preceding autumn found he had passed all examinations except that in English with the highest grades given. He led his class. This scholastic success went a long way toward ridding him of the diffidence and sense of inadequacy which had haunted him since childhood. He now felt certain that at least in academic work he could hold his own. His older brothers gave assurances that they would take care of aging parents and the ailing sisters leaving Paul free to follow his natural bent.

Two years after the immigrant, not knowing a soul in America, had landed in New York in May, 1906, he felt he now had real connections in the land — he belonged to a community, to Red Wing Seminary and the Hauge Synod. On many occasions in succeeding years he was to learn how much this meant. The teachers at the school had been friendly, helpful, and encouraging. They had faith in the young man who, awkward and green, had come to them the autumn before. Among the students he had a fairly large circle of friends, more than he had ever known. No longer was he a stranger in a foreign country.

As he called to mind the years of long ago and the school which had ceased to exist, the professor reflected on the efforts, the faith, and the hopes of the hard-working, humble immigrants from Norway and their descendants who had founded and maintained Red Wing Seminary. The church body to which they belonged, Hauge Synod, took its name from the gifted farmer in Norway, Hans Nielsen Hauge, who early in the nineteenth century had travelled widely throughout the land exhorting his countrymen to repent and seek the road to salvation. In Norway and later in America his disciples and followers were called "Haugeans" or "Haugeaners." About the middle of the nineteenth century many of the Haugeans emigrated to America. Energetic, enterprising, frugal, and sober, they combined the characteristics of German pietists, English evangelicals, and American Puritans. The Haugeans had disliked the state church in their homeland, and they distrusted the ministers trained in that church and imbued with its authoritarian spirit who came to midwestern America to organize congregations.

Among the disciples of Hauge was Elling Eielsen, who like

his master, had been imprisoned for unauthorized preaching. A restless, stubborn and zealous man Eielsen followed the early Christian precept of obedience to God rather than to man. Since the Norwegian police were constantly on his trail he left his fatherland. After a sojourn in Denmark he came to the United States and finally settled in central Illinois. Finding the Norwegians without spiritual guides there, he had himself ordained by a German Lutheran minister and organized congregations which ultimately combined into a synod. Eielsen fought bitterly against the ministers ordained in the state church of Norway who came to the Middle West.

Strongly egalitarian, the Hauge Synod opposed ritualism and the use of Norwegian Lutheran clerical vestments. It emphasized the priesthood of all believers, and it stressed piety, self-restraint, and self-discipline in daily life. In their religious practices the Haugeans came closer to those of the early American Calvinistic Protestant church bodies than did most of the other Lutheran organizations in America. And at the turn of the century the Hauge Synod attracted many recent immigrants from Norway who in their homeland had been influenced by religious movements originating in England and the United States.

At first the Haugeans were sceptical of the need for formal education for their clergymen. They were chiefly interested in securing ministers who were sincerely devout Christians, who felt certain that they had a call from on high, and who could expound the Biblical message clearly and earnestly. In time, however, the members of this Synod became convinced of the need for special training in Bible study and exegesis, in the history of Christian dogma, and particularly in the doctrines of Luther and in data for refuting the errors of other denominations. By such training their ministers would become more effective servants of God. So the property on the Hill in Red Wing was purchased, and in 1879 the Seminary opened its doors.

With the passing years the activities of the school widened. The theological seminary remained the core of the institution, but college preparatory, college, and commercial departments were added. Throughout its existence, the Seminary bore the imprint of its pious founders. Private devotion in the dormitory rooms, prayer meetings on week-days as well as on Sundays, daily chapel exercises, and periodic revival meetings formed a regular part of the school's life. It was only by slow degrees that games and athletic exercises were introduced; such activities aroused deep misgivings in the minds of the old-style Haugeans.

Rather early in the history of the Seminary some graduates of its preparatory course entered the liberal arts college at the University of Minnesota. This state institution then rated well with the Haugeans because it had daily chapel. They had learned that President Northrop led the devotions, and to earnest Haugeans it was pleasing to know that it was quiet in the University of Minnesota chapel "when Prexy prays." The pietistic farmers who supported the Seminary were proud to hear that some of its graduates won Phi Beta Kappa keys at the university, and delighted when one of them was the valedictorian of his class. He and other Phi Beta Kappas returned to Red Wing as teachers.

The Seminary represented an amalgam of things Norwegian and American, of old and new, of the religious and the secular. At religious meetings songs from Congregational, Methodist, and Presbyterian hymnals mingled with and were often preferred to those from the Lutheran books. Classes were conducted and courses organized on American rather than on Norwegian patterns. The ideas in history, literature, and science which some of the faculty members had absorbed at the state university were presented at Red Wing. Though the Norwegian language was used extensively in student discussions, the topics discussed belonged to the new world. Thus without pressure or propaganda students who were newly-arrived in America became adjusted, began to feel at home, and took root in the new country.

In all the years of its existence Red Wing Seminary's largest enrolment barely passed the 200 mark. The entire plant consisted of only the two dormitories and one classroom building. Library and laboratory facilities were inadequate even for a secondary school. It had no playing field. It was understaffed and its faculty was underpaid. Still, it fulfilled a mission. For more than half a century the school on the Hill stressed the need for a vital, living type of Christianity, one which followed the simple precepts of the Man from Galilee. Founded by men of faith, it was staffed by men of faith, and it sent out many earnest, dedicated men to widely-scattered communities in the United States and Canada. The Red Wing Seminarians who became preachers of the Gospel impressed upon hard-working tillers of the soil and factory hands the message that life is not mean and sordid, and that all of Adam's kin could become children of God and with their Master share heavenly bliss.

As the school enlarged its offerings, graduates of departments other than theology entered business or the professions. Upon them all the little school on the Hill left an imprint. They developed an appreciation of spiritual things, and a belief that life is essentially good. Their path was lighted by faith in eternal verities. Through shifting scenes and varied experiences the motto "Light and Truth" remained engraved upon their minds.

For many of those who attended Red Wing for only brief periods this was also the case. The turn-over among the students was heavy because farm boys might come for only winter terms, and immigrants often stayed but one or two years. Even upon these transients the school left its mark creating impressions which lasted throughout life. In its presentation of subjects the Seminary represented much that is fundamental in American life and thought. By so doing it Americanized both immigrants and native Americans with foreign-born parents.

In the diversity of its student body the school bore some resemblance to the famous medieval universities. At the Seminary men past thirty mingled with boys in their teens. Students came from various parts of the United States and from several sections of Norway. Among them were artisans, clerks, farm and factory workers, sheepherders, miners, sailors, and fishermen. A cheerful and friendly lot, the students often gathered in one another's rooms where conversation never lagged. Though poor in worldly goods, they were uncommonly rich in experience.

The religious atmosphere which prevailed at the school did not rule out interest in mundane matters too. Politics, both state and national, had many devotees. In the absence of important issues, political discussions centered around personalities. The Democratic governor of Minnesota, John A. Johnson, appealed to many Red Wing students. But when in 1908 his Republican opponent was a native of Norway some felt that they must support him against "Swede" Johnson. Four years later the colorful national figures, Robert M. La Follette, Theodore Roosevelt, and Woodrow Wilson, won enthusiastic followers or aroused bitter opponents. Of the three, Wilson had perhaps the strongest support among the Seminarians who were attracted to him because of his academic background and because he promised a "new freedom."

Among social questions of the day that of ridding the country of saloons seemed of primary importance to Red Wing students. On the principle they were firmly united, but on the methods for fighting the evil they were sharply divided. Some were ardent Prohibitionists while others supported the Anti-Saloon League. It was the professor of Greek who led the Prohibition forces on campus. Erick E. Espelien, known as "E. Cube", staunchly upheld the Anti-Saloon League. On days when the class in second year Greek had failed to study the assignment in the *Anabasis* someone would raise the temperance question, and the ensuing debate between the professor and E. Cube might last the entire class hour. It was great fun, but the study of Greek suffered.

Red Wing was a "wet" town with a brewery and many saloons. One spring the temperance forces mobilized in an effort to rid the city of this menace. As a first step a certain number of voters had to petition the city council for a referendum on the issue. Eagerly the students circulated the petitions and canvassed the voters, but when the issue came to a vote, the temperance forces were snowed under.

Such "outside activities" of the students disturbed "Doc" Brohough, the only Ph. D. on the Red Wing faculty. He was a professor who enjoyed the unique distinction of being also a president of a bank in a west Minnesota town. One morning when it was Doc's turn to conduct chapel he rose with great dignity and in a measured voice said, "Gentlemen, please read Nehemiah VI : 3." It was the shortest service ever known, and the students hurried out to follow his suggestion. They found that Nehemiah in response to an invitation to abandon the rebuilding of the walls of Jerusalem and to come to the plains "sent messengers ... saying, 'I am doing a great work and I cannot come down. Why should the work stop while I leave it and come down to you?' " No long sermon exhorting the students to concentrate on their studies so basic to success-ful lives could have left as lasting an impression as Brohough's brief direction.

Occasionally visiting clergymen led in chapel devotions, so in this way the students became acquainted with leaders in the Hauge Synod. Often the visitors in their prayers informed the Lord on a variety of subjects; in their talks they lectured the students about the hardships of olden times, contrast-ing them with the comforts and luxuries of the present.

Now and then visitors other than clergymen were allowed to speak at chapel. Among these the oddest character was a Frenchman who announced that he was a physiognomist, and he presented letters of recommendation from church dignitaries stating that he possessed remarkable skill in ana-lyzing people's character and discovering their aptitudes sim-ply by examining their faces. After the service he was assigned a room, and his hours for consultation were announced. Many students were taken in by this imposter. Having first paid a dollar, each of them was told in a five minute interview that his face gave clear indication of high character, unusual in-telligence, and remarkable aptitude for a clergyman's calling.

In 1910 Governor Eberhardt of Minnesota honored the school with a visit. At chapel he professed his devotion to Lutheranism and declared his profound regard for the high ethical and strict religious principles of the school. But it was known that earlier when he had addressed a convention of brewery workers he had pointed out that the Bible records only a single instance of a man asking for water, and then, said Eberhardt, he asked for only a drop of it, and besides, this man was in Hell where he ought to be. His fulsome praise of Red Wing standards failed to convince either students or faculty; it merely corroborated Eberhardt's reputation of being an insincere flatterer who tried to be all things to all people.

Perhaps because of the diversities within the student group various fads were tried in their quest for mental alertness and physical vitality. Some urged a diet of only nuts or raw vegetables; others followed Bernarr MacFadden's theories. Most pathetic were those who believed that the use of gadgets would make them good students. One poor fellow who was having trouble with his subjects bought a special chair which was equipped with swinging racks for dictionaries, a special desk lamp, a green eye shade, and a high desk at which he could stand to study. Unfortunately the equipment failed to work the hoped-for miracle!

Music was encouraged at the Seminary. Nearly every student belonged to band, orchestra, or the choral union; some belonged to all three. These were quite successful, and during the years gave a series of concerts which raised money enough to purchase a grand piano for the chapel. An octet which toured to sing for congregations of the Hauge Synod won many supporters for the school. Paul belonged to the choral union, and one year he and three friends formed their own quartet. Optimistically Mrs. Schmidt, wife of the Reverend Hanson's successor as president, undertook to train the four men. Their favorite song, "Beautiful Isle of Somewhere," was sung at a meeting of the Red Wing W.C.T.U. with some success. The women were kind, praised the young men, and treated them to ice cream and cake. When they attempted to repeat their success with the same song at a Sunday evening service at St. Peter Lutheran Church, the bass forgot to include a second "beautiful" where it was called for, and sang on ahead of the others with dire results. Never again did the quartet appear in public.

Debating and oratorical societies in English and in Norwegian flourished. "Doc" Brohough was the coach of public speaking, but his favored style of oratory with many elaborate gestures belonged to an age fast vanishing. More successful in public speaking than in music, Paul won first place in the local contest in Norwegian oratory, and second in the state competition. By his senior year he had learned his adopted country's language well enough to win second place in the English oratorical contest.

For most of the Red Wing students social life of the usual sort was non-existent. Dancing and card-playing were forbidden. The grossly underpaid faculty (annual salaries were $ 1,200 for professors of theology and $ 800 for the others) could not afford to entertain students. The local Hauge Synod congregation at St. Peter Lutheran was made up chiefly of laboring people. And the city folk of Red Wing took no interest in the Seminary. The school had been operated originally by a man named Hogg, then later bought by the Hauge Synod, so many townsfolk called the students "Hogs" instead of Haugeans and treated them in a discourteous fashion.

About 1910 Red Wing students began to agitate for coeducation. One college preparatory school operated by the Haugeans at Jewell, Iowa, was for both sexes. But daughters of most Haugeans who sought college education had to go to state schools or to schools run by other denominations. The Red Wing students argued that this might lure the young women away from the Hauge Synod. Of course the real reason they advocated coeducation was that they believed women on the campus would make life there more interesting. In 1914 the church fathers capitulated to their demand.

A mile west of Red Wing Seminary on another hill was the Ladies Lutheran Seminary. This was a preparatory school with a conservatory of music operated by the Norwegian Synod, a conservative branch of the church. Perhaps because the girls were strictly chaperoned at the time Paul was in Red Wing the students of the two schools hardly ever met. As work for the church union progressed, however, the system of rigid segregation weakened, and by 1913 Hauge Seminarians were allowed to attend "mixers" at the Ladies Seminary. The girls welcomed the young men, but entertainment was limited to childish games. What a time they had playing "Farmer in the Dell" where the young ladies, screaming with laughter, invariably chose six-foot-three, 190 pound E. Cube for the "babe."

Although successful in his other subjects Paul failed to gain real mastery of the English language while he was at Red Wing. His deficiency was due in part to the faulty early training in the subject and to the school's failure to stress English composition. Furthermore, every year from 1907 to 1913 brought a new batch of immigrants to the school, and Norwegian continued to be widely used among the students. Summers were spent mostly in Hauge congregations where Norwegian was commonly spoken. Here Paul became acquainted with that amazing aspect of American society, nations within a nation. From the members of these Norwegian-American settlements he learned more history of the immigrants, and heard many stories of men and women who though they never conquered the American idiom achieved a mighty work in building America.

It was in these settlements that Paul earned a large share of the money necessary for his six years at Red Wing. Like many of the students at that school he was wholly self-supporting. When he had first come to the Seminary he found to his astonishment that even students who were American-born lacked money for an education. This ran counter to the prevalent Norwegian belief that all Americans were well-to-do.

Unlike a number of other students Paul had no special skill

to enable him to earn good wages in his spare time at school or during the summers. His natural diffidence also handicapped him. Chances to wait on tables in boarding houses or restaurants were turned down because he feared he would be too clumsy. Though he offered his services as a handy man, he found this sort of job was irregular, poorly paid, and interfered with his school work. For a while he was a reporter for the Red Wing *Daily Republican*. Assigned to cover the arrival of night trains he could ill afford such late hours; besides, he lacked the aggressiveness of a good reporter. For brief periods he earned his meals by scrubbing floors in restaurants, but the first such job terminated when the restaurant went bankrupt, and the second he resigned to become janitor at the Carnegie Library. There he was paid the munificent salary of $ 20 a month. At the same time he earned an additional $ 4 a month by lighting the gas at 5 A.M. under the linotype machine of the *Daily Republican* and changing the date on the time clock six days a week. Since his expenses usually totalled less than $ 250 a year, Paul was then in clover. But because this windfall did not come until his senior year he had only a short period to enjoy such riches.

During those years at Red Wing the strictest economy had to be practiced. The clothes brought from Norway lasted many seasons, a boon to Paul but a source of dismay to the laundresses who were not accustomed to coping with homespun underwear. In his second semester at school he learned that by buying milk at six cents a quart and stale bread at three cents a loaf the cost of meals could be kept below even the modest charge at the Seminary's dining hall. The bread and milk with some summer sausage went far toward a day's food needs.

Savings in rent could be effected, too, by getting a room with a stove in town and buying wood from farmers. Furthermore, by living outside the dormitories a student might burn the midnight oil as often and as late as he chose, so after the first year Paul roomed out. The flexible rules of the school enabled students to carry a large number of subjects and to take special examinations for credit. By earning some academic credits for his knowledge of Norwegian, by carrying a large number of courses each year, and by taking comprehensive examinations in subjects which he studied by himself he was able to shorten his course. In September, 1907, he had entered as an eighth-grade pupil. At the end of May, 1913, he was awarded his B.A. by Red Wing Seminary where he was the valedictorian of his class.

Chapter 12

Summers, 1908-1913

Fortunately in the years 1908—1913 the Middle West was prosperous, and students could always find employment. Paul was one of the many who had to work during summer vacations. The men from Red Wing usually chose between teaching parochial school, working on the farm, or taking orders for a variety of articles in house-to-house canvasses.

Congregations of the Hauge Synod were eager to get teachers from their school to give summer courses in religion and Norwegian. They clung with tenacity to their theological beliefs and to their old-world language. During the summer classes in these subjects were held in schools or church basements. The courses lasted four weeks in each district, and as terms began in May, a teacher could give three of them by harvest time. The wage for the parochial school teacher was $ 30 a term plus room and board, a salary which equalled the monthly wages paid farm hands. If the pupils presented a program of songs and recitations at the end of the course, the collection taken up for the teacher might equal a month's salary.

Teaching finished, the student-teachers often worked at harvesting and threshing. For this work the usual wage was $ 2.50 a day, and those who could operate the engine or separator of the threshing machine earned twice that amount. But since only actual working days were counted, bad weather might materially reduce the earnings.

Students with a knack for selling made the most money.

Some of them cleared three to five hundred dollars during the summer taking orders for books, enlargements of family photographs, stereopticon views, aluminum cooking utensils, or groceries. The first was an old standby; the two last came into vogue while Paul was at Red Wing. Companies had an agent at the school who recruited and trained salesmen. Andrew Fedt had such a position at the Seminary. As a lad of thirteen he had come to the United States travelling alone from Norway with an address tag pinned to his coat. Andrew had shifted for himself since his arrival. A bright and enterprising boy he quickly caught on to American ways, and it was not many years before he had built up a successful agency. By the time he finished his own college course he had enough money to start the study of medicine. In 1908 Andrew Fedt tried to enlist Paul as a stereopticon salesman. But Paul was too conscious of his imperfect English to try such unfamiliar work. Instead he decided to get a summer post teaching parochial school.

Among the numerous duties of the Seminary president was that of training parochial school teachers. Although born in the United States, he used Norwegian more readily than English. As student and pastor he had had experience teaching classes in Norwegian and in religion. Furthermore, President Hanson, a kindly, sympathetic man who loved young people, was well qualified to train teachers for the summer church schools.

The special teachers' training course lasted six weeks. All class-work was in Norwegian, the textbooks were familiar, and Paul found the course easy and enjoyable. At its end President Hanson assured the rather timid student that he would make an excellent teacher. About this he himself was not so certain either before or after he had taught. But in reviewing his experiences during the six summers, the professor recognized that this teaching, the new contacts and impressions had all contributed in adapting him to American life.

In the summer of 1908 Paul taught in the congregations of O. O. Bergh at Volga and Artesian, South Dakota, after which he worked on the farm of Charles Fredin near Claremont. A similar pattern was followed in 1909 at Toronto, South Dakota. Then for two summers he sold aluminum cooking utensils. In 1912 he switched to selling groceries as an agent for Andrew Fedt, but failing at this, he quit the agency early in July and returned to the Fredin farm. In 1913 he first taught a term of parochial school, then he attended a six-week summer session at the University of Wisconsin. Finally he taught another term before he enrolled in graduate school. During his years at Red Wing every autumn except the first he entered school late for he had to earn as much as possible. But he always finished the school year in the spring; he could more easily catch up with the work he had missed in the autumn than pass examinations to remove incompletes in unfinished subjects.

Paul's summer activities from 1908 to 1913 were spread over nearly half a hundred scattered communities in Minnesota and South Dakota, with a brief excursion into the Red River valley in North Dakota. In both town and country most of the population had come from Norway and Sweden or was made up of sons and daughters of Scandinavian immigrants. Exceptions were the towns of Brookings and Crookston where the population was largely American. As teacher, farmhand, and salesman he learned to know a great number of people. He stayed in scores of farm homes. His hosts generally understood Norwegian; he therefore conversed with them in his mother tongue. This delighted them. They liked to hear Norwegian spoken without the admixture of English or half-Anglicized words. They were interested in conditions in the old country, and he was perhaps even more interested in what they could tell about pioneer days. Their accounts of the still unbroken prairie when houses were mere shanties or sod huts, when the market towns were far away and roads nonexistent were fascinating. Paul wanted to know how they had overcome hardships and conquered the wilderness. Rugged, toilworn farmers found pleasure and satisfaction in discussing olden times. In their humble, quiet way they liked to dwell on events of their early manhood when they had struggled hard and won. Each narrator told his simple tale while the listener lent a sympathetic ear.

As the professor conjured up friendly faces from the past and the stories he had heard, half-forgotten sensations returned. Again he felt as he had that evening on a Knaplund hilltop when he looked upon the land and sea of arctic Norway. At first only the general contours had caught his attention. Then the details took form and became associated with individuals and events. Similarly in 1936 as he travelled the road of memory the first general impressions of wide areas hove into view, then towns and farmsteads, homes and people. With surprising distinctness he recalled episodes and persons and the tales told by aged, hard-working men and women.

As a son of the soil, a fisherman and sailor, Paul had been especially interested in the physical geography of regions when he first visited them. Travelling from Red Wing to Volga in 1908 he was disappointed not to see the great open spaces and limitless plains over which the Sioux Indians had roamed, but later as he drove from Iroquois to Artesian the landscape was what he had imagined it would be. Here the homes were a mile apart and the farms a section or more in extent. And in 1911 on a train journey from Grand Forks to Grafton, North Dakota, he found the country conformed in every particular to the mental picture he had of the American West, the region of buffalo hunts and prairie fires. Here along the Red River of the North the scenery was in complete contrast to that of his childhood home. The unobstructed horizon in the famous Red River valley resembled the ocean on a calm day. He was both enthralled and oppressed by what he saw. No trees were visible except the few planted by man, no hill or gulley, only smooth, level land. He appreciated that on sunny summer days with nature in bloom and seemingly endless fields of waving grain extending in every direction this part of America would have a certain appeal. Accustomed to long winters with raging snowstorms and howling winds, he envisaged the bitterly cold days with blizzards from the north sweeping along unimpeded all the way from the shore of Hudson Bay. Roads and fences would be deeply buried in drifts, the air filled with swirling snow. He imagined the pioneer days with the settlers in rude shacks ill-suited to ward off the wintry blast. The dwellings were few and far apart and there was not even a telephone for communication with the distant neighbors. Somewhere Paul had read that the incidence of mental illness had been high among the Norwegian immigrants who had settled in the Red River valley, and when he saw the country he could easily understand why. Norwegian settlers had come from closely-knit communities where all knew each other, where ancestors had lived for many generations, and where long-established customs had provided some variety and entertainment in their lives. With high hopes the immigrants had arrived in America, the land of promise. Few could have anticipated how utterly foreign the new environment would be. Land, customs, language, everything they encountered was unfamiliar and bewildering. Americans sometimes were, if not actively unfriendly, at least condescending. Frequently they cheated the newcomers. The hardships of pioneer life were shared by husband and wife, but the loneliness and monotony bore hardest on the women. Their duties were unrelieved by trips to town and by the physical battles with the elements. For them the conditions required unusual mental balance and physical strength, rich intellectual resources, and deep religious faith. Lacking such attributes many women broke under the strain.

Walking to church one Sunday in 1908 Paul was struck by the wondrous beauty of the wheat fields. The day was bright and sunny. A light breeze created ripples like waves on the ocean over that sea of golden grain glittering in the sun as far as the eye could see. The atmosphere breathed peace. For men and beasts the day was one of rest. Only now and then was the stillness broken by the chirping of birds; they emphasized the quiet in nature. With a mind relaxed Paul felt fully attuned to this rural scene.

Later that autumn he spent a month plowing on the Fredin farm. Once more he noted the vast difference between farming in Norway and in America. Back home he had plowed with one horse. Despite the lightness of the implement, plowing had been hard work for both horse and man. The plow was poorly adjusted and had to be guided carefully. To assist the horse the man pushed on the plow which now and then crashed against hidden rocks. The fields were small and the turnings frequent. The furrows of the Fredin fields were a mile long. Five powerful horses pulled the double gang-plow. On it rode the plowman. No stone ever impeded the implement, and the horses needed no guidance until the end of the furrow. It was easy work for the plowman. On warm days he occasionally slept on his perch.

During his first years in America Paul was constantly amazed at the bounty of nature and the prodigality of man. There was no need to drain or fertilize the fields. Men just sowed the grain and harvested the crop. While the straw of barley and oats might sometimes be used, the huge piles of wheat straw were usually burned. In the evening for miles around the Fredin farm the sky was lighted by dozens of straw fires. In Norway nothing that could be used for fodder was ever destroyed.

From these general reflections Paul turned his memory to more specific episodes. The parochial school teaching came first to mind. Despite President Hanson's encouragement, Paul had been very uncertain when he started to teach. He was completely unfamiliar with this type of school, and he knew he would be an absolute stranger to the parents as well as to the children. But fate was kind. When he alighted from the train at Volga, he noticed a heavy-set man with a goatee scanning the passengers. This was the Reverend O. O. Bergh under whose supervision Paul was to teach. They instantly recognized each other, and the new teacher was cordially greeted in Norwegian by the pastor. In common with many ministers in the Hauge Synod the Reverend Bergh combined farming with his pastoral work. He had driven to Volga from his farm four miles south of town. Arriving at the farm the minister and teacher entered the large kitchen, a room which served as the family dining and living-room as well, and there they found assembled Mrs. Bergh and the nine children ranging in age from six to twenty-five. Cheerily the Reverend Bergh turned to his guest and with a sweep of his arm to call attention to his family said, "These are all Berghs, and now you are at home." In an equally informal and friendly fashion Mrs. Bergh greeted the stranger. For Paul it was a heart-warming and never-to-be-forgotten welcome.

The first week of teaching he stayed with the Berghs whose hospitality and kindness were almost limitless. Peddlers and wayfarers of every description were given lodging. The Bergh home seemed a special haven for Syrian peddlers then quite common in South Dakota. One Saturday evening such a man turned up with a young brother who had just that week arrived from Syria. On Sunday the newcomer received instructions from his brother. Early Monday morning both started out with packs and headed in different directions. Paul, who after more than two years in America was still too unsure of himself to try to sell anything, marvelled at the younger man's temerity.

While a student at Red Wing he had numerous opportunities to benefit from the wonderful hospitality of the Hauge Synod ministers. Though their salaries were low even for those days (they averaged from five hundred to a thousand dollars a year) they did much entertaining. Open house was kept for parishioners, and shelter was given not only to visiting clergymen and missionaries, but to many wandering do-gooders. Repeatedly the wives of the Haugean pastors must have performed the Biblical miracle with the loaves and the fishes. They worked unceasingly to lighten the tasks of their minister husbands and to make their homes and family lives shining examples for parishioners.

The parochial teachers were the special beneficiaries of the functional Christianity of these pastors and their wives. Often teachers were young immigrants without homes of their own.

Since they had to move around from one farm home to another they occasionally encountered that inveterate enemy of the human race, the bed-bug. Having spent a couple of nights on a chair, the hapless teacher would be forced to think up some reason for going back to the minister's home for the remainder of the week; it was essential that the shift of lodging be effected diplomatically or a contributor to the church might be offended. On the other hand, the roundsman system for parochial teachers provided splendid opportunities to get acquainted with many people and to draw from the older generation stories of pioneer life.

Light and shade mingled in Paul's experiences as a teacher. It was a delight to spend the summer in the country without having the hard work and long hours of a farm hand. Under such conditions the beauty of the landscape could be thoroughly enjoyed. Farm children welcomed the relief from chores which the school gave. But town children had a different attitude. They had had a long school year; their interest in learning Norwegian was virtually nil, and to them the church school instead of being a respite from work was an interference with vacation plans. The terms Paul taught town children he found quite unrewarding.

From a pedagogical point of view, the parochial school in the congregation's transitional period from Norwegian to English presented extremely difficult problems. The school's twin objectives, instruction in the Norwegian language and in Lutheran dogma, were hard to reconcile and well-nigh impossible to achieve in four weeks. From home the children knew a corrupt form of Norwegian, and the defects of the Norwegian primers were serious. But these problems were insignificant compared with those presented by Luther's *Short Catechism* and the summaries of Lutheran dogma which were considered essential to the course. The handbook in dogma abounded in abstract terms such as "justification" and "sanctification," terms which theologians have for centuries wrangled over. The poor children were expected to learn by heart the definitions of these terms and the supporting Bible passages. Any attempt to clarify them for young minds would have been futile.

Bible history was more easily taught. Many of the stories were full of human interest and could be told in simple language. To be sure, the greatest story of them all, that of the Man from Galilee, posed difficulties, especially the accounts of the miracles, but His gentleness and loving kindness appealed to many of the children.

Within the same class the pupils varied widely in age and language skill. A class of eighteen at Artisian had children from three to seventeen. Three-year old, blond, blue-eyed Ole Olsen knew no Norwegian, but he had an ABC for that language. Since pictures accompanied names of animals he knew like cat, dog, and cow these words did not trouble Ole. But as preparation for religious instruction, the primer included a vocabulary of short words among which was the Norwegian word for faith ("tro"). On this word little Ole had a mental block. He could roll out "trr" without trouble, but "tro" invariably became "kro" on small Ole's tongue. So it remained to the end of the term.

During recess the teacher was expected to lead the children in games. Most popular was, of course, baseball, but this game was entirely beyond the competence of the immigrant teacher. To the disgust of the bigger boys he could participate only in games like "drop the handkerchief" and "Annie, Annie over the fence."

The routine of reading and recitation was often broken by group singing which gave pleasure to teacher as well as pupils. Lutheran hymns with their majestic melodies were too heavy for young Americans, so the Reverend Brohough, brother of "Doc", had prepared a children's song-book which included both Norwegian songs and songs translated into that language. The words for these melodies were short and simple, and the tunes were lilting. Among the favorites in all the schools where Paul taught was a Norwegian version of "Far, Far Away" and "The Dying Child." Though the sad text of the latter seemed inappropriate for these children, both songs were sung with great zest. Paul's brief and transitory contacts with his pupils gave a certain charm to the recollection of their singing. After these many years the picture of a badly furnished, dingy country schoolhouse was brightened by the memory of fresh young voices lustily singing:

> Had I wings I would fly
> Far, far away
> Far, far away.

Finding that his earnings as teacher and farm hand were insufficient for the school year's needs, Paul decided in 1910 that his English was adequate for work as a salesman. Toward the end of May he set out to sell Wear Ever utensils. Cautious as ever, he secured a territory in Brookings County, South Dakota, where he had connections. Some of the housewives there had already used aluminum pots and pans. One of them, a Mrs. Johnson, had complained to the company about a tea kettle which leaked after only two years use. Paul was instructed to inspect this kettle and replace it if the metal were at fault. He found there had been impurities in the cast aluminum, so he promptly replaced the kettle with a new sheet aluminum one. The grateful Mrs. Johnson not only allowed Paul to use her name as a reference, she lent him to use for demonstration purposes an aluminum pan still serviceable after fifteen years of hard wear. In addition she gave him free breakfasts for a week; it was an encouraging and profitable deal for the new salesman.

Volga and Brookings were friendly to the student, but the rural areas had strong sales resistance. To trudge country roads where houses were about half a mile apart, and to carry the heavy sample case was hard and slow work. One day he hired a livery rig, but not a single sale was made, so he never again indulged in such extravagance. However, the Reverend Bergh, kindly as always, lent Paul a pony and cart with which he covered the neighborhood, and the venture brought fairly good results.

Even the hard facts of economic need failed to cure Paul

of his diffidence. He was too shy to stage demonstrations of the use and superior qualities of aluminum ware at meetings of ladies aid societies and similar gatherings. More or less mechanically he told prospective customers that the utensils would neither chip, corrode, nor rust, and that as a metal aluminum was an excellent heat conductor, was very malleable, and had great tensile strength. Some of these phrases were not understood, and frequently the listeners were sceptical of his statements. One housewife bluntly announced, "I don't believe you that aluminum doesn't rust." The agent's rejoinder, "I am sorry, Madam, but your disbelief will have no effect on the metal," failed to bring about a sale.

Early in his career he learned that salesmen were disliked by many householders. Their attitude was summed up with brutal frankness by the Reverend Henrik Voldal of Volga who said, "When students turn agents I have absolutely no use for them." Wham went the door in Paul's face! Some days the salesman was so unnerved by rebuffs that he felt relieved when no one answered the bell.

Although he had learned his sales talk well, in general conversation he occasionally stumbled over English words. Sometimes he was tolerantly corrected, at other times his accent and pronounciation provoked laughter. In explaining the merits of an aluminum percolator to two young teachers one day Paul noticed that one of them could hardly control her merriment. When the other made further inquiries and used the word "percolator," the former burst out laughing and said, "My dear, that thing is called a perforator." At this point Paul explained that perforated aluminum was used in the percolator, and so was able to turn the tables on his critic. But all such scoffing left its mark and added to the difficulties of the immigrant learning to make a place for himself in his adopted country.

Among the things which amazed the reserved young Norwegian was the readiness with which some women would unburden themselves to a perfect stranger. Several times when he suggested that the husband would approve of the splendid aluminum utensils, a wife would burst into a dreadful tirade about what a skinflint her spouse was. Another type of woman who perplexed Paul was the kind who expressed enthusiasm for the Wear Ever utensils, but who by pure chance was out of cash when he came to deliver the pans she had ordered. Might she have them and pay next week? Twice he granted this request to women reputed to be pillars of the church only to learn when he called for his money that the purchaser would not pay him the price agreed upon. Though the pans showed clear signs of hard usage, he recovered them and sold them to someone else at a reduced price; never again did he leave the goods until he had received the cash payment.

Such instances were, however, exceptions. Other housewives were exceedingly kind to the aluminum agent. He recalled with gratitude Mrs. Green who had given him magazines because she was sure he felt lonesome evenings, and Mrs. Knappen who had served him coffee and cookies in the middle of a hot morning because she thought he must be weary trudging along with the big sample case. Gifts in kind were the more readily accepted because until the first set of orders had been delivered he was penniless. At one time when he changed rooms he had to go without food for two days; when the utensils he had ordered arrived, he could collect on his deliveries and eat once more.

When the market in Brookings County was exhausted, he tried without success to sell his wares to housewives in Pipestone, Slayton, and Windom, Minnesota. At Windom he looked up Dr. Louis Sogge, a graduate of Red Wing. Dr. Sogge advised him that the farming community in Jackson County was progressive and prosperous. The Hauge Synod was strong in the area and farmers' wives might react favorably to a sales talk by a Red Wing student. Dr. Sogge's sister who had music pupils in the neighborhood offered to give Paul a ride to her old home and introduce him to relatives and friends.

So the salesman went with Miss Sogge to Belmont township where she introduced him to her numerous relatives and put him in touch with a buttermaker who had a horse and buggy which he let Paul use on week days free of charge. Miss Sogge's uncle and aunt, Mr. and Mrs. Hans Sether, invited him to be a guest at their home while he canvassed the community. One of their daughters had just married the Reverend Peder Wee, brother of Red Wing Seminary Professor M. O. Wee, and they were interested in the school and its students. Thus Paul was well launched. Soliciting orders in a ten mile radius around the Sether farmstead he achieved a good deal of success especially with the various branches of the Sether family. All in all the summer of 1910 netted him nearly $ 200, and he resolved to continue as an aluminum salesman the next year.

In 1911 Paul chose the territory around Crookston, Minnesota, because he wanted to visit a cousin married to a farmer living about thirty miles east of the town. Arriving in the area he found a community more impoverished than any he had hitherto seen in America. The gravelly soil of the farms ill-requited the labor spent on it, and Crookston itself was a languishing lumber town. For two weeks he rang doorbells and explained the superior qualities of aluminum utensils without getting a single order. Finally he shifted to Becker County where business was a little better. There, too, he became acquainted with the beautiful resort country of the area, and had the good fortune of learning to know the Reverend H. H. Knudsvig and his wife. This friendly and jovial clergymen was a Red Wing graduate. Less austere than most Hauge Synod ministers, he had worked successfully in and around Audubon for several years. His home became headquarters for the salesman who often accompanied the pastor on calls and to services in the two congregations outside the village. He made little money in his 1911 vacation, but the summer brought returns of another sort. He met many people and learned a great deal about life in Minnesota communities.

Deciding to abandon his career as an aluminum salesman, Paul tried his luck with groceries in 1912. But after covering hundreds of miles criss-crossing Becker and Clay counties and obtaining very few orders, he gave up selling and returned to his South Dakota employer, Charles Fredin. The Fredins welcomed him cordially, and for the remainder of the summer Paul engaged in the hard but rewarding work of haying, harvesting, and threshing. Because of his familiarity with the Fredin farm he was paid what then was the top farm wage of $ 50 a month for a two months period.

As the professor re-lived those student years he became aware that he had learned from the grass roots, so to speak, about the land of his adoption. It was from the lips of the pioneers that he had heard the tales of the early days. Neither regret, self-pity, nor bravado tinged the accounts of hardship and privation told by those scores of narrators who had been the first to break the tough prairie sod and turn the wilderness into flourishing communities.

In the fading daylight, the vision of a farming district near Bricelyn, Minnesota, rose before him. It had been a thriving area in 1913 when Paul taught parochial school there. Outstanding among the well-to-do farmers were the Amlies and the Silrums, three brothers and a brother-in-law. They had followed the confusing custom of Norwegian immigrants in choosing their names from the different farms held by ancestors in Norway. The result was that of the three brothers two were Silrums and one was an Amlie. The other Amlie had married their sister. Together they owned and farmed about 2,000 acres of good Minnesota land. The parents of these families had come from the Trondheim district in Norway. They had settled on virgin soil, worked hard and prospered. In 1913 nearly all the children were grown up. The families had large comfortable homes and owned expensive automobiles; there were many cousins all of whom were musical, and they had a pleasant social life with lots of group singing and gay family gatherings.

The patriarch of this little clan was "Old Joe" Silrum, a man in his late sixties. He had been the pathfinder for the rest. Despite his years Old Joe was still vigorous in a quiet sort of way. His long sinewy arms, deep chest, and broad frame conveyed the impression of great physical strength. He might well have served as prototype for the hero in Knut Hamsun's *Growth of the Soil.* Like Isak, Joe Silrum had been a pioneer, and he, too, was built "like a barge of a man."

One evening as they sat in the parlor of Silrum's home Paul asked his host about conditions in that district when he took land there. "Yes," said Old Joe in his deliberate way, "it was kind of hard for a few years. The nearest railroad was forty miles away. We had no roads and the prairie was treeless. For five years we lived in a dugout in the little hill you see back of the house. We were quite snug there, but when the other members of the family arrived from Norway thirteen of us were in that dugout one winter. Then we were rather crowded. And in fall and spring we had trouble keeping the roof from leaking." It was a simple straightforward story with no heroics in it. The Silrums and the Amlies had sprung from yeoman stock. Because they loved the soil and the life thereon the old folk did not want the children to go away to school. They feared that they might be weaned from the land where the parents had persevered and succeeded.

Another story of courage, hardship, and eventual success was told by Mrs. Napstead of Clay County. Paul, then a grocery salesman, arrived at her farm on a June evening in 1912. The house and farmyard were neat and tidy. Two men in their thirties were finishing the chores as he came into the yard. Sensing that they were Norwegian-Americans, he addressed them in his native tongue, they answered in the same language. When he asked if he might get lodging for the night, they referred him to their mother who was just coming out of the house. She had a serene, sweet face, and she greeted the agent kindly. He soon learned that both she and her husband (who, gored by a bull, had died the year before) had come from Norway. In 1876, the year after their arrival from the old country, they had learned of homesteads in this area south of Hawley. From Alexandria a hundred miles distant, she and her husband had walked all the way leading a cow. With high hopes they broke land and sowed the grain. But for four successive years grasshoppers came and devoured everything that they planted except the potatoes. It was the potatoes and the milk from the cow which kept them alive during those four calamitous years. A similar account of the grasshopper plague Paul had heard in 1910 from Lars Sogge, father of Louis. The elder Sogge had walked from Goodhue to Jackson County, sleeping in hay and straw stacks on the way, in order to reach the land where he would homestead. He, too, had seen the "hoppers" destroy every spear of his grain and corn those first four years on the land. But like the Napsteads, Sogge had stayed on. Eventually both families had prospered. To them the years of trial seemed but an evil dream. In no way had their early failures embittered them or warped their lives.

Other pioneer tales dealt with blizzards on the open prairie when neither roads nor fences were there to guide the traveller, and when fierce winds and swirling snow destroyed all sense of direction of men and beasts. One such night Mrs. Jacobsen sat in a homesteader's shack a few miles south of Frost, Minnesota. That morning her husband had gone to town, but the snow was so deep that he was delayed by the hard and slow going. In the afternoon the blizzard struck. Hours passed and no husband appeared. Finally Mrs. Jacobsen acted on a sudden impulse. Grabbing the dishpan and a mallet she went outside and banged away with all her might. The husband who had just passed the house and was headed for an un-settled stretch south of his home, heard the noise of the dishpan, turned his horses back and steered for the sound. He was saved. "It was God's finger," said Ole Jacobsen, "that moved my wife to act as she did that night."

Other tales of blizzards had less happy endings. When the famous blizzard of 1888 struck the southwest corner of Brookings County, a Swedish immigrant-homesteader was nursing his young wife, ill with pneumonia. For two days and nights the storm raged with diabolical fury. The first night the wife died. Numbly the bereaved husband kept vigil at the bier of his childhood sweetheart. As the wind shook the flimsy cabin and the snow beat against the window he recalled happy days in the homeland. Mechanically he put wood in the stove; otherwise he just sat and stared at the beloved face now so calm and peaceful. The cattle in their shed a stone's throw from the shack were forgotten. "I was so heartsick," the man told Paul twenty years later, "I didn't care what happened." On the third day the storm abated, but by then the animals had perished from thirst and exposure.

Almost equally harrowing were the accounts of the great depression of 1893 when thousands of farmers in Brookings and some of the other fertile counties of South Dakota would sell a farm of 160 acres for a pair of harnesses. Some just abandoned their property and left. The Ole Larsons living five miles north of Artesian stuck it out. They bought deserted farms, and at one time owned 1,760 acres. In 1908, when Paul stayed at their home, they still held 1,440 acres then worth nearly $50 an acre. "Believe me," said Mrs. Larson feelingly, "we struggled in those depression years." Indeed she had, for in addition to caring for her six children and maintaining a clean home, she had worked with her husband in barn and field, and scoured the pasture for dry cowdung, the only fuel available to use in their stove.

That the need for hard work had not vanished with the disappearance of the frontier and the lifting of the depression was often evident. Large families were still an asset. At five or even younger, farm children performed assigned chores. On the Hetland farm between Artesian and Iroquois a boy of eleven dragged the fields with a twelve-foot harrow pulled by six three-year-old horses. Father Hetland raised horses which he broke at two and sold at five, a system which gave him power for virtually nothing. When Paul remarked that it was risky to let a mere boy drive so many young horses, the father replied, "Six young horses are not apt to start off all at once, and the lad can steer as well as a grown-up man." Callous though this sounded, Hetland was really an indulgent and considerate husband and father. In 1908 his was the only farmer's household where Paul saw a washing machine.

In many instances the hard toil left its mark. At fifteen Oliver Selvig of Elmore, Minnesota, walked and talked like an old man. His father was always on the road buying and selling. From the time he was twelve Oliver had done a man's work and had carried a man's responsibility on the family farm. In 1908 when Paul worked for Charles Fredin he discovered that often farmers in America were worn out as early as were factory hands. A Swedish immigrant, Fredin had married a Swedish-American farm girl. Early in the century they came to the neighborhood of Claremont and bought the 480 acre Pladsen farm for $ 28 an acre. The following year a tornado blew down the big barn. Discouraged, Fredin approached the former owner with a proposal to turn the farm back to him. Pladsen was willing provided Fredin would forfeit the entire down payment. This he refused to do. His wife stood by him. In 1908 the farm was paid for but Fredin, still in his forties, was so worn out that he was no longer able to do a full day's work. In 1915 when Paul visited the Fredins again he found both husband and wife completely broken in health. Financially they were well off, but in their case the price of success had been too heavy.

Although a poor judge of his own and his wife's strength and endurance, Fredin could gauge that of his horses with amazing accuracy. Balky horses that seemed completely useless he bought and made of them obedient draft animals. When grain elevator operators replaced their blinded horses with gasoline engines, Fredin bought two of them. Difficult to handle because of their blindness and their long experience walking only in circles, the horses were re-trained by Fredin and became excellent work animals. He used only rein and voice. No whip was found on his farm. Among Fredin's twelve horses Old Dan, the first horse he ever owned, was the favorite. By 1908 Dan, slow and spavin-legged, was used as the children's horse. He would take them to school and return home without a driver. In the afternoon he was hitched up and sent by himself to fetch the children. But when some of the older school boys began to drive Old Dan, he stopped a quarter of a mile short of the schoolhouse and there waited for his charges.

In many ways Charles Fredin was the exact opposite of Hans Christ. First of all he was an excellent horseman who, unlike Hans, had never had a runaway. Secondly, in marked contrast to Hans who spent a day each week going to town, Fredin reduced his trips to a minimum. From Sears, Roebuck he stocked an ample supply of spare harness parts. Before harvest started he and Paul examined all harnesses with great care. Worn buckles and straps were replaced with new ones and the harnesses were carefully oiled. Thirdly, Fredin made little of handling farm machinery. Whereas Hans Christ had impressed on the newcomer that it would take years before he could learn to drive a harvester, when harvest time came in Dakota, Fredin simply told Paul to take one of the two eight-foot binders and drive it. To Paul's remark that he had never before driven one Fredin answered, "There's nothing to it. You can do it easily." And he was right.

Returning one noon from an inspection of his wheat fields, Fredin said that he was going to town to hire two men for the harvest to begin the next day. Sure enough, at Claremont he picked up two itinerant farm workers who with hundreds of others had just arrived in that little town from farther south travelling on railroad box cars. A small army of such workers followed the wheat harvest in this fashion from Texas to Canada. Many of these men had other employment in the winter. Of the two whom Fredin hired one worked in a machine shop in Illinois, and the other was a Colorado miner. Both were Swedish immigrants and steady, hard-working men.

In harvest and threshing the farm work went forward at a fast and strenuous pace. On the Fredin farm harvesting was done with eight-foot machines pulled by four horses. The standard for the working day was twenty acres of grain harvested with one man to shock that amount. Experienced hands let the machines make several rounds before they went to work, but the greenhorns who grabbed sheaves off the bundle carrier on its first round were soon lost. A group of city-bred men from Cincinnati came to the Dakota fields that year hoping for big wages. But not only did they find the work too hard, they could not endure the humiliation of being made fun of by the country yokels, and nearly all of them quit at the end of the second day. Stories about those Cincinnati boys furnished lots of laughs that autumn when farmers of the Langford-Claremont region met.

Work in the field started at six and lasted until sundown. Barn chores before and after the field work extended the laboring day from five in the morning till nine-thirty at night. There was an hour's break at noon, and farmers of German and Scandinavian ancestry gave their hands coffee and sandwiches in the middle of the afternoon. A few even provided a forenoon snack. But American and Irish farmers who were less considerate were unpopular especially with the student harvest hand contingent. The long stretch from noon to the evening meal was an endurance test. The heat, the heavy work and the alkaline water of the area sometimes forced even strong and experienced men to quit. During the war of 1914–1918 Paul read about strikes in the wheat fields engineered by the Industrial Workers of the World. When he saw the farm hands described as "I Won't Work" men, he felt that for many of them the label was false.

At the time Paul worked in the wheat belt the threshing was generally done with large, clumsy machines, the engines of which were fired with straw. Into the maw of the separator four men pitched sheaves as rapidly as possible. Ten or twelve teams with wagons or racks accompanied the machine. Sometimes two men went with each wagon; at other times the one man on a wagon was assisted by extra hands in the field. The standard for such an outfit was 2,000 bushels of wheat per day.

Part of the threshing crew might be resident farm hands, but many were migrants who followed the machine and slept in barns or strawstacks during the season. Meals were served at the "chuck" wagon which was hauled from place to place with the threshing "rig." The meals were more remarkable for quantity than for quality. It took vast amounts of food to keep a twenty-five or thirty man crew satisfied. Speed counted for much at meals, and students who carefully washed before dinner found that supplies had run short when they arrived. After one such experience they adopted the custom of the crew and rushed straight from field to table.

Since hauling grain from the machine to the elevator in town was done by the farmers themselves, they usually co-operated and pooled their help for the work. Paul always represented the Fredin farm on the trips to the elevator. All he had to do was back the wagon box to the machine, fill up, and then drive to town where the load was weighed and the box emptied automatically. The trips enabled Paul to get pretty well acquainted with the migrant laborers of the wheat belt. They were a companionable and industrious lot who certainly never should be described as lazy.

Returning to the same area in later years Paul was able to gauge how the Dakota wheat farmers had fared from 1908 until the time of his visit. He was shocked to find that in spite of the hard work, the long days, and the meager wages they had paid their help, most of the farmers had almost no return on their investment. In 1912 one of his best friends in the area, Gilbert Gullickson, told Paul that four years earlier he owned his 480 acre farm and had $1,500 in the bank. By 1912 the cash was gone even though most of the work on Gullickson's farm was done by the farmer and his sons. In an effort to eliminate the middleman's profit and, the farmers thought, get fairer grading of the wheat and less dockage for weeds, a farmers' cooperative elevator company had been organized. But inexperienced management yielded only failure, and the stockholders' investment was lost.

The pall of the 1893 depression still lay over the wheat belt in 1908. The farmers of the region generally voted Republican because, they said, the Republicans had been against slavery, Abraham Lincoln had been a Republican, and Cleveland's victory in 1892 had brought on the depression. In June, 1912, when Paul hitched a ride to town with Tom Anderson, he asked the farmer, "How are you going to vote this year?" "Republican, of course," was the answer. "Why?" queried Paul. "If you had been here in 1893 you wouldn't ask such a foolish question," was the retort. "When did the bottom drop out of the wheat market?" was the student's next question. "In the autumn of 1892," Tom replied. "But since President Cleveland did not take office until March, 1893, how could he have been responsible for the drop in wheat prices?" Paul persisted. There was no reply. As the farmer and Paul entered a Hawley store the storekeeper asked, "Well, Tom, how are you going to vote this year?" "For the Democrats," Tom answered.

The old-world conflicts which culminated in the break-up of the union between Norway and Sweden had repercussions in the Midwest, especially in Minnesota. But when the statesmen of the two kingdoms settled the delicate political issues peacefully, tempers cooled both in Scandinavia and in the States, and soon friendly relations were restored. Most of the time Norwegians and Swedes in the Midwest co-operated in politics. This was particularly apt to occur if Irish Roman Catholics were involved in the contest. Friction between Scandinavians and Irish settlers, caused in part by religious bigotry, was intensified by the fact that the bosses of railroad gangs were often Irishmen while the common laborers were Scandinavian immigrants.

When he was Fredin's farmhand Paul was treated like a member of the family. Fredin, too, was an immigrant and the men found pleasure in comparing customs, superstitions and traditions of their homelands. Time and again Fredin would exclaim, "Truly, Swedes and Norwegians are brothers!" The American-born Mrs. Fredin hardly ever said a word. But when Paul left for school in September she drove him to the Claremont station. As he said good-bye he saw to his surprise that she had tears in her eyes. In her quiet way she also let him know she appreciated the friendship her family had formed with him. "Our house will seem very empty tonight," she said.

As Paul worked with men of different economic and social backgrounds he learned to know and to like people not of his own blood. He found that national diversities were greatly outweighed by similarities. Experiences as a farm worker in succeeding summers multiplied his attachments to the native-born Americans no matter from what country their ancestors had come. Plowing the land he subconsciously formed a connection between that soil and himself. He was helping to make it productive; he and the land were cooperating together. A mystical allegiance sprang up between the two providing for him a new anchorage.

Chapter 13

Apprenticeship Years

Oɴ Jᴜɴᴇ 1, 1913, Paul received his Bachelor of Arts degree from Red Wing Seminary. In six years he had completed the work from the eighth grade to the baccalaureate. He felt curiously numb on the day of his graduation. Other members of the class had relatives or fiancées to help them celebrate. Not so he. In his loneliness he was faced with an important decision. He must choose what his life work should be. His mother wanted him to become a minister, and friends who also urged him to study theology promised him financial assistance if he would do so. But the inner "call" was lacking. Other offers had come his way. A Norwegian engineer had told him that at the British Columbia mine where he worked it was easy for college graduates to earn $ 100 a month even though they had no technical training. A hundred dollars seemed big money to one who had lived on $ 20 a month for several years. But to go that far away to a mine in the mountains was too much of a gamble for cautious Paul; he would have to elect something else.

Finally he chose teaching. To teach in secondary schools, however, one needed a minimum of twelve credits in special courses. Seven of those credits had been taken at Red Wing; the rest must be obtained elsewhere. From university catalogues he discovered that he could earn the necessary credits in a six-week summer session at the University of Wisconsin, so he decided to go there. In the weeks between commencement and summer school he taught parochial school in Elmore, Minnesota.

At Wisconsin, Paul for the first time in his life was a student at a great university. The buildings, the library facilities, and the size of the student body seemed overwhelming. The courses he took were the sort usually chosen by summer school teachers. They were extremely thin in content, and Paul had trouble with them because he was not used to spinning out words in examinations for which no factual knowledge was required. But he finally managed to get through with satisfactory grades. After the session he again taught parochial school, this time at Frost and Bricelyn, Minnesota.

During the summer he had hoped against hope that a position in a secondary school might turn up. Nothing did, so once more a choice had to be made. Again he was urged to study theology, but he decided that he would first consult Dr. Sogge, the Windom friend who had aided him in his cooking utensil venture of 1910. Dr. Sogge suggested that Paul enter a university for graduate work, promised he would sign a note if he had to get a bank loan, and advised taking out life insurance. The terms of the Windom bank were rather stiff — 10 per cent interest. But Paul borrowed the money, and off he went to the University of Wisconsin. There he encountered a little difficulty. No holder of a Red Wing degree had ever before been granted full graduate standing. After some hesitancy the registrar and Dean Comstock of the graduate school agreed to recognize the Seminary's B.A.

During the summer Paul had noticed a room in the library set aside for students in European history. This had greatly attracted him. He had always been fond of the subject so he decided that European history would be his choice in working for a master's degree. Professor A. L. P. Dennis, the professor of British history, became Paul's mentor and guide during that first year of his graduate work. In selecting a subject for his master's thesis Paul recalled that as a boy he had been much interested in the Boer War. He had recently read

that the states conquered by the British during that war had
been given self-government and had combined with two other
South African colonies into a union. What were the factors
behind the formation of the Union of South Africa? A study
of this subject met with the approval of Professor Dennis, and
Paul soon was launched on his investigations.

The work at the university called for a seminar, a course
in historical method, and two lecture courses. The lectures
were given by Professors Coffin and Sellery. The seminar was
under Professor Dennis's direction. It was a small group the
members of which had come from various institutions. The
seminar work was entirely new to Paul, but he quickly learned
that to make satisfactory reports it was necessary to examine
the sources of British history. For the first time he had
access to stenographic reports of speeches in Parliament
and the official publications of the British government known
as the *Parliamentary Papers.* The London *Times,* of which he
had heard so much even as a boy, was now available too. He
spent long hours working on the topics for the seminar, hours
which he thoroughly enjoyed.

Much as he liked his studies, he was constantly worried by
the need to keep expenses down. From his undergraduate days
he still had a debt of $ 350, $ 200 of which had been borrowed
from Hans Christ at 7 per cent interest. The new loan at
10 per cent substantially increased the burden. During the
1913 summer session he had made friends in Madison. One
of these families rented rooms; they took pity on him and
let him have a room in their home for a dollar a week. They
were kind people, who every now and then would even give
him breakfast. But unfortunately the room was inhabited by
some of his old enemies, and it was almost impossible to get a
good night's rest. Yet in spite of the handicaps of bedbugs
and financial worries, he was able to read more than in any
previous year, and he counted the first term at Wisconsin a
highly rewarding one.

At the opening of the second semester Paul had the greatest
surprise of his life. One afternoon as he was reading in the

library the chairman of the history department, Professor Dana C. Munro, came and asked Paul to report at the office for an interview. With some trepidation the student went. There to his amazement he was offered a part-time assistantship in ancient history. He was to teach two quiz sections a week, and the salary would be $ 20 a month. To this offer Paul replied, "But I have had no special training in that field." Munro's answer was, "You can learn ancient history; I know that." So the assistantship was happily accepted.

This small appointment in the department of history at the University of Wisconsin proved a turning point in the life of the young man who eight years earlier had first entered the United States. It helped him to get the proper training for his life-work, and it settled the question whether he should seek a position in a church school or try for a post in a state university.

The immediate effect of the history department's offer was to give him a great psychological lift. That in his first year of graduate work at the large institution he should have been asked to assist, to be placed on the roll of university instructors even though the position was the very lowest one on the academic ladder, was enormously encouraging. In his native Norway university professors had high standing; they were always treated with great respect. Although in 1914 he had no idea that some day he might join that charmed circle, it seemed a fine thing to be, even for a short period, listed as a member of a university faculty. As soon as he received this appointment from Professor Munro, Paul sent the thrilling news to his parents. They later told him how elated they were with word of his appointment. They had worried over their youngest son who was so far away in a foreign land, but when they learned that he had been given a position as a university assistant, they knew he was making his way and would be all right. Some slight embarrassment arose when the appointment was erroneously reported in an American Norwegian-language paper as that of an assistant professor, and the Bodö paper then listed the rank as professor. The readers there came to the conclusion that it must be easy to become a professor in an American university where, evidently, not much training was needed.

The salary of $ 20 a month meant Paul could move from the uncomfortable dollar-a-week room to another at $ 10 a month. Later in the semester a member of the history faculty learned about the 10 per cent interest on his loan. One day in the history office Professor Munro courteously inquired whether it was true that Paul paid such a high rate. To the affirmative reply Munro exclaimed, "I think that is an outrage. I don't want to interfere in your private affairs, but if you are in need of money, just come to me." A few days later he renewed the offer saying, "Today I have received my salary. Won't you let me write you a check?" Professor Dennis made him a similar offer. Though Paul was touched by the generosity of these men he decided that with the assistantship salary and the refund of the non-resident fee he had paid he would be able to finish the semester without going further into debt. But this tangible proof of the kindliness of his professors and their sympathetic interest shown to a stranger warmed the cockles of his heart.

The new part-time assistant was assigned to Professor Westermann for his second semester course in Roman history. To supplement his inadequate training in the field, he studied the works of the famous German historian, Theodore Mommsen. This gave him a good background, and by attending the lectures, taking copious notes, and listening attentively to the directions Westermann gave each week, he was able to handle the quiz sections. Since the professor carried one section himself Paul, by going to that session, could observe Westermann's method. The first time he faced his own class was both interesting and trying. Among the older students in the section was an elderly widow. This woman, well in the fifties, insisted on calling the new assistant "professor." It was impressive but it was also embarrassing. The students were, on the whole, a friendly lot who did not seem to mind his foreign accent. They readily came to him for conferences and advice.

In many respects that first semester of teaching was one of the most pleasurable periods during the time when he was both student and teacher.

With a master's degree from Wisconsin safely in hand Paul obtained a position in the high school at Decorah, Iowa. There he taught history and Norwegian from 1914 to 1916. The town was a center of Norwegian-American culture and intellectual life. Like the surrounding area, it had been settled by Norwegian immigrants. Luther College, the oldest Norwegian-American college, was there. Also at Decorah was the publishing house for the Norwegian Synod of the Lutheran Church, and the offices of the Norwegian language newspaper, *Decorah-posten*. Men from the college, the publishing house, the newspaper, the two Norwegian Lutheran churches of the town, and other interested persons had organized "Symra" a literary Society at whose meetings Norwegian was usually spoken and Norwegian-American cultural problems discussed. The new teacher was adopted by this group, and the association with the members of Symra he found especially enjoyable.

One of the older teachers at the high school warned Paul that he must maintain control of his classes from the very beginning. Despite the fact that corporal punishment was permitted, his predecessor had failed to keep order, and was virtually run out of the school. Paul, determined to make good, let his pupils know from the very first day that they could not get away with anything. He quickly got a reputation for strictness, a reputation which made it fairly easy for him to carry on the teaching.

The high school was small with only about 200 pupils, and the courses were the traditional ones. The European history course covering the entire period from the dawn of civilization to present-day events was to be taught in three semesters. Though the school library was poor, and not much reading could be assigned outside the text, some of the students had books at home for supplementary study. Paul, who had always been eager for an education, found it difficult to appreciate the attitude of high school pupils who tried to get by with as little work as possible. Nor did he understand those parents who felt that the most important thing for their children was a high school diploma rather than a real education. More than once he was stopped by parents who were concerned about their children's low history grades. They would begin, "Of course I know you will do all you can so that my son will graduate —" whereupon the teacher would reply, "I shall do all I can to insure that your child will learn history, but if I certify that he is ready to graduate before he has obtained an education, I would be dishonest." By and large, however, he found that most parents and pupils were reasonable, and he was happy in his work.

One really distressing aspect of school teaching was the system of annual appointments. This made the position of the older teachers so insecure that they compromised with standards and accepted slovenly work in order not to offend the pupils' parents who had influence in the community. Though Paul was not old enough to be affected by the fear of no renewal of his contract, the system decided him to abandon secondary school teaching and equip himself to teach at the college level.

His Decorah salary of $ 800 the first year and $ 850 the second enabled him to pay off his college debt and accumulate sufficient funds to visit his parents in Norway. Upon his return in the autumn of 1916 he went to the University of Wisconsin where he had been granted a history assistantship. There he could work toward his doctor's degree. He was assigned to assist his former mentor, Professor Westermann, and he continued work in the history of the British Empire with Professor Dennis. With a thesis entitled "Intra-Imperial Aspects of Britain's Defense Problems, 1870—1914," he was awarded his doctor's degree three years later. These years, 1916—1919, were disturbed ones at the university because of the war. The teaching staff was so depleted that Paul assumed duties beyond those of the average graduate assistant. In 1917—1918 he held the post of acting instructor, teaching ancient and modern European history. These courses covered such widely separated periods that Dennis quipped good-naturedly, "Paul is the Colossus of Rhodes." In 1918 the university appealed to the draft board that he be exempted to instruct members of the Student Army Training Corps, and during that academic year he again taught both ancient and nineteenth century European history.

In June, 1919, it was a strange and interesting sensation to walk in the academic procession for his Doctor of Philosophy degree. Pleased though he was, his pleasure was tempered by loneliness and sorrow as it had been in 1913. In May, as soon as he learned he had passed the oral examination for his degree, he cabled his parents. But the news came too late — both Mother and Father had died that spring.

Present at the commencement exercises was one of his old friends from Decorah, Dr. Stabo, whose son was getting his B. A. degree. Dr. Stabo seemed so elated over Paul's achievement that his loneliness was mitigated. And when several of his former students came up and told him that they were proud of him, he was heartened and surprised. Somehow he never expected that anyone in America would take such an interest in him. When graduation was over, the Stabos invited him to be their guest for dinner. At the commencement exercises Dean Sellery had told Dr. Stabo that Paul would be retained on the staff as a regular instructor, and the news had pleased the good doctor almost as much as if it concerned his own son. The dinner was truly a gala affair.

When Paul wrote his old friend and benefactor, the Reverend H. J. Berg, that he had his doctor's degree, he immediately received an invitation to spend a week-end at the hamlet where he had lived when he first came from Norway in 1906. Ostrander had changed. Paul, of course, had never really been a part of the community there. For a little over a year he was just an immigrant hired man on the farm of an eccentric in the neighborhood. But even taking this fact into account, the changes were many. By 1919 Hans Christ was dead, as were a good many other people Paul had met when he worked on the Hans Christ farm. Others of the old farmers had sold out, gone to town, or moved farther west. New men had come in from Iowa or Illinois. Only the kindly Bergs were the same. Paul felt pretty much a stranger in Ostrander.

The next three years were extremely busy ones for the new history instructor, years which tested his ability as a teacher. The end of the war brough a vast influx of students. Paul was put in charge of the freshman course in English history; it was a course new to him, and his first class was a huge one with 440 students enrolled. The very first lecture proved a nerve-shattering experience. The classroom was crowded and many students were standing in the aisles when all of a sudden in the midst of the lecture alarm clocks began to go off in various parts of the room. Taken aback for a moment, he grew angry and ordered one of his assistants to collect the clocks and throw them out of the window. The noise stopped as suddenly as it began. After class he learned that the alarm clock episode was just a stunt imposed on freshmen by the sophomore class. But for him it was an especially cruel incident because he was anxious that in this, his first lecture, no untoward event should occur.

Beginning in 1920 Paul was asked to give the freshman course in English history then required of all students majoring in commerce. With its greater emphasis on economic factors this course differed from the one of the previous year. And the composition of the class was different too. Many of the students were veterans of the World War, and nearly all of them planned to enter business. As one man frankly confessed to the instructor, his aim at the university was just to train for a business career, get his degree, and then marry. But he, like many others who were taking the course simply to work off that requirement, eventually became interested in the story of the peoples of the British Isles through the ages. These two different types of large freshman courses introduced Paul to teaching problems of many kinds, but the work was evidently satisfactorily done for in 1921 he was promoted to assistant professor.

Living at the University Club which housed about 100

graduate students and instructors, he learned about the other university departments, and their methods of handling students. The history department had a long record of success in teaching and in creative scholarship. It was democratically organized, and the young instructor could take part in all discussions at the meetings of the department. From the very beginning he was treated as an equal by the older and more experienced men. Because members of the history staff participated widely in the administrative affairs of the university, general university problems were often discussed, and thus Paul learned about the traditions and policies of Wisconsin. It was highly satisfying to discover what made things move, and since he was older than most of the instructors, he was early placed on university committees. In this way he soon became closely identified with the university community and felt entirely at home with students and faculty members.

The only real vacation Paul took during these apprenticeship years was in 1920 when he spent the summer in Alaska. Brother John, after a year in Chile, had gone to the state of Washington. There he married and had two children. In 1916 he fell on hard times. That winter he met at the Tacoma wharf an old shipmate who had bought a motorboat and was ready to leave for Alaska. He asked John to join him. Moderately successful in Alaska, John soon brought his family to Ketchikan where he built his own little home. In 1920 he invited Paul to come and spend the summer with him at the fishing station, Port Alexander, on Chatham Strait.

The beautiful inner passage to Alaska reminded Paul of the coast of Norway. The scenery was magnificient, mountainous like the Norwegian coast with the addition of the lovely mystery of dense forests growing right down to the water's edge. There was virtually no sign of human habitation for miles and miles on end. In Ketchikan John met Paul. The moving reunion was heightened by the realization of how much the other had aged during the intervening years. Those years had not been easy ones for either of the brothers.

For the first time Paul met Olga, John's wife, and their

young son, Carsten. Their little daughter had been killed three years before by the only automobile on the island. From Ketchikan the brothers travelled in John's boat to Port Alexander where they spent the summer. Those months on the fishing boat trolling for salmon along the western shore of Baranoff Island were marvellous; clear sky, sunshine every day, and the mighty Pacific calm and placid most of the time. At this camp there were about 200 fishermen. Most of them were old prospectors, adventurers from nearly every country of Europe and most states of the American union, as well as a number of Indians and Filipinos. The cheaply built shacks of the fishermen nestled under gigantic trees. The harbor, so sheltered that no storm could possibly damage the fleet, was an excellent one. As old prospectors, many of the fishermen were unskilled; their catches were small, but the majority were bachelors so they were not much concerned.

From old-timers Paul learned about the Alaskan fishing industry and heard tales of how greedy packing companies had blocked spawning streams with their traps and ruined the fishing in the area. It was surprising to discover that most kinds of fish other than salmon and halibut were considered valueless. One day he went out with a cousin who had a halibut schooner. The redsnapper, caught on the halibut lines, were simply shaken off and left floating all over the sea. How different from those days when he had fished with Father in Norway! Then they were happy if they could catch twenty or thirty redsnapper in a long day of toil.

Among the many interesting types of men was the sourdough, the real old-timer who had been in Alaska for many years. One of these men had a motorboat called the *Bull Moose*. No one seemed to know the owner's name; the fishermen always referred to him as the Bull Moose. He went about by himself, fishing in the summer and trapping in the winter. Oddly enough he was a bibliophile. One day John and Paul pulled up to the edge of a big snowbank that came down to the water's edge to get snow to preserve their fish. The Bull Moose was there ahead of them. In conversation with him

Paul learned that he had been born in the Baltic area of Sweden, and that this strange man was extraordinarily well-informed on a great variety of topics. They discussed together everything from the tides in the Baltic to conditions in Washington lumber camps. In the cabin of the *Bull Moose* was a large library with many books on philosophy, and a copy of Bacon's *Essays* of which the sourdough was especially fond. Also there were many recent magazines, not trashy ones but the *Atlantic,* the *North American Review,* and *Harpers.* The Bull Moose would go to town once or twice a month, and there he would buy all the latest magazines. Then he would anchor in some secluded harbor and spend a week or two reading. The morning after John and Paul had met this man the two boats started off for the fishing grounds at the same time, but the Bull Moose soon shied away and went off by himself. He had had enough of conversation and social life to do him for a long while.

As might be expected, the adventurers at camp had tried many projects — and had failed. For their failures they blamed society and the social system. Some were admirers of the Bolshevist experiment and wished America would adopt the Soviet ideas. One Sunday a delegation from camp came to ask Paul if he would talk to them. They wanted him to discuss capitalism and socialism. Instead he said he would talk about the newly-organized League of Nations and the need for international cooperation. Though the men listened politely and asked a few questions, there was no sharp exchange of opinion as there undoubtedly would have been had the talk dealt with the principles of capitalism and socialism.

Many of the fishermen were friendly and had lots of stories to tell. There was an old Scot named Stewart who had worked for the Hudson's Bay Company many years. At Port Alexander he operated a store; not much of one, it had only a few of the necessities which he kept in a shack. Stewart quizzed John's brother about his work, where he came from, and what he did in the winter. When Paul told him that he was a university instructor in history, Stewart made no reply. He just walked away. But a day or two later when Paul happened to see Stewart again, the old storekeeper, primed for talk, began, "Caesar and Alexander, Xerxes and Napoleon had great armies didn't they?" Surprised by such an approach, Paul discovered that Stewart had carted along with him old history textbooks which he had used in his school in Scotland fifty years earlier. After he had met the university instructor, he had dipped into those books for suitable topics of conversation with the visitor.

Then there was John Jacobsen, a man well in his fifties. As a lad of seventeen he had left his home in Denmark and gone to Australia. From there he visited New Zealand, the Fiji Islands, Hawaii, and finally landed in Alaska as a prospector. At one time he spent four years with a partner in the foothills of Mt. McKinley. The prospectors would draw lots to see who should go out in the summer to get provisions. They were 500 miles from the trading post, and 100 miles from the nearest camp of other prospectors. It took the whole summer, of course, to go down the Kuskokwim River and then up again with the supplies for the coming winter.

Having heard lurid tales of life in the mining camps, Paul was anxious for first-hand information, so he asked Jacobsen about the miners and inquired if they were really a lawless lot. "No," said John, "they were all very nice boys." Then he paused a moment and observed, "Well, there was one man I knew who was kinda rough." "But," he added hastily, "he was a half-breed. His name was Campbell, father Scottish and mother Mexican." "Besides," said John, "Campbell was a coward." This interested Paul so he asked John to tell more about Campbell who was "kinda rough" and also a coward.

Here was the evidence. One night Campbell had a fight with a big Swede in a saloon. The Swede picked up Campbell and threw him against the stove, broke down the stove, picked him up again and threw him against the door. That sent Campbell to the hospital for three months; afterwards he behaved himself for quite a while, sure proof that he was a coward. As for his being "kinda rough," — when two young Swedes who were believed to have money quit the camp they slept on the bank of a river. Campbell spotted them, and shot them with a high-powered rifle from a distance of 100 yards, which, of course, was rather conclusive evidence that he was "kinda rough." That he had used a high-powered rifle for his foul deed confirmed the suspicion that he was a coward.

A prominent figure at Port Alexander in 1920 was Billy Allen from Alabama. Allen had prospected for many years in western United States and in Alaska. He was a big, powerful man who suffered from a form of hydrophobia — he disliked using water externally, and he shaved only once every two months or so. Billy Allen was not exactly well-groomed, but he was a kindly and intelligent man, and an interesting one. On the Fourth of July the Knaplund brothers attended the annual stockholders meeting of the Alaska Fishermen's Union Cooperative, an organization formed to market the fish caught at Port Alexander. As president Allen presided at the meeting. The picturesque gathering included men of many nationalities, an audience that was rough-looking but very well behaved. In addressing them Allen violated every known rule of English grammar; yet by force of character and personality he dominated the group, and the proceedings went well.

Throughout his long and checkered career Billy Allen had acquired qualities of leadership and an interesting philosophy of life. One day in the middle of the 1890's Allen had been prospecting somewhere in Idaho. It was hot, and as he crossed a dusty open stretch on his bicycle, he grew thirsty so he stopped at a wayside saloon. There was only one other customer in the place. As Allen gave his order, the customer noticed Billy's Southern accent, and immediately he began to be abusive calling Allen a rebel and using other nasty names. A good-natured man, Billy at first paid no attention to the other fellow's vilification, but finally it got under Allen's skin and he started to note the size of the room — would there be space enough for a good honest fight? The bartender observed this, and hustled the other customer out of sight. Billy finished his beer, mounted his bicycle, and rode away. But as he peddled along he started to think of all the nasty names he had been called by that unknown man. His anger rose. He stopped and argued with himself; should he return and give him a thrashing? For several minutes he debated the issue. "Then it came to me how foolish it all was," Billy told Paul. "Why should I fight a complete stranger because our fathers happened to have fought on opposite sides in a war that was over more than thirty years ago? The two of them were dead. The case was settled. Why should we fight because our parents had fought?" He added, "I decided that would be just silly, so I got on my bicycle and went my way." Billy Allen, short though he was of book knowledge, had learned a lesson in wisdom which the nations of the world would do well to ponder. Most of the ills of our age come about because the past is eternally carried on our backs.

The motley crew assembled at Port Alexander was remarkably orderly. The nearest police were in Sitka some sixty or seventy miles away, yet in 1920 there was no serious disturbance at the camp. Another outstanding characteristic of these men was that everyone stood by his fellows in any emergency. John Jacobsen told how he had had to speed a hundred miles on snow-shoes in the dead of winter to get aid for a companion who had been injured at the mining camp. He covered the hundred miles without resting. He took with him only a few slivers of bacon, some tea leaves, and a tin can. Every so often he would pause, light a fire, brew himself a little tea, fry some bacon, and then be on his way. The heroic effort paid off; he brought help in time, and his companion recovered. This same rule of immediate and unquestioning aid applied at the fishing grounds too. If the motor on any boat stalled, the whole fleet would pull up gear and steer to the one who was in trouble whether they knew the man or not. The spirit of comradeship and mutual help among the rough untutored adventurers strengthened Paul's faith in the common man. Regardless of race, nationality or social background, these men all had an innate sense of fair play and human worth.

During the first three years as a regular member of the staff at Wisconsin, Paul worked hard at his teaching and tried to make himself generally useful in the university community. Promoted to the rank of assistant professor in 1921, he resolved to add scholarly research to his other activities. So in the summer of that year he re-wrote sections of his doctoral dissertation, and the resultant article was published by the *Canadian Historical Review*. To see for the first time a monograph of his own published in a historical journal was a real satisfaction. But for additional and worthwhile research in the field he would have to work in the British archives. Three visits to England proved interesting and fruitful. There Paul became acquainted with English people, established valuable connections, and gained access not only to the British public archives but also to private manuscript collections which yielded a rich harvest.

The first trip to Britain in 1922–1923 was the longest and professionally the most rewarding. He left the United States in August and except for a week in France and a trip to Brussels to read a paper at the meeting of the Fifth International Congress of Historical Studies, he spent all his time in England until the following June. The summer of 1923 he visited his old home in Norway. His second European trip, that of 1926, started immediately after his marriage in June. Going straight to Norway he proudly introduced his bride to his brothers and sister. After a brief period of travel on the continent, he and his wife went to England for six months of research and writing. The trip of 1933 was made alone. Leaving his wife and two children behind, he went north for a short visit with his Norwegian relatives, after which he returned to England to collect material for his book on Gladstone's foreign policy.

Viewing these European trips in retrospect, the professor realized how important they had been in his life work. Observing the soil and climate of Britain, France, and the Low Countries he could easily understand why these lands had been so attractive to Scandinavians of the Middle Ages, and why the West European countries had grown rich. The magnificent cathedrals were awe-inspiring monuments to the religious devotion of the population of medieval times and mute testimony to man's eternal quest for a state of blessedness and security. Convinced that the true temple of God is not made by hands, he found his admiration for the cathedrals tempered by the uneasy feeling that perhaps human pride had motivated their construction. Both in the erection of the cathedrals and in the building of the enormous castles much hard and unrequited toil had been demanded from the masses; many of those from whom sacrifices had been exacted had dwelt in hovels, eaten meagerly, and lived but briefly. Since Paul himself had sprung from the common people, he had deep sympathy for the common man, and profound respect for the dignity of every human being. Reverently he stood in the famous cathedrals, but no less reverent did he feel when he visited the little Lea church north of London, a country church, very old and very plain, whose flagstone floor and worn pews gave evidence of its use by humble country folk for generation after generation.

As a teacher of English history, Paul was eager to find out as much as he could about the English people. He explored the highways and byways of London. He frequented meetings at Hyde Park and Trafalgar Square, attended sessions of Parliament, and watched the enormous crowd which had assembled in Oxford Street to learn the returns from the general election of 1922. In 1926 there was the public reaction to the long drawn-out coal strike to be observed, and the important imperial conference of that year, the conference which adopted the famous report of the Committee on Status. In 1933 he obtained special information about the political changes of 1931, and about the British recovery program which was then well advanced.

As the center of Britain's far-flung empire London offered

unique opportunities for contacts with scholars from the dominions. There were many such in the Public Record Office, at the British Museum, and the Historical Institute in Gower Street. For several months in 1922–1923 Paul lived at the Duchess of Connaught Memorial Hostel which accepted visitors from the dominions and the United States. Through his association with South African students at the hostel he became a member of the South African Student Club. From these unofficial representatives of the British dominions came first-hand information about conditions in their countries and their attitude toward Britain. In that period many Canadians were inclined to resent the patronizing attitude of Britons. One Canadian doctor after a visit in an English home returned disgusted because his host always referred to Canada as "our colony" and to Canadians as "colonials." The Afrikaners were even more touchy on imperial questions, and especially resentful because fellow countrymen of British ancestry neglected to learn their language. Though the Afrikaners while in England wanted to be considered pro-British, they were often heard to mutter under their breath "Verdamnte Engelskman."

In addition to his contacts with students and scholars from the dominions Paul also benefitted by the activities of organizations formed to promote friendship between English-speaking peoples. At a reception given by the English-Speaking Union in 1922 to introduce Americans to Lady Bryce, widow of that famous friend of the United States James, Viscount Bryce, the secretary of the Union inquired the purpose of Paul's visit to England. Learning it was to study British Empire history, she immediately said, "Then you should meet Colonel Mills. I'll write him about you." Paul put this down as just polite conversation, but to his surprise he shortly afterwards received a letter from Colonel Dudley Mills inviting him for dinner at the Athanaeum Club. The invitation was eagerly accepted, and a life-time friendship between the two men was begun. The very next day when he returned from the Record Office Paul found a message from

Colonel Mills again inviting him to dine — this time at the home of Lady Dunn. The dinner was a delightful and memorable experience for Colonel Mills had followed the interesting English custom of borrowing a friend's London house in which to entertain while he was up from the country. That night Paul and an English school-master were the Colonel's guests, and the three men were sumptuously dined and wined in Lady Dunn's home.

Colonel Mills was very fond of America and Americans as well as of Norway and Norwegians. His interest in Norway had originated because his maternal grandfather, Sir Thomas Dyke Acland, had been interned as an enemy alien in that country from 1807 until 1814. Sir Thomas's experiences during those years when he was treated more as a guest than a prisoner had been so satisfying that the contacts he had made in Norway were maintained by his descendants for more than a century. In addition to this dual bond between Paul and the colonel there was the third and most important one — their common interest in British imperial history. Colonel Mills who for many years had been in the British colonial service, had personal acquaintance with many sections of the empire as well as a Brycean interest in peoples and places. To his new friend he was a never-ending source of information.

The American University Union gave Paul an introduction even more far-reaching for his apprenticeship training. While examining colonial office records for 1846 Paul became convinced that the eminent Liberal statesman, W. E. Gladstone, had been misjudged as an imperial statesman. Discussions of Gladstone's imperial policies had often been deeply influenced by party prejudices. Moreover, this topic had been treated lightly by John Morley, Gladstone's biographer. A fuller study was needed, but to give Gladstone's imperial policy a fair and complete treatment it would be necessary to examine his private papers. Paul consulted the director of the Universities Union in London, Dr. MacLean. He knew Lord Haldane who, in turn, was a close friend of Lord Gladstone, the youngest of the former prime minister's four sons. Briefly Paul stated his reasons for wishing to examine the Gladstone papers. This statement Dr. MacLean forwarded to Lord Haldane, who enthusiastically endorsed it in a letter to Lord Gladstone. Next Paul was interviewed by Mr. Bassett, cataloguer of the Gladstone papers. A month later he received not only permission to examine this collection but also an invitation to stay as the guest of the Gladstone family at St. Deiniol's Library and Hostel at Hawarden where the collection was housed. Since St. Deiniol's was a semi-ecclesiastical institution at which religious services were held several times a day, he was asked to attend one of these services, the compline, at ten o'clock each night. The invitation was happily accepted, and during the winter and spring of 1923 he worked many weeks there.

At St. Deiniol's Paul had a study in the library and free access to the Gladstone papers. Though he had permission to examine the entire collection of more than 300,000 documents, he was told that before he published anything he must submit his selections to the trustees of the collection. At that time the trustees were the sons, Mr. Henry Gladstone the occupant of Hawarden Castle close by the village of that name, and the Viscount Gladstone, formerly governor-general of South Africa.

Almost reverentially Paul first entered the strongroom which held the private papers of the great statesman. As he was working with the documents he heard a knock at the door. Opening it he saw a handsome and smiling elderly gentleman who introduced himself by saying, "I am Mr. Gladstone." This unexpected meeting with the son of the famous Liberal prime minister was an exciting moment. After a brief conversation in the study Mr. Gladstone invited Paul to have luncheon at the castle with him and Miss Helen Gladstone, one of his sisters.

Gladstone's home, Hawarden Castle, was an eighteenth-century country house of substantial proportions. About a quarter of a mile distant from this modern dwelling stood the ruins of the small border stronghold dating back to the thirteenth century. At the luncheon the host and hostess showed the keenest interest in the project concerning their father's imperial policies. They were clearly devoted to their father's memory, they felt that he had been misrepresented by political opponents, and until now those misrepresentations had been taken at face value by historians. The Gladstones showed Paul through the house with its large library, and their father's study known as the Temple of Peace. This study had been kept just as it was at the time of Gladstone's death in May, 1898. There were the two desks used by Gladstone, one for his everyday work and the other for Sundays when he wrote on ecclesiastical matters. Among the furnishings in the study which attracted Paul's special attention was a bust of Gladstone's political rival, Benjamin Disraeli. Attached to the study was the Octagon, built by W. E. Gladstone during his lifetime to house his vast collection of private papers.

In 1923 and again in 1926 Paul met the Gladstones on a number of occasions both at Hawarden Castle and at their London homes. Lord Gladstone who spoke cautiously about most of the problems of South Africa was emphatic in defending his father's retrocession of the Transvaal in 1881, and he was convinced that a tactful handling of the points at issue between Briton and Boer would have avoided the Anglo-Boer War and resulted in a peaceful union of South Africa. That, he said, was also the view of General Botha with whom Lord Gladstone had often discussed these questions. All the Gladstones, especially the Viscount and his sister, Mrs. Drew, felt strongly that their father had been misrepresented by his political enemies, their apologists, and their biographers.

Despite her crippled condition Mrs. Drew (Mary Gladstone) followed with the keenest interest developments in British politics, and delighted in reminiscing about events and personalities of her father's time. She judged David Lloyd George kindly, even though he had treated her younger brother very roughly. Mrs. Drew asserted that the charge of

inconsistency against Lloyd George was due to a superficial
study of his career. The Labor Party interested her a great
deal. She expressed sincere sympathy for Miss Ishbel Mac-
Donald whom she knew well and who at an early age had
had to assume the responsibilities of hostess at No. 10 Downing
Street. In 1926 on Paul's last visit to Mrs. Drew she talked
delightfully about her friends, Lord Grey of Fallodon, Lord
Balfour, and Lord Rosebery. Although she thought very
highly of Lord Grey and admired his ability and integrity,
she considered it a real misfortune that he did not know
foreign countries, statesmen, and languages. She criticized the
Balfour family because they were not interested in people
and had "no hold" on life. Said Mrs. Drew, "The Balfours
do not care whether they are living or dead." When Paul
mentioned that both at the Paris Peace Conference and again
at the Washington Naval Conference Arthur Balfour had
won a reputation for affability, Mrs. Drew tartly replied,
"Then he was a humbug. He really doesn't care for people
at all." From the *Mirror of Downing Street* Paul quoted the
statement that Balfour did not know the names of his own
servants, and Mrs. Drew agreed. "That I believe," she said,
"my maid has often spoken of how radically the atmosphere
in the Balfour household differs from that in the household
of Lord Rosebery."

It was Mrs. Drew who arranged the interview with Lord
Grey of Fallodon early in December, 1926, when Paul wanted
Grey's permission to edit and publish his speeches on foreign
affairs. As Sir Edward Grey he had been British foreign
secretary during the eventful years, 1905–1916, and was one
of the most powerful men in the world during that period.
Lord Grey lived very simply in a small house not far from
the Parliament buildings at Westminster. He proved a charming and delightful host. With his ruddy complexion and
rumpled tweed suit he looked what indeed he was, a country
squire fond of the out-of-doors. The Roman cast of his
features was softened by his friendly smile. Before a blazing
fire in his living-room Lord Grey talked simply and frankly

with his American visitor. In the course of the conversation the latter mentioned some of the continental statesmen of the pre-1914 era. About one of them, Count Isvolsky who as Russia's foreign minister had participated in the negotiations of the Anglo-Russian treaty of 1907, Lord Grey said with significant emphasis, "He was quite all right *then*." Fridtjof Nansen, Norwegian explorer, scientist and humanitarian was also mentioned. Nansen had been Norway's first diplomatic representative in London after the dissolution in 1905 of the Norwegian-Swedish union. Concerning him Grey showed a curious reserve, but he did tell one little story. When Nansen visited England after his polar expedition, Gladstone, then living in retirement at Hawarden, expressed a desire to meet the famous explorer. As Nansen left the room after the interview Gladstone remarked admiringly, "What a magnificent specimen of humanity!"

In 1926 Grey's mind was much occupied with the League of Nations, and with the urgent need for British social legislation. Success of the League Grey considered a *must* for the survival of civilization and humanity. Though neither the general strike of May, 1926, nor the coal strike still in progress was brought up Grey expressed himself strongly on Britain's long-neglected social and industrial problems. Solutions must be found, he said, or Britain could not maintain her position as a leading world power.

His visitor's request to edit and publish Grey's speeches was readily granted. But Grey refused to write an introduction for the edition. The two reasons he gave for his refusal were failing eyesight and the fact that he had never read and corrected published reports of his speeches. During the conversation with Grey the thought often recurred to Paul of what tremendous responsibilities had been carried by this quiet modest man in the early days of August, 1914. The events of those days were not referred to, but no evidence exists to indicate that Grey ever felt that the wrong road was chosen. As Paul left Grey's house and walked into the London fog, he wondered whether the ideals represented by Grey and his generation had gone forever.

Among other leading British statesmen whom the historian had the good fortune to meet was the Right Honourable John Burns who had been a colleague of Grey in the British government from 1905 till 1914 and who in the latter year resigned on the war issue. Paul met Burns several times at the National Liberal Club. In many ways the exact opposite of Lord Grey, Burns was not at all reticent about his actions as a minister or as a labor leader. He was quite willing to admit that he had played a prominent role in various important epochs of British history, particularly in the inauguration of the new unionism when unskilled laborers were organized and their unions admitted to the British Trades Union Congress in 1890. Burns knew of the work done at Wisconsin in labor history by Professor Commons and his associates. Concerning the events of 1914 Burns was emphatic that by resigning on the war issue he had done the right thing and he said, "I have never regretted my action at that time."

These direct contacts with some of the people who had helped to shape British imperial policies in critical periods enlivened and gave color to the information found in public and private records. Especially interested in British imperial history in the nineteenth century, Paul examined vast quantities of Colonial Office, Foreign Office, and War Office material. In addition to the private papers of W. E. Gladstone much attention was also given to those of Lord Granville, Lord John Russell, and Sir Robert Peel, men who did much to direct the course of history in the last century. The perusal of such confidential manuscript material is essential to any aspiring historian's work, and Paul found this study more valuable than all the books he had read or lectures and seminars in historical methodology he had attended. It was these public and private confidential documents which revealed the inner workings of the British governmental machinery. From them he discovered facts about the interplay of the complex forces and motives which shape governmental actions and policies. The private papers demonstrated why scholars should often suspect printed government documents which sometimes were selected to prove a particular point or justify certain actions. They also disclosed that most ready-made generalizations and hasty historical judgments were false.

Paul was particularly interested in the British administrators as human beings. He found them far less complex than they are commonly believed to have been. Detailed examination of documents revealed the care which men of high intelligence and integrity had given to the issues at hand, and showed that frequently mere chance helped to determine the action taken. Moreover, they pointed up the folly on the part of historians, endowed with the wisdom of hindsight, in assuming an arrogant and hypercritical attitude toward past ages and their leaders.

By a curious bit of good fortune in 1923 Paul was able to clear up an important point in Anglo-Norwegian relations. Browsing through British Foreign Office documents on smuggling activities of British merchants near his home town of Bodö, he discovered that a certain John Rice Crowe had been discharged in the 1830's from his office as British vice-consul at Hammerfest because of his alleged connection with the Bodö Affair. The accused official defended himself so successfully that not only was he reinstated but he was promoted in the British consular service. In the course of these events Crowe called the attention of the British Foreign Office to the possibility that Russia might seize northern Norway and from that vantage point threaten British naval supremacy. The British foreign secretary, Lord Palmerston, heeded this warning. As a result of Crowe's reports Palmerston in 1855, when he had become prime minister, took the lead in securing French support for an Anglo-French treaty which guaranteed the protection of Norway and Sweden against Russian attacks. The question of the origin of this treaty of guarantee, known as the November Treaty, 1855, had long engaged the attention of historians. Various theories concerning its origin had been propounded, theories which seemed perfectly logical. Most of them attributed the origin to actions taken by the French emperor, Napoleon III. Paul was able to prove, however, that the real father of that treaty was John Rice Crowe. He derived much satisfaction in clearing up this problem, especially since as a youth he had been comforted by the existence of that very pact.

In Britain Paul was generally considered an American, and his research won for him recognition as an American historian. A fellowship from the Guggenheim Foundation in 1926 enabled him to complete his first book, *Gladstone's Imperial Policy*. One September evening in 1927, the year of the book's publication, the chairman of the University history department, Professor Frederick Paxson, called on the Knaplund family in their newly purchased home. As he entered he addressed the head of the household as "professor" and told him that his promotion to that post had been approved. This was exciting news indeed. The immigrant had found a truly snug harbor in America with a family, a home, and a recognized academic position.

Chapter 14

The Home Port

As events
of bygone years passed in rapid review the professor recalled the old saying, "you may take the boy out of the
country, but you can't take the country out of the boy."
In this case "sea" might replace "country" for though Paul
had never been much of a sailor, the sea had figured so prom-
inently in his early life that with the advancing years
nautical terms kept coming to mind as he considered his
departure from Norway and his gradual adjustment to America and American ways. He had weighed anchor and left
the home port. A new harbor with a good anchorage had been
found, but the change had been very gradual. Cables had not
been slipped. Instead they had been strained and broken
strand by strand until the old moorings were severed.

Meanwhile he had become firmly attached to the land of
his adoption, but not by the quick process of dropping anchor
and fastening strong hawsers to bolts ashore. On the contrary,
the mooring had progressed so slowly it was as if those
famous maidens of Norse mythology, the Norns, had patient-
ly spun a myriad of the finest threads which when twined
had, though soft as silk, become bonds strong as steel. Only
when he had a home and a family of his own could the
anchor really hold. Only then would he be firmly moored
until life's last day.

In his first years in America he had been closely associated
with Norwegian-Americans. Many of these lived *in* America

but were not *of* the land. No matter how long they had been on this side of the Atlantic they had not become real Americans. Their failure to assimilate could be partially blamed upon Americans of the older stock who, contrary to the Declaration of Independence so proudly read at Fourth of July celebrations, refused to recognize the principle that men are born equal. The Negro charwoman at Ellis Island, who had watched the immigrants with such obvious scorn, had many spiritual kinsfolk among white Americans. But their arrogant nativism had not often troubled Paul who embraced the creed of Robert Burns:

> The rank is but the guinea stamp;
> The man's the gowd for a' that.

Furthermore, the intelligent concept of what constitutes true Americanism shielded the foreign-born in university circles from the vulgarities of professional patriots.

Among those who kept hyphenism alive, American politicians were the worst offenders. Political parties had their foreign-language divisions, and made special efforts to attract the unassimilated citizens and to appeal to their European prejudices. By so doing the politicians played right into the hands of foreign pressure goups and governments who sought support from expatriates in America.

Norwegian immigrants, unlike those from many other lands, brought few old-world hatreds to their new home. But because they came from a small country which until recent years had produced few men of world fame, some were inclined to be apologetic about their national origin. Those who failed to integrate with American society formed cliques and strove to straddle the Atlantic. Their pathetic efforts were usually so unsuccessful that they became literally people without a country. Others could not believe that Norway had changed since they left. They were like the mail carrier in Brookings who argued heatedly that he knew all about conditions in Norway because "I lived there fifty years ago." For many immigrants the hard economic conditions in the land they had left were forgotten. They remembered only the pleasant aspects, the beauty and the friendliness of life in the old country. Farm wives shed nostalgic tears for the old home across the water. Time failed to assuage the pain of sundering old ties.

A visit to Norway often dispelled some of these illusions. Karl Staaf, retired Minnesota farmer, diagnosed his own case when he said, "It took three trips to Norway to make me satisfied with America." Paul had a similar experience. He had returned to Norway four times, and during these visits he had grown increasingly aware that he was a stranger in the land of his birth. With each arrival back in the United States he felt more conscious of coming home, and in 1933 when his return was awaited by wife and children the feeling had become a certainty.

By 1916 he had been away from Norway for ten years. His parents were old, his mother seventy-seven and his father eighty-four. Soon their lives would end. Sisters Constance and Katherine had both died. There were still a daughter and three sons living in Norway, but the parents wanted very much to see the other two sons who had been away these many years. Unfortunately it was impossible for John to make the trip. But Paul was free; he had paid off his college debt and saved enough to cover the necessary expenses of the journey. An appointment to an assistantship at Wisconsin with a salary of $400 for the 1916—1917 academic year gave him a certain amount of security for the immediate future.

A freak of fate forced Paul to retrace part of the route he had travelled ten years earlier when he came to Ostrander. The day before he left Decorah a flash flood disrupted the regular railroad connection to Chicago. He therefore had to take a local train which connected at McIntire, Iowa, with a Chicago line. So once again he was in the little station at McIntire where in 1906 he had spent a night as a lonely and bewildered newcomer. How safe and settled he now felt! The impression grew as he journeyed to New York. In Chicago two friends from Red Wing met him, and the three spent the day together. On the way east he passed through Harper's Ferry, Washington, and other places which because of his study of American history now had meaning for him. During his two days in New York he visited points of interest, not as a foreign tourist, but as an American eager to learn something about his country's greatest city.

From New York to Christiania (later Oslo) Paul travelled on a Danish ship, the *Hellig Olaf*. As it entered the open ocean he went up in the bow so that he might better sniff the salt air. He had not much missed it in the years he had lived in the Middle West, but breathing it anew excited him. At long last he was headed for home and Mother and Father. The following morning, awakened by a song from the next cabin, he was again exhilirated by its haunting familiarity. Just for a moment he failed to place it; then all of a sudden he caught the words. The unknown neighbor was singing the old ballad about Holger the Dane who, always proudly displaying Denmark's coat of arms and its national flag, wandered through many lands far from home. The song conjured up scenes from the one-room schoolhouse at Knaplund, the maps on the walls, and the children singing songs of the north.

Most of the passengers aboard the *Hellig Olaf* were Norwegians or Danes returning to visit their homeland after a few years in America. Many of them showed a childish eagerness to display their knowledge of English which was often quite meager. They spoke such a curious jargon that a sturdy Norwegian sailor was prompted to observe, "These people will cause their parents much grief. They have forgotten their mother tongue and they haven't learned any other."

Aboard the ship one small group of swarthy men kept to themselves singing songs in a strange language. They were Armenians on their way to join the Russian army to fight their hereditary foe, the Turk. There was something both fascinating and melancholy about these determined, serious men headed for a forlorn mission.

Several memorable events occurred on this Atlantic crossing.

The first day out a passenger died. He was a Norwegian sailor who, in the last stages of tuberculosis, had implored the captain to take him aboard so that he could die in his homeland. But life flickered out a few hours after he had boarded the ship. The following afternoon he was buried at sea. The day was calm; the ship stopped; solemnly two clergymen, one from the church of England, the other from that of Sweden, conducted the appropriate services in accordance with their rituals; the ship's orchestra played softly. As the roughly-made coffin was committed to the sea, the sun broke through the overcast. For a moment a bright ray played on the casket. Then the ocean closed over it. The unknown sailor had gone home.

The other unusual episodes related to the war then raging. Although the *Hellig Olaf* belonged to a neutral country, it faced war hazards. Shortly before it left New York, the English cruiser, *Hampshire,* with Lord Kitchener aboard, had struck a mine and sunk in waters traversed by the *Hellig Olaf.* Passengers recalled the fate of the *Lusitania* in 1915. To insure safety for the *Hellig Olaf* the Danish flag had been painted on its sides. The night it entered the dangerous waters northwest of Ireland bright spotlights illumined the ship's sides. Many passengers, afraid to retire, stayed on deck. Paul who had gone to bed was awakened from sound sleep when the ship's engines stopped. Dressing hurriedly he went up on deck. The *Hellig Olaf* was in the center of a clear patch of ocean about five miles in diameter; beyond the fog hung like a heavy curtain. Within the circle a sinister-looking gray cruiser slowly steamed, its guns trained on the Danish vessel. Those aboard had an eerie, helpless feeling. Having ascertained that this was a genuine passenger ship the cruiser launched a boat which rowed to the *Hellig Olaf.* The boat's crew was literally armed to the teeth. From it two men carrying what appeared to be rolled-up maps clambered aboard. It soon became known that the new arrivals were British officers who would pilot the ocean liner through the mine-fields west and north of Scotland, and the passengers were much relieved.

Not until evening did the ship reach Kirkwall; by then the entrance to the harbor had been closed so the night was spent in the outer roads. But all vessels bound for the Netherlands and the Scandinavian countries had to be inspected by British naval authorities so early Sunday forenoon when the steel submarine nets were drawn aside the *Hellig Olaf* was brought into the harbor. In New York its cargo had been examined and its hatches sealed by British consular officials, but at Kirkwall the ship's and the passengers' papers, stores and luggage were inspected. One passenger with a vast amount of luggage was taken ashore. It was six o'clock Monday evening before the *Hellig Olaf* was allowed to proceed on her way. The first glimpse of the Norwegian mountains sent a flutter of excitement through the hearts of returning Norsemen, and they sang the national anthem with gusto. As Paul watched Norway rise out of the sea, disturbing thoughts entered his mind. Soon he would be in the land of forbears, childhood, and youth. Was this land still his own? Here he had been something of a misfit. For him no door of opportunity had existed. To find such a one he had had to leave Norway, to go beyond the high mountains and the broad sea. He had found opportunity's door in America and there had pried it open. The land of which he was now a citizen had given him much. His loyalties were divided. Where would the dominant ones ultimately lie?

These perplexing questions were soon pushed aside. In common with other returning natives Paul looked forward to the landing on Norwegian soil. Peaks and skerries seemed to welcome the travellers. On a warm sunlit June morning the *Hellig Olaf* steamed up the lovely fjord which leads to the capital of Norway. Shores and islands were clad in summer finery. From knolls and cabins flags fluttered and people waved in friendly greeting to the ship from America.

In 1916 few formalities hampered Americans entering Norway. Passports were not required, and the customs officials examined the baggage in cursory fashion. Again Paul heard his mother tongue spoken everywhere, all signs were in Norwegian, everything should have made him feel at home, but he had the odd sensation of being a stranger in this place. The travel procedures of America were now familiar to him; those of Norway he did not know. After some fumbling he found a porter, secured a hotel room, and sent a telegram to his parents. The one day in Christiania he did little sight-seeing; he was busy trying to re-orientate himself and excited over the prospect of being reunited with his family. From the capital he travelled through the Eastern Valley of Norway to Trondheim. His compartment was shared with several young men who, spotting him as an American, inquired how to pronounce the name of the recently nominated presidential candidate, Charles Evans Hughes. They were keenly interested in various phases of American life, and showed an amazing knowledge of American politics. Both then and on later trips Paul was always impressed with the extent of Norwegians' information about America. Some of this interest may have been due to ties with emigrants there, but a large share of their knowledge had to be credited to the excellence of the country's educational system.

When he was young Paul had longed to see Norway's fertile agricultural area and the big farms and extensive forests of the famed Eastern Valley. In 1916 when this dream could be realized he stayed awake all night so he would miss nothing. Although he now judged the farms by American standards, he found they fulfilled his expectations. While the fields were not so large as those of the Middle West the farm buildings and the standards of cultivation were better. As the train approached Norway's north-south divide, the valley narrowed, the farms were smaller, and the pines less majestic. At the little coppermining town of Röraas on the Divide, trees were stunted and vegetation sparse. From thence the descent was steep and swift to the railroad terminus at Trondheim.

It was the eve of St. John's Day when the *Kong Harald*, the express coastal steamer, left Trondheim. As the ship steamed out of the fjord Midsummer-night fires blazed from the hills. They stirred old memories, and when Paul retired he dreamed of white nights, bonfires, and the fragrance of birches. The next morning, half-awake, he smelled the salty air, seaweed and fish drying on the rock, and he heard the quacking of eider ducks and the screaming of gulls. Was he dreaming still? He peered through the open porthole. The ship was passing through a narrow sound. There were all the familiar scenes — cliffs, sea fowl, fish spread on rocks, rows of boat houses, and salmon traps. Yes, now he was in Norway and on his way home.

That day on the coastal steamer was clear and warm. Nature was in a Midsummer Day mood vastly different from that gloomy April day ten years earlier when he had travelled in the opposite direction. On this sunlit morning islands, mountains, and waterfalls welcomed the homebound traveller. Glorious peaks were silhouetted against a cloudless sky, sparkling waterfalls came tumbling down glistening mountainsides, the sea was mirrorlike, islets and skerries seemed like birds resting on glass, and even the humblest of human habitations appeared snug and inviting. In a gay good humor Paul mingled with the friendly passengers.

Among those aboard, a group of teen-age girls caught his attention. They kept close together, and seemed to have a guide with them. Then he realized they were blind — students at a school in Trondheim now homeward-bound for their summer vacation. Nature's mighty panorama was hidden from them. But as the ship passed the Arctic Circle its whistle blew. The blind girls were assembled in the bow. With their sightless eyes turned to the north where infinitely far away a golden ball lay floating on the sea they sang in praise of the sun whose rays they had never seen. Their voices were young and fresh, but the tune was in a minor key, haunting and melancholy. The pathetic little group, the time, and the occasion created for one of *Kong Harald's* passengers a never-to-be-forgotten picture.

As the boat docked at Bodö there was Brother Julius waiting to greet Paul. But ten years in America had left such a mark on the younger brother that Julius failed to recognize him. Later in Lofoten Brother Bernt had the same experience.

The summer of 1916 was for Paul quite unlike any other. It marked the return of a native after many years absence, and old friends sought him out. But it was the joy of being reunited with his parents which made that summer truly unforgettable. To an extraordinary degree nature co-operated to make the visit festive. For six weeks running the sky was cloudless day and night. With astonishing regularity the diurnal change of winds — a morning breeze from the mountains, a sea breeze in the afternoon — suffered no break. The weather's customary tendency to fickleness was held strictly in check.

Ebullient optimism prevailed everywhere. No ocean-going shipping belonged in Bodin; few young men then sailed in overseas traffic so no local sailor had yet been lost in the war. The rationing and shortages caused by the world conflict came a year later. In 1916 the Lofoten fishery, so important to the economy of northern Norway, had yielded unprecedented wealth. During that winter Britons and Germans bid against each other for the fish so that by the end of the season prices had reached dizzy heights. Ten years earlier fishermen considered themselves fortunate if they had 150 kroner after the winter's fishing; in the spring of 1916 they might have as much as 3,000. Those who bought fish for curing found a similar bonanza in the skyrocketing prices; so did the herring fishermen that autumn. The large amount of money in circulation was, of course, a boon to boatbuilders and merchants. With thousands of kroner in their pockets, fishermen felt like millionaires and spent freely on finery and on rides in the few taxis of which Bodö could boast. When Paul hinted that this prosperity was but a flash in the pan, he was laughed down. The people in Bodin assured the American Cassandra, "The old hard times will never come back. Prosperity is here to stay."

Since Paul was now the only unmarried one of their children, his parents looked upon him in a special way as their own. Realizing this he spent most of the summer with them. Invitations from friends were turned down and when he visited Sister Julianne at Skjerstad and Brother Bernt in Lofoten his parents went with him. The Lofoten trip was the high spot of the 1916 summer. Father had felt apprehensive about the journey to Kalle because there would be so many changes of conveyances — a boat across the fjord, overland to Bodö, six hours on a coastal steamer, and perhaps a change in Svolvaer to a local steamer before Kalle was reached. Even on the short trips to Skjerstad the noise and confusion aboard the steamer made his head ache. But in the end Father's objections were overcome.

When visiting Bodö in former days, the parents had always walked between the landing place on the north shore of Saltenfjord and the town. This time the overland journey was made by automobile. The comfort and the speed astonished them. The one drawback was that the car went so fast they were unable to see the changes along the route. The state-room on the upper deck of the steamer was comfortable and quiet, so quiet in fact that Father wondered if they were the only passengers. Mother rested well content, while Father switched the electric light on and off marvelling at this wondrous new illumination. His memory went back to the days before the kerosene lamp. In his childhood all work in the long winter evenings had to be done in the flickering light from the open fire, the feeble rays from a fish-oil lamp, or the glimmer from a tallow candle. Should the fire go out in the night, the first chore next morning would be to run to borrow a brand from a neighbor, for not even matches were known in his early days. Much, indeed, had changed during his life-time. For forty years he had crossed the turbulent waters of the Vestfjord, always in a small square-rigged open boat. Now he travelled that route in luxury, his first experience of the comfort of a cabin. All the apprehension he had suffered proved groundless. The journey was an easy and exciting one.

At Svolvaer Bernt met his family with a motor boat. Not until well past midnight did they reach Kalle, but the old people had rested on the steamer and the perpetual daylight created the illusion of no night. To stay up into the early morning hours did not bother even the octogenarian father.

The succeeding two weeks were quite perfect. The spacious mansion of the Kalle fishing station provided plenty of room for the seven guests and their hosts, Bernt, his wife, Gunhilda, and their foster daughter, Marit. The guests included Gunhilda's sister, her half-brother, his wife, and teen-age son. The easy routine of the household enabled everyone to follow his own inclinations. Bernt and Paul spent much time fishing in Lake Kalle. Father explored the surroundings, the fishermen's cabins, and the warehouses. In the winter of 1847, as a "half-share" fisherman only fourteen years old Father had been stationed at Kalle. There seventy years later he discovered the foundation stones of the cabin his boat crew had used that winter long ago, and he located their landing place and the site of the fish-drying racks. Without nostalgia or regret, he reminisced about life in those far-off days. Mother enjoyed the magnificent scenery in the midst of the Lofoten Alps, marvelled at the luscious blueberries which grew so abundantly on the slopes of Kalle Mountain, was happy to be with her family, and enraptured by the stories which Gunhilde's brother, Heide Aas, told. For some years he had taught in out-of-the-way places in sections of Norway with a mixed population of Norwegians, Lapps, and Finns where the confusion of language and the clashes of race and culture often resulted in amusing episodes. A peerless raconteur Heide Aas poured forth an endless stream of tales which kept his audience roaring with laughter.

When they left Lofoten Father insisted on staying on deck all the way from Svolvaer to Bodö. There he could spot fishing grounds and stations, peaks on both islands and mainland, and watch the Lofoten "Wall" recede from view. It pleased him mightily that he was able to locate and name the various places where he had fished from the days of his youth till the threshold of old age. In 1847 there had been no light-houses to guide mariners, the boats were small, and at the fishing stations the tiny cabins had only dirt floors and bunks under the roof. Father had often rowed for his life against a rampaging nor'wester or had scudded before the gale to Skrova or the mainland. He had never "ridden the keel" of a capsized boat, but he had seen boats overturn and men drown in the churning Arctic without a chance of rescue. The fishing comrades of Father's early years were no more. A number of them had found their final resting place in the kelp of the Lofoten Sea. In silence he surveyed for the last time the scene of many manhood struggles and stark tragedies. Respectfully Paul watched his white-haired father as on that bright August day he sat on the deck of the express steamer recalling men and events of long ago.

Hoping against hope, Mother had asked Paul as she embraced him after their ten years separation, "Have you come home to stay?" The answer had to be a negative one. He was trained for a career in America. During that long and beautiful summer, the prospect of a final separation hung like a pall over the visit. Inexorably the day of his departure drew nearer. Finally it came. Slowly Mother and Father walked with him to the boat which took him across the fjord. None spoke. It was a silent farewell. Mother broke down. Father looked grim and pale. Such are partings in the vale of life. Less than three years later both parents passed away.

In some respects the Bodö-Trondheim trip of late August, 1916, was a repetition of that in April ten years earlier. The dazed, numb feeling returned. But the general situation had changed immensely. Paul would not again face the unknown. That fact had consoled his parents in the dark moment of parting, and it made a tremendous difference to Paul, too. At the University of Wisconsin he had made a place for himself; at the University of Oslo he would have been an absolute stranger. Though he had found the two months spent in the old familiar surroundings thoroughly enjoyable, he had also been conscious of the fact that he no longer had a home in Norway. True, the house wherein he was born and where he had spent childhood and youth was unchanged. But it was no longer *his* home. It belonged to Brother Julius, his wife, and children. The parents now were lodgers in that place. Paul was but a guest there. He had occupied his old bedroom. As formerly, every morning a skylark rose from the lawn beneath his window and poured out its soul in joyful song. The lark was the same. The mountains, the hills, the moors and glens, the fjord, and the tide current were all unaltered. But the people had changed. Or perhaps it was he who had changed more than his relatives and old friends. For ten years he and they had travelled different paths. Paul's intimate friends were now in America. There he had a port; in the land of his birth he had none. His anchorage was beyond the sea.

The return trip was made on the *Bergensfjord* of the Norwegian-America Line. In some ways the passengers on this voyage were an even more heterogeneous lot than those aboard the *Caronia* in 1906. To be sure, *Bergensfjord* had no steerage, but the third-class had a strange assortment of Scandinavian and non-Scandinavian passengers. Some were evidently escapees from German and Russian prisoner-of-war camps. Others were religious objectors and radicals of various stripes fleeing from their warring homelands. Still others were adventurers of one sort or another.

When the Statue of Liberty and the New York skyline came into view Paul was thrilled and happy. Hearing that the American citizens were to go ashore ahead of the rest, Paul, ignorant of the rule that those on third should wait until the first and second-class passengers had disembarked, was one of the first off the ship. His haste aroused the suspicion of the customs inspector. Bags were examined thoroughly, and even diplomas from Red Wing and Wisconsin underwent close scrutiny. These documents seemed as strange to the customs inspector as they had to Paul's Norwegian family when he had displayed them at his old home, but here they were examined in quite a different way. Finally, and with obvious reluctance, the inspector cleared Paul's scanty luggage, and he was free to entrain for Madison.

All during his journey westward Paul was elated by the feeling of being no longer a stranger in America. This sense of belonging was heightened on his arrival in Madison when his landlady of the spring of 1914 welcomed him back with enthusiasm. She even hustled out another lodger to give Paul the room he had formerly occupied. Except for Professor Munro who had gone to Princeton, the history department was unchanged.

In the summer of 1923 Paul again visited Norway arriving at Christiania in June. His parents were now dead and he was in no hurry to return to the north. There was research to be done in Norwegian archives in order to complete his study of the origins of the November Treaty. There he met several Norwegian historians, and visited museums and art galleries as he explored the beautiful capital and its environs. He found his greatest pleasure in the company of his two nephews, Karl and Harald, sons of Sister Julianne. Toward the end of June he left Christiania for Nordland. On the trips to Norway he made special efforts to study its people and their conditions of life. This study became more meaningful as he learned more about other West European countries. The winter of 1923 he had spent in England. In London he had occasionally seen ice on ponds in the mornings, but by noon it had vanished. On his visit to Hawarden in January, 1923, he crossed England from London to Chester. Pastures were green, cattle and sheep were out grazing. In mid-April when he went to Paris, the apple trees were blossoming in northern France. The scenes from these favored lands came to his mind as he travelled from Christiania to Trondheim through the Gudbrand Valley. Though it was past Midsummer Day, fields and meadows were far behind those he had seen a month earlier in Denmark. At the Opdal station north of the Dovre Mountain in what appeared to be a prosperous farming community, remnants of the winter's snowdrifts were still glistening by the railroad tracks. Upon arriving at his old home, Paul learned that here even at sea level there had been snow on the ground until June. Nature treated this northern land harshly. No wonder that in the Viking age Norsemen sought new homes in England, France, and Ireland. Yet starting literally from scratch in 1814 the people of Norway had in a hundred years reached a high cultural level. They had developed a truly democratic system of government, founded excellent schools and extensive public services, and established a general standard of living far superior to that of many richer and more favored lands. Paul rejoiced in these achievements of his native country and felt proud of kith and kin.

The summer of 1923 was a sharp contrast to that of seven years earlier. It was cold and rainy. The westerlies with drizzle or downpour blew as steadily as trade winds. Gray clouds hid the mountains. The drabness in nature was matched by the prevailing gloom of men's minds. The prosperity of 1916 had vanished long ago. The price of fish had slumped disastrously; a large percentage of the Norwegian merchant marine lay idle. Banks by the score had closed their doors; even old and well-established business houses had gone bankrupt. The severe economic depression set deep marks on Norway's political life. Under these conditions the quacks and "blue-print men" had good innings. Deadbeats and dreamers vied with each other in offering panaceas which had in common the theory that more and more of the good things in life could be had by doing less and less if only a new economic system were adopted. Idlers found it profitable to mouth catchy slogans, wave the red flag, and shout "onward toward dawn." Communists had organized cells in Norway, and were suspected of arming and drilling. The government found it necessary to spend large sums to relieve the unemployed.

While Paul was in the north he again took pleasure in being with his sister and three brothers. But they, too, were affected by the economic depression, so it was difficult to make the reunion a cheerful one. He helped his family as much as his limited resources would permit, and gave money to his eldest nephew so he could complete his preparation for the university. Because of the death of his parents, however, he was more aware than ever that he no longer had a home there. Having been away from teaching for a year, he longed to return to it. In the dawn of a late August morning he left Bodö for the third time to journey to America. Brother Malfred stood on the quay waving goodbye. He was the most optimistic of the family, and he made Paul's departure less difficult than former ones had been, for he was certain that the brothers would meet again.

With a feeling of confidence in the future Paul embarked in Liverpool for New York. As a second-class passenger he travelled in comparative comfort. For the first time he read Kipling's *Captains Courageous*. As luck would have it, on a calm bright day his ship passed right through the fishing fleet on the Grand Banks, and with his interest in fishing and his imagination fired by the yarn just read, he watched with admiration the mother vessels and their bobbing dories. He knew what brave and hardy men plied this dangerous trade. What a contrast it was when the liner later that day came upon the rum fleet hovering at a safe distance off Long Island! That flotilla of law-breakers appeared sinister and ugly.

The University Club was a home of a sort to return to when Paul reached Madison. Here he had roomed since the autumn of 1919. The residents formed a congenial group, and the semi-monastic atmosphere did not preclude good fellowship. Still, neither his university work, absorbing and interesting though it was, nor the agreeable association with colleagues and friends fully satisfied him. An innate home-lover, he had for many years dreamed of the time when he would have a place truly his own, a place where he was loved and wanted, where he was accepted and understood.

Shortly after his return from Europe in 1923 Paul fell madly in love with one of his students, and on June 19, 1926, he was married to Dorothy King of Wilmette, Illinois. Their hope of a European wedding trip was realized with the award of a Guggenheim fellowship for research in England. After a month on the continent the newlyweds settled down in a London hotel where the next six months were devoted to research and the writing of Paul's book on Gladstone and Britain's imperial policy. For the first time in his life he experienced the joy of having a collaborator; his wife took a deep and genuine interest in his work. The research in the Gladstone manuscripts at Hawarden, and their weekend holidays enabled them to visit various parts of England, renew old friendships, and form new ones. At Hawarden the Henry Gladstones and Mrs. Drew made the stay in that secluded Welsh village a delightful one. Colonel and Mrs. Mills at Beaulieu showed the same friendly hospitality toward the newly-married couple that they had shown to Paul three years earlier. The cordiality of fellow historians enriched visits to Oxford and Cambridge. Christmas at the Oxford home of Mr. and Mrs. Robert Mowat who with their six young children welcomed the Knaplunds like members of their own family was a truly happy occasion. Everywhere the British were friendly and hospitable, and in London where Dorothy and Paul spent most of their time, they were made members of an English club to which Paul had been elected a member *in partibus* in 1923.

Paul's marriage had, of course, immeasurably strengthened his ties with America. Because of his wife's American nationality both of them were always referred to as Americans, even by their English friends who knew Paul well. At the hotel, where they showed an American preference for warmth and comfort instead of the English predilection for drafts and colds in the head, they left no doubt as to their nationality. Moreover, their closest family connections were now with America. In that direction went the frequent letters, and in that country their arrival home was awaited with great eagerness.

Back in America early in 1927 the completion of homemaking followed in short order. In June, soon after their return the first child, Katherine Barbara, was born; the next autumn a small home was bought, and in August, 1928, the second child, Paul William, arrived. For twenty years Paul had been a wanderer upon the face of the earth; now he had at last attained his long-desired goal. In work and play he had a partner. Jointly they met life's problems, watched the children grow and develop, rejoiced in their progress. This unity and companionship in happiness and in solicitude, more than any house built with hands, created that spiritual atmosphere which is the essence of a home. With such a haven in America Paul's childhood home in Norway receded into a dream-like memory.

As the children grew older their father saw America in a new light. The earth those children trod, the soil sifted through their little hands became to him more hallowed than the places where his ancestors had toiled and found their last resting place. The living were for him more significant than the dead. In the lives of his children his own life would continue.

The completeness of his own transplantation became abundantly clear during a visit to Europe in 1933. A research grant enabled him to spend a summer in England. The children were too young to travel easily, so he went alone. On the eastward voyage Paul's gaze was fastened on the ship's wake; the golden path which the setting sun made on the ocean was a trail leading home to his wife and children. As during his first year in America when every night he recalled the hour of Mother's evening prayer in which she remembered him, so now he called to mind sweet little voices saying, "God bless Daddy." In 1906 Paul had soared on the wings of dreams eastward; in 1933 he flew westward to be with his family. His home and his treasures were in America; his heart was now there and not in the land of his ancestors.

In the autumn of 1933 as his ship sailed toward America and approached New York it passed the *Bergensfjord* headed for Norway. He rejoiced that he was not aboard her. Her course lay to a foreign land. He was homeward bound. Rushing through the landing formalities he hurried to his train and joyfully sent the message "Home tomorrow night." He was moored in America.

Chapter 15

Review and Reflections

THE EVENING'S REVERIE made the professor realize how full of contrasts his life had been. He had known a wide variety of people and environments. The differences between the land of his birth and that of his adoption were indeed striking. No less dissimilar were the people whom he had known — unlike in background, education, social status, and occupation. Yet, their similarities were far more fundamental than their dissimilarities. Their disparity in rank had been "but the guinea stamp."

In profound admiration Paul had listened to the straightforward tale of Joe Silrum as he related how he had lived and faced the hardships of the Minnesota frontier. The dugout which had been his home assumed the character of a holy place. Courage, determination, steadfastness had carried the Silrum family through the hard years; they had triumphed at last. Equally memorable was Paul's recollection of a scene in a large country house. There a son and daughter of Gladstone had told of events in the life of their famous father, that earnest, singularly gifted statesman who from his position of power had wrestled with the problems in government, society, and religion. In many respects the farmer and the statesman differed as widely as is humanly possible. But as they were with "God's sigil" upon their brow they were alike. Both were men of character, fortitude, integrity, and the will to achieve. Both had walked humbly before God.

Equally diverse had been the lives of that brave pioneer

woman, Mrs. Napstead, and of Mrs. Drew. The saga of the Napsteads' efforts to overcome the trials of life on the wild prairie and build their home in a foreign land had been simply told. Though she was bent with toil, her life's tribulation had not broken her spirit nor dampened her zest. She still looked forward and planned improvement of farming methods and living standards. Hopelessly crippled, unable to move save in a wheel chair, Mrs. Drew, close friend of some of the most famous people of her era, was just as intrepid. In 1926 the party which her father had led so long and gloriously was shattered; his ideals had been discarded. But Mrs. Drew neither indulged in self-pity nor bemoaned the fate of the British Liberals. She lived in the present. Keenly interested in social reform she turned her attention to the prospects of the Labour Party. Clearly, qualities of heart and mind — dauntlessness, hope, and sympathy — are not restricted by barriers of class or nationality, time or place.

The recollection of these diverse episodes brought into juxtaposition two others. On August 5, 1914, Paul was working on the Hillestad farm near Ostrander. At the noonday meal Farmer Hillestad read to the threshing crew the latest news. Germany had broken a solemn pledge and invaded Belgium. A signed document had been treated as a scrap of paper. Justice had been flouted, rights violated. Gathered around the long dinner table were twenty ordinary American farmers. To a man they bristled with indignation at the news. If lawlessness were to dominate the relations between the countries of the world, then, they felt convinced, humanity was doomed. Twelve years later one of those present at that August dinner had an interview with Lord Grey of Fallodon who in 1914 had striven to avert the calamity of a world war. During the conversation two pictures flashed through the mind of the visitor. The one was of Sir Edward Grey on the eve of that same August day standing before a window gazing over London and saying, "The lamps are going out all over Europe; we shall not see them lit again in our lifetime." The other was the scene at the dinner table of the Minnesota farmer with Hillestad, elderly, bearded, and very grave reading slowly the startling news of events in a far-off country; the listeners, roughly clad, horny-handed, weather-beaten laborers, waxing indignant at what they heard and filled with foreboding about the future.

In the enveloping darkness, the professor saw the steeple of yonder church clearly outlined against the western sky. The silhouette summoned likenesses of famous cathedrals as well as of humble places of worship. Beautiful and awe-inspiring as were Salisbury or Notre Dame, they had not warmed his heart as had the small Hauge church in Perry township, Wisconsin. It was erected in 1853 by Norwegian immigrants, few in numbers and poor in material goods, who so much wanted to worship in the manner of their ancestors that they built in imitation of the churches they had known in Norway. The Perry church was tiny, almost a toy church, but in the arrangement of seats, altar circle, pulpit, and gallery it was a true copy of places of worship in the old country. Far from an architectural masterpiece, it was the best the builders could do, and into it they had put their devotion, labor, and thought. Here lonely, hard-working men and women had found solace in grief; here they had been uplifted and felt the nearness of God. Their devotion and worship had given them strength to face hardships, overcome loneliness, and persevere in life's struggle.

From these recollections the professor's imagination traveled back to the church at Knaplund. It was a summer day. Light poured in through the high windows in the choir. At its entrance stood the deacon's pew. Minister and congregation were invisible; Paul saw only the stall with Mother and Father. They were happy together in God's house. Their religious faith was direct, earnest, and simple. In common with the worshippers in the Lea and Perry churches, they believed implicitly in the fatherhood of God and the brotherhood of man. In such places man-made distinctions in creed and ritual mean little; it is the basic human needs and longings which are of vital significance and unite all mankind.

This concept of a common humanity had facilitated for Paul the change of anchorage from the land of his ancestors to that of his children. As the professor scanned his log he found grief on the voyage but also triumph. All in all he had had a good trip. When he rose from his seat by the window "cowled night" had descended on hillside and town. A bright star hovered over the steeple on the near horizon. It reminded him of tomorrow. Tomorrow he would go and fetch the family home.

Genealogical Appendix

Father: Martinus Johnsen (1832—1919)
Mother: Kristine Andreassen Johnsen (1839—1919)
Siblings:

   Astrup (1862—1893)
   Constance (1864—1909)
   A stillborn son (1865)
   Jensine (1867, died in infancy)
   Malfred (1868—1945)
   Julius (1870—1955)
   Bernt (1873—1945)
   Julianne (1875—1961)
   Katherine (1878—1911)
   Johannes (John) (1881—1951)
   Paul (1885—   )

Norwegians generally use as their surname either the patronymic or the name of the place of birth. Surnames may vary within a single family or during the lifetime of individuals. The author's eldest brother and his sisters used the patronymic "Johnsen." His brother Bernt when he was eighteen chose "Knaplund." Elder as well as younger brothers later followed Bernt's example.

INDEX

Aalesund, Norway, 45, 51, 134, 136

Alaska, 232-237

Andersen, Conrad, 185

Andreassen, Johan, 78, 79, 83

Artesian, S. D., 201, 203, 208, 216

Audubon, Minn., 212

Bakken, Karl, 262

Balfour, Lord, 244

Beck, Ole, 71

Berg, H. J., 157, 161, 162, 177, 179, 230, 231

Berg, Mrs. H. J., 157, 161, 231

Bergen, Norway, 37, 38, 44, 45, 51, 78, 133-138, 163, 167

Bergensfjord, 261, 266

Bergh, O. O., 201, 205, 209

Bergh, Mrs. O. O., 206

Björnson, Björnstjerne, 50, 76, 102

Blue Man's Ice, 17, 24, 89, 119

Bodin, Norway, 59, 67, 70, 87, 99, 185, 257. Until 1896 "Bodö" applied to both town and parish; when the town became a separate parish, the rural area was called "Bodin." *See also* Bodö.

Bodö, Norway, 18, 32, 33, 58, 67-69, 76-79, 87, 88, 97, 98, 109, 131-134, 147, 156, 157, 166, 185, 226, 247, 256-260, 264

Bodö Affair, The, 97, 98, 247

Boekman, Peter W. K., 54, 67

Boer War, 51, 72, 224, 243

Bricelyn, Minn., 213, 224

Brohough, G. O., 194, 196, 208

Brookings, S. D., 202, 209, 211, 215, 216, 250

Bryce, Lady, 240

Bryce, Lord, 240

Burns, John, 245, 246

Canada: British attitudes toward, 240; attraction for immigrants, 23, 132

Caronia, 144, 145, 147-152, 261

Catholicism: in Norway, 61, 66, 68

Christ, Hans, vii, 130, 147, 152-182, 184, 218, 225, 230

Christiania, Norway (later Oslo), 17, 252, 255, 262

Christiansen, Ludvig, 159, 181

Christiansund, Norway, 45, 104, 107, 134, 136

Claremont, S. D., 202, 217, 218, 221

Coffin, Victor, 225

Comstock, George, 224

Crookston, Minn., 202, 212

Crowe, John Rice, 247

Dass, Petter, 100-102, 110

Decorah, Iowa, 169, 228-230, 251

Denmark: Norwegian Union with, 75, 76, 87, 98

Dennis, A. L. P., 224, 225, 227, 229, 230

Drew, Mrs. Harry, 243, 244, 265, 268

Eastwold, Ole, 176, 177

Eberhardt, Adolph O., 195

Eielsen, Elling, 189, 190

Ellis Island, N. Y. x, 147-151, 250

Elmore, Minn., 217, 224

Elstad, Hannah, 147, 152-157, 160, 173, 179

Espelien, Erick E., 193, 197

Fedt, Andrew, 201, 202

Finland, 50, 86, 97, 146

Finnmark, Norway, 35, 48-50, 74, 104

Finns, 18, 74, 259
Fox River Settlement, Illinois, 2, 167-169
France: foreign policy of, 49-50, 247
Fredin, Charles, 202, 205, 213, 217, 218, 220, 221
Fredin, Mrs. Charles, 217, 221
Frost, Minn., 215, 224

German-Americans, 219
German theologians, 56-57
Germans: Norwegian attitudes towards, 51, 76, 98
Gjerset, Knut, 1
Gladstone, Helen, 242
Gladstone, Henry, 242, 265
Gladstone, Lord, 241-243
Gladstone, W. E., 241-246, 265-268
Grafton, N. D., 203
Grand Forks, N. D., 203
Granville, Lord, 246
Great Britain: foreign policy of, 38, 50, 51, 94, 98, 240, 243; history of, 224, 225, 229, 231, 238, 239-247, 264-266
Grevstad, N. A., 164
Grey, Sir Edward, 244, 245, 268
Grötöy, Norway, 38, 41
Guggenheim Foundation, 248, 264
Gullickson, Gilbert, 220

Haldane, Lord, 241
Handlin, Oscar, vii
Hanseatic League, 37, 38, 77, 137
Hanson, Martin, 184-186, 195, 201, 205
Hauge, Hans Nielsen, 56, 189
Hauge Church, Wisconsin, 269
Hauge Synod, 162, 183, 186, 189, 190, 194-196, 200, 205, 206, 211, 212
Haugeaners, 56, 189-191, 196, 206. *See also* Lutheranism.

Hayfield, Minn., 151
Heg, Hans, 4
Heimsness, Ole, 152, 153
Hellickson Family, 169, 170, 176-178
Hellig Olaf, 252-254
Hillestad, Ole, 268, 269
Hofstad, Ole, 184
Holter, Olaus, 73, 185

Ibsen, Henrik, 76, 118
Irish-Americans, 159, 219, 221
Iroquois, S. D., 203, 216
Isvolsky, Count, 244, 245

Jacobsen, John, 235, 237
Jacobsen, Ole, 215
Jacobsen, Mrs. Ole, 215
Japan: Norwegian attitudes toward, 49, 50
Johansen, Ellen Jeremiassen, 114
Johnsen, Astrup, 57, 61, 62, 110, 114
Johnsen, Constance, 17, 110, 111, 114, 131, 177, 251
Johnsen, Katherine, 114, 131, 251
Johnsen, Kristine Andreassen, 12, 19, 40, 56-61, 64, 68-70, 76, 84, 94, 104-119, 131, 132, 165, 177, 223, 230, 251, 252, 258-260, 266, 269
Johnsen, Martinus, 17, 19, 21, 22, 28, 29, 31, 35, 38-41, 43, 45, 57, 59-61, 70, 76, 80, 83-85, 88, 92, 97, 101, 104-119, 131, 135, 137, 177, 230, 233, 251, 252, 258-260, 269

Kalle, Norway, 52, 54, 258, 259
Knaplund, Bernt, 20, 23, 37, 91, 114, 132, 143, 256-259
Knaplund, Carsten, 233
Knaplund, Dorothy King, 264, 265
Knaplund, Gunhilda Kolstad, 259

Knaplund, Haakon, 32, 33, 92

Knaplund, Johannes (John), 12, 20, 28, 29, 60, 61, 64, 65, 68, 72, 105, 114, 138, 141, 142, 144, 179, 232-234, 251

Knaplund, Julius, 84, 110, 112, 114, 132, 256, 261

Knaplund, Katherine Barbara, 265

Knaplund, Malfred, 110-112, 114, 116, 264

Knaplund, Olga Tvenstrup, 232

Knaplund, Paul William, 266

Knaplundöy, Norway, 96

Knappen, Mrs. George F., 211

Knudsvig, H. H., 212

Kolbeinsen, Katherine Arnsberg, 19, 60

Kristensen, Harald, 262

Kristensen, Julianne Johnsen, 59, 60, 114, 258, 262

Lapps, 68, 74, 83-87, 97, 259

Larson, Laurence M., vi

Larson, Ole, 216

Larson, Mrs. Ole, 216

Lea Church, England, 239, 269

LeRoy, Minn., 165, 173, 176

Liverpool, England, 131, 138, 140-144, 147, 264

Lofoten, Norway, 18, 27, 30, 34-55, 58, 66-69, 80, 92, 101, 104, 110, 134, 146, 167, 257-260

Louis Philippe, King of France, 60, 100

Luther, Martin, 3, 51, 69, 100, 190, 207

Luther College, Iowa, 1, 169, 228

Lutheran Church, 3, 4, 56-61, 67, 69, 73, 99-101, 157, 159, 162, 169, 183, 190, 200, 206, 269

Lutheran Denominations, 3, 149, 190, 197, 228. *See also* Hauge Synod.

Lutheran Education, 4, 5, 71, 162, 169, 179, 183-199, 200, 201, 206-208, 228. *See also* Luther College, Red Wing Seminary, St. Olaf College.

Lutheranism, 3-5, 54-67, 71, 73, 99-101, 110, 111, 142, 162, 169, 183-201, 206-208, 269

Madison, Wis., 169, 225, 261, 262, 264

McGregor, Iowa, 176

McIntire, Iowa, 151, 251

Methodists, 3, 57, 66, 191

Mills, Dudley, 240, 241, 265

Mills, Mrs. Dudley, 265

Minnesota, University of, 161, 162, 191

Morrisen, Jakob, 72, 104

Mowat, Robert, 265

Munro, Dana C., 226, 227, 262

Nansen, Fridtjof, 76, 245

Napstead, Mrs. J. O., 214, 215, 268

Nelson, Knute, 5

Northrop, Cyrus, 191

Norwegian-Americans: and American Civil War, 4, 163; and Catholicism, 159, 221; political attitudes, 163-164, 193, 195, 220-221

November Treaty, The, 50, 247, 262

Olav Haraldson, King of Norway (St. Olav), 66, 135

Olav Tryggvason, King of Norway, 22, 96, 135

Oscar II, King of Norway and Sweden, 30, 94

Ostrander, Minn., 147, 149, 151, 152, 157, 161-165, 180, 181, 230, 231, 251, 268

Palmerston, Lord, 247

Paxson, Frederick L., 248
Pedersen, John, 40, 97
Pedersen, Matilde, 154, 156, 160, 179
Port Alexander, Alaska, 232-234, 236, 237

Queensland, Australia, 23, 132

Raud the Strong, 96, 106
Red River Valley, N. D., 2, 202-204
Red Wing Seminary, Minn., 5, 179, 180, 183-203, 211, 212, 223, 224, 251, 261
Röst, Norway, 40, 53, 99, 105, 117
Russell, Lord John, 246
Russia: emigration from, 144, 146; foreign policy of, 244, 247, 252; influence in Finland, 49-50; Norwegian attitudes toward, 49-51, 72

St. John's Day (Midsummer Day), 12, 255, 256, 262
St. Olaf College, Minn., 183
Salomonsen, Adolph, 53
Salomonsen, Ingvald, 53, 54
Salomonsen, Salomon, 40, 41, 99
Saltenfjord, Norway, 26, 30, 43, 87, 96, 97, 258
Scandinavian Seamen's Missions, 14, 131, 141-144
Schmidt, Mrs. Edward, 195
Schytte, Erik Gerhard, 99, 100
Sellery, George C., 225, 230
Sether, Hans, 212
Sether, Mrs. Hans, 212
Silrum, Joe, 213, 214, 267
Skjerstad, Norway, 68, 258
Skrefsrud, Lars, 111

Sogge, Clara, 211, 212
Sogge, Lars, 215
Sogge, Louis, 211, 212, 215, 224
South Africa, Union of, 240-243 passim
Spring Valley, Minn., 165, 171
Stabo, Trond, 230
Stavanger, Norway, 138, 139, 156
Storting, 5, 17, 52, 88, 94
Sulitjelma: mountain, 17, 97; miners, 30, 32, 79
Sweden: relations with Norway, 17, 49, 94, 98, 162
Swedish-Americans, 193, 215, 217-218, 221
Swedish theologians, 56-57

Tasso, 136-139
Tegnér, Bishop Esaias, 101-102
Toronto, S. D., 202
Troms, Norway, 49, 74, 167
Trondheim, Norway, 66, 131-136, 141, 163, 213, 255, 256, 260, 262

Utröst, Norway, 99

Vestfjord, Norway, 36, 37, 39-42, 258
Volga, S. D., 201, 203, 205, 209, 210

Wee, M. O., 212
Wee, Peder, 212
Wergeland, Hendrik, 76, 102
Westermann, W. L., 227, 229
Windom, Minn., 211, 224
Wisconsin, University of, 5, 6, 127, 129, 202, 223-232, 238, 248, 251, 260, 261, 264
Wold, O. R., 184

Zakariassen, Ingeborg, 83, 84